'Berry's perspective on the controversy (still) surrounding the composer is clear-eyed, empathetic, and pleasingly free of polemics of its own . . . Berry's survey of the individual works is comprehensive and exemplary.'
– *BBC Music Magazine*

'It's a book that needed to be wr   dge and passion, it makes required   es alike . . . Berry wields the swor analysis but with a full underst told here of Schoenberg's American years is full of   ring witness to a monstrous ego, a bad sport and a terrible grudge-holder.'
– *Gramophone*

'Arnold Schoenberg lived a "critical life" by any standards, and his entry here into the Critical Lives series of compact volumes devoted to leading cultural figures of the modern period is very welcome. No composer has ever earned quite such a bogeyman reputation, one still widely held if concert and opera programming is any evidence, yet for those of us who actively crave the sound of his music there is also the fascination of the figure himself – and a deeply human side of the composer, to which those who knew him still testify.' – *Opera*

'Berry is a masterful advocate for the composer's quality and importance. His writing has the elegance, energy, warmth, and wit that come from a complete command of his subject matter and the confidence that his view and conclusions are right . . . an ideal introduction to the composer.' – George Grella, *Brooklyn Rail*

'The thrust of this book is distinctly partisan. Mark Berry is a Schoenberg champion. He describes him as not only the most controversial of all 20th-century composers but also the most important – the true founding father of heroic modernism.' – *Catholic Herald*

'Mark Berry's gentle and confident account is the best explanation yet of how the lush Wagner-inspired composer turned into a supposedly ornery modernist inventor. It is a convincing, concise tale of what was in fact brave integrity and powerful creativity in the face of cloth-eared prejudice and dangerous anti-Semitism that changed the conversation about the future of music.' – John Deathridge, Emeritus King Edward Professor of Music, King's College London

'A superb piece of writing: informative, engaging and compact. It wears its considerable research with a winning lightness of touch. The best introduction to the composer.' – Thomas Hyde, composer and Lecturer in Music at Worcester College, Oxford

Titles in the series Critical Lives present the work of leading cultural figures of the modern period. Each book explores the life of the artist, writer, philosopher or architect in question and relates it to their major works.

In the same series

Arnold Schoenberg

Mark Berry

REAKTION BOOKS

To my nephew, Aran

Published by

REAKTION BOOKS LTD
Unit 32, Waterside
44–48 Wharf Road
London N1 7UX, UK
www.reaktionbooks.co.uk

First published 2019, reprinted 2021
Copyright © Mark Berry 2019

Printed and bound in India by Replika Press Pvt. Ltd

A catalogue record for this book is available from the British Library

ISBN 978 1 78914 087 3

Contents

Photograph of Arnold Schoenberg taken in a Berlin photo booth, *c*. 1930.

Introduction

Arnold Schoenberg was the twentieth century's most violently controversial composer. He remains so in the twenty-first. Was he the greatest? Perhaps – although there will always be several other deserving pretenders to the title. His music is certainly not the most performed, the most listened to. Indeed part of his 'greatness', certainly of his controversy, lies in confrontation with a world that often will not listen, that sometimes does not even know. Schoenberg, however, was not only the most controversial of twentieth-century composers; he was also, by any reasonable historical measure, the most important. He embodied and continues to embody the essence, like Beethoven at the beginning of the previous century, of the heroic – in this case modernist – composer. *Contra mundum*. And yet, whereas both the original 'contra mundum', Athanasius of Alexandria, and Beethoven would quickly enough – for us, if not necessarily for them – become accepted as pillars of the Western tradition, what of Schoenberg?

Schoenberg's life is in many ways a tragic story that yet awaits its true catharsis. Again like Beethoven, the degree of Schoenberg's influence dwarfs that of any other twentieth-century composer, Igor Stravinsky included. The latter's *Rite of Spring, Les Noces, Symphonies of Wind Instruments* and other works may have changed the face of twentieth-century music, but Schoenberg's break with the tonal universe within which Western art music had operated for roughly three centuries, and his subsequent adoption of the 'method of composing with twelve notes [or "tones" in u.s. English] related only to one another', transformed its course utterly. That transformation went quite beyond mere 'influence'. When the soprano in Schoenberg's Second String Quartet tells us that she feels the 'air of another planet', not only do we feel it too; we also know that, once we have breathed that air, nothing will ever be quite the same again – even if, perhaps especially if, we elect to return to tonality, be it that of earlier or later music.

Even those resistant to or uninterested in those two defining steps in the course of musical history have found themselves compelled, sometimes against their better judgement, to confront them. Take this imaginary, admittedly caricatured exchange:

> *A: Is it not as absurd now to write tonal music as it is*
> *to build a Gothic cathedral? Even if you could do it,*
> *why would you answer the questions of the fourteenth or*
> *the seventeenth centuries, rather than your own?*
> *B: Neither is absurd, for are not beauty and truth eternal?*
> *Why mistake your inability to match your predecessors for*
> *'progress' or the demands of a nebulous 'spirit of the age'?*

Or as Pierre Boulez, one of the most ferocious and yet ambivalent of Schoenberg's successors, put it after the composer's death: 'Any musician who has not experienced – I do not say understood, but truly experienced – the necessity of dodecaphonic [twelve-note] language is *useless*.'[1] Such *enfant terrible* fighting talk inspired and repelled, much in the line of Schoenberg's hardly less fanatical words.

Recent academic musicology and history alike have sought to chip away at the role and the very idea of 'great men'. (Women, alas, have rarely been considered 'great' composers.) They have sought more often to consider, even to dwell on, the plateaux rather than the summits, and to question our motives and suppositions in designating the terrain as such. Nevertheless, if we are honest, we remain fascinated and even spellbound by those lofty peaks. In the world of musical performance, that is how concert halls and opera houses operate. Ironically, it is how they operate even when, as in the case of Schoenberg, much of that world elects to give vast swathes of his music a wide berth. For every sigh of relief when Schoenberg's music, yet again, fails to appear on the season's programme, there will be another angry 'Disgusted of Donaueschingen' response to its near-criminal neglect. Schoenberg, as man and as composer, has from the outset both inspired slavish devotion and provoked instinctual – sadly, often downright anti-Semitic – aversion. The composers Alban Berg and Anton Webern abased themselves in correspondence in ways that extend considerably beyond the hierarchical conventions of that time or indeed any other. Even his American pupils spoke in awe of him, as we shall see. They admired – even worshipped – him but they also feared him. The same might be said of us, their successors. Any distinction perhaps lies in the proportion of admiration to fear rather than in the degree of obsession. At any rate, neither side – few do not feel compelled to take sides – seems able or willing to escape Schoenberg's shadow.

That goes for audiences, too. We might argue, in high modernist style, about how much a composer needs an audience, even a performer. The music itself is still there, is it not? In some ways, yes; in other ways, no. Music is something more than mere notes on a page, even notes in performance. What of its role in bringing us together, even dividing us? In that sense, and not only that, it is abidingly political. What of its role in making us laugh and cry, in making us think as well as feel? The arguments are as old as music itself, yet some come to seem more important at certain times and in certain cases than in others. Maybe we do not want to be made, or even asked, to think; maybe we do not want to be made to feel, either. For Schoenberg's music is not, whatever some may tell you, dry or merely intellectual. Its expressive range and power are perhaps sometimes too much for us, the violence of its changing moods too extreme; it harnesses such emotional power to great intellectual power, and vice versa, that we feel drained. In short, it makes demands of us. One of the composer's most revered predecessors, Richard Wagner, wrote of his own artistic desire, well achieved in practice, to induce 'emotionalization of the intellect'.[2] He might have written with equal justice of the 'intellectualization of the emotions'. In the intensity of those relationships, as in much else, the proud German, Schoenberg, stands very much as Wagner's heir.[3]

Why else would audiences flee, seeing Schoenberg's name on the programme? A few years ago the Philharmonia Orchestra, when performing *Gurrelieder* in Birmingham – anything but a difficult, forbidding work – offered to refund the cost of the ticket to any audience member who did not enjoy the music.[4] Is the prospect of half an hour of music one merely does not like very much enough of a reason to miss more than an hour of Brahms and Mahler? Such certainly seemed to have been the case when, as a student, I caught the train to London to hear Schoenberg's Violin Concerto at the Proms. The Royal Albert Hall is a cavernous beast; nevertheless, it usually fills up for Mahler, several times a season. But on this occasion it could barely have been 20 per cent full. Why else, on the other hand, would performances of Schoenberg's music inspire a fanaticism among devotees that perhaps compares with that of the followers of Wagner himself? Why did I not only make that journey, but later show myself willing to travel across Europe for the express purpose of seeing rare stagings of Schoenberg's operas? I am speaking personally here, I know, but the quality of 'specialness', born partly yet not entirely of rarity, will often prove a more popular phenomenon than sceptics would suspect. Nietzsche once wrote, with equal measure of devotion and disgust, that Wagner summed up the modern world. Schoenberg, we might say, sums up the modernist world.

Having offered a brief outline of the case, not so much for or against – although there are strong elements of that – but also concerning singularity and extremity, I should like to put it a little to one side. Controversy can be good and healthy; it certainly helps our world go round. It can also blind us, though, and deafen us, or at least obscure our hearing, when it comes to music. There are sensational, even sensationalist, elements to Schoenberg's life and work. They make great set pieces, such as the Vienna 'Skandalkonzert' in 1913, which was abandoned on account of visceral audience response in a dispute that ended in the courtroom, but there are many other such events that, more or less arbitrarily, have failed to attract quite as much attention. There is unquestionable extremity in Schoenberg's music: not just of emotion or difficulty, but of beauty and humanity too. It is all there in the gigantic, late Romantic choral cantata *Gurrelieder*, beloved even by those who normally keep their distance from Schoenberg's music. It is all there, too, in the unfinished opera *Moses und Aron*, too often considered a harder nut to crack (especially by those who, sadly, never try).

For that reason, I decided in the end not to complete my planned final chapter on the reception of Schoenberg's music after his death. His is a mansion with many fragments; my particular fragment may wait until another day. Here I wish to concentrate on his life and work. Not that I think there is something pristine, authentic, to be reached, somehow beyond the distorting grasp of reception; far from it. My Schoenberg, your Schoenberg: neither of them is his, any more than those of Boulez and Karlheinz Stockhausen were. Schoenberg in the 1950s and '60s, Schoenberg in the twenty-first century: those and others are also fascinating stories, very much part of who he has become.

There are, however, other stories to be told, perhaps stories that are less mythologizing – or do we kid ourselves? Schoenberg's life and work have narratives of their own, too readily forgotten, or at least obscured in later, violent partisanship. In any case, they have enough violent partisanship of their own. It is perhaps a vain hope, if not entirely an undesirable one, to allow the great events of his life – illustrated by, yet also embodied in, his musical work – to tell their own, more interesting tales. They find their context in, yet also contribute to our construction and understanding of, broader historical narratives. Schoenberg remains the great modernist composer, forbidding and heroic, in life *and* work a standing, intransigent rebuke to the commercialist imperatives of his time and ours.

But he was much more than that, too. Schoenberg was also a Viennese Jew who converted to Lutheranism and back again, the reconversion a sign at least as much of solidarity with his fellow Jews as of religious conviction – whatever that might mean. He lived his life largely between Vienna and Berlin. Then, following the Nazi seizure of power, he lost his job, his bearings, his life, and became an exile, eventually settling in Los Angeles, far from the culture and the soil in which he had grown up. He was born and raised in the vanished world – a world always with us in its art and in its history – of Austria-Hungary, where there stood an anti-Semite on every street corner. He died not only having lived through the trauma, which he had long foreseen, of the Holocaust, but having witnessed the creation of the State of Israel, a Zionist project towards which he felt and voiced the strongest yet most difficult of connections.

Schoenberg was also a husband and a father, dearly beloved in both cases. He was a teacher to a host of pupils across the world: not just to honoured and honouring disciples, such as Berg and Webern, but to more 'difficult' pupils, such as the committed Marxist Hanns Eisler, whose politics were, as we shall see, very different from Schoenberg's. He taught Hollywood film composers and American experimentalists whose concerns were in many respects quite alien to his own, to those of Old Europe: composers such as John Cage and Lou Harrison. Even Dave Brubeck had a couple of consultation lessons with Schoenberg, although those seem not to have been happy encounters.

I have no intention of avoiding the music; it is an integral part of Schoenberg's life, and is ultimately the reason this life is being told. However, I wish to set it in a broader context than like or dislike, love or hate, advocate or eschew. Some works will, alas, have to pass with less discussion than others, completed works as well as a host of fragments (not that every fragment will be ignored). I have, however, taken to heart – or rather I was reminded of this, having tried in any case to consider as much as I could – Schoenberg's admonition, in a centenary tribute to Liszt in 1911, that 'the personality of an artist can hardly be typified by the single work, but by the sum total of all his works.'[5] Schoenberg's way, like Liszt's and Wagner's, like that of many although not all composers, was to build on what had gone before, his art and artistic path helping to create and structure narratives that are very helpful to a biographer. This is intended as a critical life, with music at its heart: it is not a series of musical analyses, partial or full; nor is it a call to action. If it proves not entirely without use to such related endeavours, all the better; if not, there remain many more books to be written.

1

Birth and Transfiguration

No one, not even a charismatic hero such as Wagner's Parsifal, is conceived in or born into a vacuum. We must start somewhere, though – even if we then find ourselves starting again a few times. Let us therefore consider what it meant for Schoenberg to be born when, where and to whom he was, before beginning to construct a story of his life on those foundations.

Arnold Schoenberg was a son of Austria-Hungary. That is more unusual than it might sound. Many say 'Austria-Hungary' when they mean all manner of other things: the Habsburg monarchy, the Austrian Empire, Austria, Hungary and so on. In fact, to be a child of Austria-Hungary entailed being born during a relatively brief period, between the *Ausgleich* or compromise of 1867 that formed the 'Dual Monarchy', *kaiserlich und königlich* (imperial and royal), and its dissolution in the aftermath of war in 1918. Schoenberg would always remain a monarchist, fiercely loyal, as were many Austro-Hungarian Jews, to the House of Habsburg, a surer guarantor of their rights than most alternatives and successors. The political, social and cultural identity of the state and society in which Schoenberg grew up was in many ways particular to that period; its particularities, as well as its continuities, shaped the upbringing of a composer whose story is founded upon and contributes to the history of that society. It now seemed that Austria was unlikely in the foreseeable future to become part of a German state, whose leadership had fallen to Prussia as a consequence of military victory rather than overwhelming popular sentiment. The Habsburg lands would continue to pursue a difficult, if far from impossible, balancing act between Austria and Hungary, known at the time and since as 'muddling through'. Such counsel was one of despair, perhaps, yet also one of strength in accommodation, between West and East, Christianity and Judaism, monarchy and democracy: all manner of tendencies gathered under the hallowed name of *Mitteleuropa*, 'central Europe'. It not only sounds more prosaic, but is considerably less meaningful in English.

Go to Vienna today and you will see road signs, depending which way you look, pointing to Prague or Brno (Brünn to Schoenberg), to Budapest or Graz. Like Schoenberg, *Mitteleuropa* has survived Austria-Hungary; after the end of the Cold War, it has more or less been reborn. We could thus start again by saying that Arnold Schoenberg was a child of Vienna. Unlike so many composers whom Vienna has claimed as its own – Mozart, Beethoven and Brahms among the most notable – Schoenberg, like Schubert, and indeed like Berg and Webern, actually was Viennese by birth. It escapes no one's attention that, with the partial exception of Mozart, Vienna treated the sons by adoption named above rather better than it did its sons by birth. However, it can scarcely be denied that, gracious or ungracious, Vienna was more than merely the city of Schoenberg's birth. His biography and his music – even the twelve-note opera *Moses und Aron* – waltz more often than many would imagine. At any rate, Vienna was then, much as it is again becoming today, the beating heart of Europe: not a frontier city, not the cold, grey setting for *The Third Man*, but the gateway to so many of those lands, cultures, musical tendencies and, perhaps above all, mutual connections that had been lost, obscured or suppressed for decades.

We might start once again and say that Arnold Schoenberg was born a German. Or was he born an Austrian? Or was he born a Jew? By most reasonable understandings he was born all three, although, following Bismarck's division – popularly considered 'unification' – of Germany in 1871, the claim of 'German' might be considered a little more contentious. It was not, however, contentious enough for Schoenberg to feel any difficulty in often identifying, as we might now say, as such. He also spent productive years in Berlin. Moreover, following his departure from both Vienna and Berlin for the New World, Austria would turn (or return) to the German fold in 1938, under a regime that would vigorously contest any claim that one could be both German and Jewish. That came after the composer, born an Orthodox Jew, had both converted to Protestantism – an eccentric move in Roman Catholic Vienna – and, in 1933, reconverted to Judaism. Part of the answer to questions of identity, then, will be that it depends when, and on whose terms.

There is, perhaps, any number of alternative openings to this story. How about this, in more tabloid, sensational style?

On 13 September 1874 the most celebrated and most influential triskaidekophobe in musical history was born. Unlucky for some? His legion of detractors might well have sensed something in the stars: Schoenberg's numerology would certainly always retain a good proportion of the occult to the 'mathematical' caricature those detractors would often present.

As it happens, Schoenberg's undoubted superstition concerning the number thirteen, often invoked to explain his fondness instead for twelve, was probably no greater than that of many others; his daughter Nuria described it to me as having been akin to not walking under ladders. What, though, of him meeting his death on Friday 13 July 1951?

We must make some progress, however tempting it might be to remain forever in the year in which Schoenberg's fellow Viennese satirist Karl Kraus and his fellow musical pioneer Charles Ives were also born, and in which Wagner completed *Götterdämmerung* (Twilight of the Gods) and thus his magnum opus, *Der Ring des Nibelungen* (The Ring of the Nibelung). Let us start again, then, for one last time, and leave hanging those questions – there will be more – of identity and begin to work them out, which does not mean resolve them. For, of all composers, Schoenberg does not permit easy, formulaic resolutions; nor, indeed, does he permit easy, formulaic beginnings.

On that thirteenth day of September 1874, in Brigittenau 393 (now, following the incorporation of Vienna's suburbs into the city proper, Obere Donau 5) in the Jewish Quarter of Vienna, a boy, Arnold (Franz Walter), was born to Samuel and Pauline Schönberg, a Jewish shoemaker and his wife (née Nachod).[1] Arnold was the first Schönberg child to survive. A sister, Adele, had died that May, several months short of her second birthday; another sister, Ottilie, would be born two years later, followed by a brother, Heinrich, six years later. The three surviving Schönberg children were soon joined by orphaned cousins. Samuel had been born in the Hungarian town of Szécsény, but his family had soon afterwards moved to Pressburg (now Slovak Bratislava), and at the age of fourteen he had taken up a job in Austrian, German, nearby Vienna. Whereas Samuel was, to quote his son, a 'freethinker' (*Freisinniger*), closer to a Reform Jew as we might understand the term, Pauline seems to have been more conventionally pious, even Orthodox.

Those two strands in Arnold's inheritance would do battle until the end: not so much between Reform and Orthodox as between syncretic, historicist thinking and the authority of tradition, or between the rational and the mystical. Following that conversion of the suburbs, the Leopoldstadt had since the seventeenth century been home to a substantial number of Jews: first as an actual ghetto, then as a focus for social and religious life, despite having been named after Leopold I, the viciously anti-Semitic Holy Roman

Emperor who had expelled them from the city of Vienna proper. The nineteenth century brought a wave of migration from other Habsburg lands, and both sides of Schoenberg's family were among the newer inhabitants of what would become Vienna's Second District. A list of those who lived there reads almost like a Who's Who of Viennese Jews, with quite a few Viennese of Jewish ancestry, too: Sigmund Freud; Arthur Schnitzler; the violinist Fritz Kreisler; Alexander von Zemlinsky (later to be Schoenberg's brother-in-law, and the only real composition teacher he ever had); Johann Strauss I and II; the Hollywood composer Max Steiner (*King Kong*, *Gone with the Wind* and others); Theodor Herzl, the founding father of Zionism; and others.

There was, typically for a son of Vienna, and of Jewish Vienna, music on both sides of Schoenberg's family. However, as often seems to be the case with especially musical offspring, that tendency was not at its strongest in the parents' generation. For instance, they do not seem to have owned a piano; they were certainly not wealthy.[2] These things are relative; in common with so many working men of his time, Samuel enjoyed his choral-society singing and fraternity. Moreover, the Nachods had produced a number of synagogue cantors (in Prague, then very much a German city in Austrian Bohemia). At any rate, Arnold's younger brother Heinrich and his cousin on his mother's side, Hans – who would create the role of Waldemar in Arnold's *Gurrelieder* (Songs of Gurre) – became professional singers. Hans's father, Fritz, was perhaps more instrumental to Arnold's later intellectual life; a poet himself, he taught Arnold French and introduced him to a variety of literature, especially poetry (some of which Schoenberg would later set as a song-composer) and drama, of which Schiller in particular was a model for the morally strenuous opera composer of later years.

The first but not the last piece chosen, in 1882, for the honour of being Schoenberg's 'opus 1' – all budding child composers have been there – was, in a nod to his uncle, entitled in French: '*Romance (ré mineur), pour deux violons et alto, par Arnaude Schönberg*' (Romance (in D minor), for two violins and a viola, by Arnold Schoenberg). The odd instrumentation was born of what was available to him, but in retrospect it offers a strange anticipation of Dvořák's *Terzetto*, op. 74, written five years later. The key, D minor, would prove a favourite, not only for Schoenberg but for the Second Viennese School more generally. Moreover, one of Schoenberg's most celebrated early yet 'mature' works, the string sextet *Verklärte Nacht* (Transfigured Night, 1899) (adding another viola and a couple of cellos), would take the same tonal journey from D minor to D major. That is not to imply 'influence' or straightforward recollection, but Schoenberg was beginning to work out certain musical and technical problems – the piece is endearingly full of *tremolandi*. It is certainly worth a glance, even an occasional aural glance. It would be interesting to hear it performed once as a preface to *Verklärte Nacht*, as much to show the difference between apprenticeship and mastery as anything else, but perhaps not just for that reason.

Another trope in composers' childhoods has parents, especially fathers, wishing them to pursue a more sensible career. Leopold Mozart's touring of his prodigy son is anything but typical. In the case of Schoenberg, engineering lost out. He did not face strenuous opposition to exploring his musical talents and, even if he had, his early success at the violin (in which he had lessons from the age of eight) and his childhood compositions would have militated ultimately against any alternative career. He was no Mozart or Mendelssohn *Wunderkind*, but it was music that captured his interest most of all. His record at the secondary Realschule was far from impressive on its narrow terms: it was not something he discussed much as an adult. However, he lived in Vienna, which was arguably the capital of the musical world and certainly that of the Western instrumental musical world.

Photograph of Arnold Schoenberg with his mother, Pauline, and sister Ottilie,
Vienna, 1879.

By the standards of mere mortals, Schoenberg made far from negligible progress. Looking back at his childhood in 1949, he would recall: 'There was not, as has generally been the case with families of musical prodigies, a music enthusiast in mine. All my compositions up to about my seventeenth year were no more than imitations of such music I had been able to encounter: violin duets.' Among the compositions were a *Sunshine-Polka*, a *Karoline Waltz* (for Pauline's mother, Karoline Nachod) and a *Birthday March*, 'and duet arrangements from operas and the military band pieces played in public parks'. They are not necessarily pieces we should play today, save out of especial interest in Schoenberg, yet such dances and marches show a keen ear for picking up popular – yes, *popular* – styles, such as would continue to haunt his later 'serious' music. That aspiration was certainly there from the start, too; the elderly composer would proudly recall that he had come 'so far as to compose once a kind of symphonic poem, after Friedrich von Schiller's drama, *Die Räuber* [The Robbers]'.[3] Doubtless Uncle Fritz would have been delighted.

However, once Schoenberg had befriended a boy named Oskar Adler at school, the musical world began to open up in ways the young composer could never previously have imagined, and which would yet be crucial for his development. 'Through him,' Schoenberg recalled, 'I learned of . . . musical theory . . . He also stimulated my interest in poetry and philosophy, and . . . [I played string] quartets with him, for even then he was already an excellent first violinist.' Another friend, David Joseph Bach, 'greatly influenced the development of my character by furnishing it with the ethical and moral power needed to withstand vulgarity and commonplace popularity'.[4] After Samuel Schönberg's death from influenza and subsequent complications during the epidemic of 1890, friends such as these increasingly took on the role of a secondary family: playing chamber music (Schoenberg's own included); taking walks in the Aurgarten and Prater parks; and discussing literature, politics and philosophy, as serious-minded boys and young men in that milieu had a tendency to do. Schoenberg learned to play both viola and cello, settling ultimately on the latter as 'his' instrument; here, unquestionably, are the seeds of the importance of string chamber music for his mature output and his strong gravitation to the music of 'Viennese' Classicism and Romanticism once he knew it, up to and including that of Brahms. Indeed, it would, famously or notoriously, be in the Second String Quartet (second numbered, that is, for there were many juvenile efforts) of 1908 that Schoenberg would make his fateful break with tonality. These things are perhaps easier to accomplish, or at least to accomplish well, when one knows the musical forces from the inside.

Still more important than either Adler or Bach to our story was a third childhood friend, Alexander Zemlinsky. Older by three years than Schoenberg, Zemlinsky was the son of a Viennese of Slovakian-Catholic descent, who had the previous year converted to Judaism, and the daughter of a mixed Muslim and Sephardic marriage. Let it never be said – and this is a serious, highly relevant point – that the Vienna, the Austria-Hungary and the *Mitteleuropa* of Schoenberg's life were anything other than multicultural, albeit with some cultures far more equal than others. Nor should it be thought that such a plethora of identities was anything but fluid, since in fact 'unusual' conversions were less unusual than we might suspect. Full citizenship for Jews helped; it had been bestowed by Emperor Francis Joseph in 1867, not far off a century after Joseph II had taken the first – by European standards, very early – steps on the road to emancipation. It enabled both a greater possibility of professional and cultural standing, and a certain degree of coexistence between different strands of identity, which yet also served to sharpen certain dividing lines between them.

However, Zemlinsky was crucial to Schoenberg in far more than the sense of a vague cultural model. Having benefited from a formal conservatoire musical training such as Schoenberg

Schrammelmusik (invented 19th-century Viennese folk music) quintet, Payerbach, Lower Austria, 1900: Louis Savart (horn), Fritz Kreisler (violin), Schoenberg (cello), Eduard Gärtner (violin) and Karl Redlich (flute).

would never receive, he managed to impart some of that learning to the enthusiastic, wilful young cellist he encountered playing in Polyhymnia, the amateur orchestra Zemlinsky conducted. In Polyhymnia, Schoenberg and his friends were more properly able to acquaint themselves, again from the inside, with a number of works from the orchestral repertoire. By that time Schoenberg had gained some facility on the piano, and had even written a few, somewhat stilted, Brahmsian pieces for the instrument. He never really had the experience, though, typical for many young nineteenth-century musicians, of learning much of the symphonic and operatic repertoire through playing versions for piano duet at home.

Zemlinsky noted that the autodidact Schoenberg could not even hold his instrument correctly; it was hardly surprising, given that he had long had to make do with what he called a 'violincello', an outsize viola procured for him by Adler and fitted by Schoenberg with zither strings.[5] Yet Zemlinsky more or less immediately saw something in Schoenberg. He acted as unofficial teacher of counterpoint and musical form, and also, more importantly, as friend, model and interlocutor. He even programmed a Schoenberg *Notturno* for solo violin and string orchestra, in March 1896, perhaps the earliest public performance of a Schoenberg work, and if not, certainly more than a single step up in terms of prominence. We must accept that there is a surprising amount we simply do not know about these early years, even though they are not so very far removed from our own time.

Zemlinsky knew the elderly Brahms, who was always interested in the work of young composers, and showed him the draft of a string quartet by Schoenberg. Brahms generously offered to pay for a conservatoire education for the struggling young composer who, out of a pride that would only become more pronounced as he grew older, felt that however great and unexpected the honour he must decline. Zemlinsky introduced the young composer to complete works by Wagner – as opposed to mere highlights heard in the park – and thereby set in motion a productive conflict, mirroring that in German musical life as a whole, between 'conservative' Brahms and 'revolutionary' Wagner that would persist throughout the whole of Schoenberg's life and work. Schoenberg now began to lap up opportunities afforded by the Court Opera, avidly attending several performances of Wagner's music dramas. Indeed, Zemlinsky's unusual receptivity towards the music of both composers itself proved a model for his young charge.

Moreover, Zemlinsky offered a key, partly via Brahms, to the Austro-German historical tradition in which Schoenberg would so proudly place himself: 'Zemlinsky told me,' Schoenberg would recall, 'Brahms said that every time he faced difficult problems, he would consult a significant work of Bach and one of Beethoven [:] . . . how did they handle a similar problem . . . In the same manner, I learned from . . . [Beethoven's] *Eroica* [Symphony] solutions to my problems.'[6] There may be an element there of rationalization after the event. This nevertheless seems very much to have been the method in which Schoenberg, prompted by Zemlinsky, instructed himself. Just as important, Zemlinsky seems to have been instrumental in introducing Schoenberg to various other cultural luminaries on the Viennese coffee-house scene – it really was akin to our understanding of a 'scene', often centred on wild enthusiasm for Wagner's *Tristan und Isolde* – as well as to the work of writers who would soon inspire a number of musical works. Hans Nachod looked back on this experience in a memorial piece for *The Listener* in 1952:

> They are nearly all dead now. One of the last to join them was my cousin and dear friend, Arnold Schönberg. They are all gone. Zemlinsky, Bodansky, Edmund Eisler, Piaud, Carl Weigl, the brothers Jonas, and many others. They were rebels, attractive rebels, especially attractive to the younger generation to which I belonged . . . because they were unconventional in the conventional surroundings of the old traditional Vienna. They met in the old Café Grinsteidl or in the Winterbeerhouse, discussing their problems night after night until dawn, coming home intoxicated.[7]

The feature has a number of typographical errors, perhaps owing to Nachod's account deriving from an interview with a journalist, but the persons referred to are Artur Bodanzky (conductor); Edmund Eysler (an operetta composer); Walter Pieau (a singer and later Schoenberg's Lutheran godfather); Karl Weigl (composer); and the brothers Jonasz, of whom Anton was a Polyhymnia member and later an army doctor. The Café Griensteidl was nicknamed the Café Megalomania on account of its nightly clashes of egos.

Zemlinsky also introduced his protégé to the works of a number of writers who would soon inspire some of Schoenberg's most celebrated compositions, including Richard Dehmel (*Verklärte Nacht* and various songs) and Stefan George (songs up to and including the song cycle *The Book of the Hanging Gardens*), as well as, from further afield, Maurice Maeterlinck (the tone poem *Pelléas et Mélisande*) and Jens Peter Jacobsen (*Gurrelieder*). 'We were all very young,' recalled the poet and dramaturge Arthur Kahane. 'The very youngest and the one with the least money was Arnold Schönberg.' He was the one, Kahane continued, who wanted to conquer the world.[8]

In the meantime, following his father's death, Schoenberg had needed to give up on schooling – no serious blow in itself – to take up an apprenticeship at Werner & Co., a bank in the First District. When the firm collapsed in 1896, he resolved that his banking days were behind him, much to the consternation of his mother and the rest of his family, who needed the money, with the exception of the encouraging Uncle Fritz. It was from his work as a conductor of choral societies that he first made a little money as a musician, initially in Mödling, just outside Vienna, where he would live for a while following the First World War. Other positions followed, either outside or in the suburbs of Vienna. He was called *Genosse* (comrade) by the men, as was the custom, and he seems for a while to have sympathized with the socialist ideals of these organizations. He soon realized, however, that the more straightforward political commitment of his friend David Bach was not for him, and would later recall:

> In my early twenties, I had friends who introduced me to Marxian theories . . . at this time, when the Social Democrats fought for an extension of the right of suffrage, I was strongly in sympathy with some of their aims. But before I was twenty-five, I had already discovered the difference between me and a labourer; I then found out that I was a *bourgeois* and turned away from all political contacts.[9]

Writing from McCarthyite America, Schoenberg perhaps had reason to exaggerate. It is true, however, that his later political interests would be of a very different nature – and not just of a different ideology. Moreover, money, always to be a problem in Schoenberg's life, was never enough; he never acquired on any instrument the performing skill required to give lessons. He had to supplement his income through tedious, though not necessarily useless, work for music publishers: copying, reducing full orchestral scores to piano versions (such as Zemlinsky's opera *Sarema* in 1897) and, the other way round, orchestrating operetta scores by composers who had simply written them in short score (which would prove an especially important source of income when he first moved to Berlin). At any rate, he had made up his mind that he would make his way in the world as a musician, however difficult that might prove.

Schoenberg had also found love, at least of a kind, for the first time: unrequited, as would befit so serious-minded a sixteen-year-old Romantic. His cousin Malvina Goldschmied, also from the Leopoldstadt, might have offered relief from the drudgery of his life at the bank. Yet reality inevitably disappointed, his composition of a *Song without Words* for her notwithstanding. The first two of his surviving letters were both to her; in the second, from 1891, he writes in that clumsy, hectoring style so typical of teenage intellectuals:

> Ma chère cousine! Your letter did not satisfy me in any way
> . . . You . . . say that you have only disputed the amount
> of nonsense that is in the Bible; now I must oppose you,
> as an unbeliever myself by saying that nowhere in the
> Bible is there any nonsense. For in it all the most difficult
> questions concerning Morals, Law-making, Industry and
> Medical Science are resolved in the most simple way.[10]

Very much his father's serious, freethinking son, Schoenberg insists, with seemingly unintentional comedy, that the Bible 'really gives us the foundation of all our state institutions (except the telephone and the railway)'. Malvina (or 'Malva') would later marry Robert Bodanzky, the anarchist playwright, journalist, writer of operetta libretti and brother of conductor Artur Bodanzky; a better match, it seems, and a great admirer of Schoenberg and his music.

Schoenberg's unfashionable insistence on the contemporary importance of Scripture and his intensive rereading – many of his bibles are full of scribbled marginalia – and artistic reworking of its stories and ideas would persist to the end of his life, whatever his changing, complex and even sometimes quite unclear theological views. In 1898 our Jewish 'unbeliever' was received into the Lutheran Evangelical Church, in its Stadtkirche congregation on the Dorotheergasse. There is pleasing symbolism here, in that the church had been rededicated in 1783 as a direct consequence of Joseph II's Edict of (Protestant) Toleration two years previously; in 1782 Joseph had similarly initiated the process of Jewish emancipation, of which the lives of Schoenberg, his family and so many of his friends and colleagues were very much part. Zemlinsky followed suit the following year: already, influence ran both ways. Schoenberg's precise motives at this time may never be established. Genuine conviction seems to have played the principal role, at the very least; in his case, it almost always did. This was certainly no career move; had it been so, he would have opted, in Vienna, for Roman Catholicism, as Gustav Mahler had the previous year. If anything, this particular conversion was perhaps indicative of a broader identification with German culture. Luther's Bible – the Bible itself was always central to Schoenberg's outlook – stood as a monument to German language and literature. Lutheranism was also the creed of J. S. Bach; that may or may not have been relevant quite yet, but it would certainly inform Schoenberg's later exploration of his faith.

Let us now consider compositions from the years 1897–9, among which stand the first that receive regular performance today. The final one, *Verklärte Nacht*, remains Schoenberg's most popular work. The D major string quartet that Zemlinsky had shown to Brahms is not officially 'numbered', yet is generally held to merit inclusion in complete quartet 'cycles'. It is a thoroughly accomplished, if not yet quite characteristic, work, its charming 'Bohemian' inflections closer to Dvořák – an unsurprising model for Brahms to approve – than to anyone else. There are also certain characteristics (no more than that) suggestive of the strong, Brahmsian tendency for 'developing variation' – that is, well-nigh permanent ongoing motivic development – that would mark much of Schoenberg's later music. After considerable revision so as to meet with Zemlinsky's complete approval, in March 1898 the quartet received a private premiere from the Tonkünstlerverein, a society dedicated to new music, on whose board Zemlinsky sat. In December that year it was heard in public, again in Vienna, at the Bösendorfersaal in the Herrengasse. The redoubtable conservative music critic Eduard Hanslick was impressed; he even spoke, if perhaps not entirely without irony, of a 'new Mozart'. The conductor and writer Nicolas Slonimsky later remarked sardonically that it was fortunate that Hanslick never lived to hear the new Mozart's later music.[11]

For Hanslick's *bête noire*, Wagner, was also beginning to assert himself in Schoenberg's music. An orchestral tone poem – very much a genre of the Wagner-Liszt-Richard Strauss school – was begun, yet never finished, in 1898. Its inspiration, Nikolaus Lenau's poem 'The Death of Spring', was also suggestive of increased interest in Strauss, who was at the time seen as a post-Wagnerian avant-gardist. Schoenberg had most likely heard Strauss's *Don Juan*, itself after Lenau, as early as 1892, but had come only recently to more of his music. Two sets of songs, Schoenberg's official opus 1 and 2, were composed, and a third set (op. 3) begun. The Wagnerian chromatic eroticism of the second set in particular was partly a response to Richard Dehmel's verse, yet would have been inconceivable without the example of *Tristan* in particular.

Moreover, there are signs of a parallel to the music of Claude Debussy, post-Wagnerian harmonies being relished for their own sonorous sake as opposed to drawing their primary justification and meaning from placing in progression (where they have come from and where they are heading). These are prophetic straws in the wind for the later, freely atonal composer, although their prominence can readily be exaggerated, since such effects can largely be explained in terms of word-setting. Developing variation is, even in this vocal music, perhaps more apparent, and certainly more important. All three sets would be published in Berlin in 1904. 'Your poems,' Schoenberg would later write to Dehmel, 'have had a decisive influence on my development as a composer. They were what first made me try to find a new tone in the lyrical mode. Or rather, I found it even without looking, simply by reflecting in music what your poems stirred up in me.'[12]

Verklärte Nacht was perhaps the first piece by any composer truly to attempt a reconciliation of chamber music in Brahms's 'Viennese' tradition with the programme music of the so-called New German School (Wagner, Liszt, Berlioz and Strauss). It was here also that Schoenberg's interest in Dehmel's verse reached its culmination. *Verklärte Nacht* may, as Schoenberg owned retrospectively in a programme note of 1950, 'be appreciated as "pure" music. Thus it can perhaps make you forget the poem which many a person today might call rather repulsive.' That, however, will surely only whet today's readers' – and listeners' – appetites, for, as Schoenberg stated quite clearly in that same note, 'it is program[me] music, illustrating and expressing the poem of Richard Dehmel'; and he continued to believe that 'much of the poem deserves appreciation because of the highly poetic presentation of the emotions provoked by the beauty of nature, and for the distinguished moral attitude in dealing with a staggeringly difficult human problem.'[13] Schoenberg wrote the piece very quickly, over a period of just three weeks in September 1899, while on holiday in the Lower Austrian town of Payerbach, about 65 kilometres (40 mi.) southwest of Vienna, with Zemlinsky and his sister Mathilde. His compositional career tended to alternate between intense periods of composition like this and then bouts of difficulty in writing, or at least completing, anything at all, resulting in an unusual number of unfinished works among his legacy.

The 'Transfigured Night' of the title is also the title of Dehmel's poem, whose form the sextet follows closely, with five contrasting musical sections mirroring its five stanzas. The odd-numbered sections present the forest, so long a favoured scene of German Romanticism, literary, visual and musical; a place of redress and of justice (think of the fairy tales of the Brothers Grimm). There is certainly sepulchral darkness to the opening, as our (aural) eyes adjust, but also the sense of a gateway to something unknown, dangerous perhaps, yet also exciting, certainly imbued with Fate. The second and fourth sections present the words of a woman and a man respectively. Walking through that forest in the moonlight of silvery string music, ethereal harmonics and all, the woman confesses that she had married a man she did not love. Desirous of a child, she had therefore yielded to another, a stranger, whose child she now bears. Transfiguration is a Wagnerian idea if ever there were one, and was also familiar to Schoenberg from Strauss's *Death and Transfiguration* (1889); here it is effected through the man's nobility of soul, manifested not in a self-denying act of charity, but in a violin and cello duet of love. It expresses 'the warmth that flows from one of us into the other', transfiguring the child to become his own, and thus transfiguring the night itself. The 'miracles' that follow are explicitly those of Nature, not of hidebound bourgeois morality, whose necessary outcome would surely have been tragedy, not numinous transfiguration. Twists and turns in individual lines aurally suggest those of a *Jugendstil* drawing; in their general tendencies, individually and in combination, the leaves, branches, lightness and darkness of the forest, both material and metaphysical, emerge and transform before our ears. Is it the creature of the man and woman, or vice versa? 'Two people walk through the high, bright night.'

Music that sounds, according to the late nineteenth-century operetta composer Richard Heuberger, 'as if someone had smeared the score of *Tristan* while it was still wet' is actually tightly constructed in something akin to, or perhaps nostalgically reminiscent of, Classical-Romantic rondo form.[14] Heuberger's friend Brahms might or might not have appreciated that; he had died two years earlier. Developing variation works its distinguishing and combinatory wonders the whole time: new motifs always have their roots in what has been heard before, and always have within them the seeds of what is to come. For all the clarity of the work's sectional division, its marriage of poetic narrative and self-transforming semi-traditional form lies in the connections, the cumulative experience. Schoenberg seems to have drawn that primarily from Viennese instrumental tradition, at least consciously; yet he must surely, if only subliminally, also have complemented that tendency with the complex relationship between narrative and music that Wagner sets forth in his later, 'symphonic' music dramas, *Tristan* foremost among them. Musical Vienna and much of musical Europe continued to be riven in conflict between aesthetically radical (tending towards extremes of political Right and Left) Wagnerians and allegedly conservative (yet often politically liberal) Brahmsians. Schoenberg's aesthetics, perhaps also his politics, already stood out as intriguingly integrative – or transcendental. The dissolute yet earnest boys from the 'Café Megalomania' (as Café Griensteidl was nicknamed) and, indeed, his greater experience of life in general had already helped Schoenberg to move some way away from the world of that excruciating teenage love letter to his cousin.

The sextet received its first performance from the Rosé Quartet and two other musicians from the Court Opera Orchestra, the violist Franz Jelinek and Schoenberg's exact contemporary the cellist and composer Franz Schmidt (born in 1874, in Samuel Schönberg's Pressburg). That Vienna premiere in 1902 aroused considerable hostility. 'It shall not be forgotten', recalled Schoenberg, that it 'was hissed and caused riots and fist fights. But very soon, it became very successful.'[15] It becomes a little more difficult once again when one listens motivically rather than merely atmospherically, but one might say the same about almost any piece of Beethoven or Brahms too. The 'late Romantic' sound still offers a seductive entrée, at least for many concert listeners' ears. In a lecture given in English in Denver, Colorado, in 1937, tellingly entitled 'How One Becomes Lonely', the composer summarized his attitude to what remains the most frequently performed of all his works, the work for which even those who profess to loathe, or simply not to understand, his music will make an exception:

My *Verklärte Nacht*, written before the beginning of this century – hence a work of my first period – has made me a kind of reputation. From it I can enjoy (even among opponents) some appreciation which the works of my later periods would not have procured for me so soon. This work has been heard, especially in its [1917] version for [string] orchestra, a great many times [a second version would be made in 1943]. But certainly nobody has heard it as often as I have heard this complaint: 'If only he had continued to compose in this style!' The answer I gave is perhaps surprising. I said: 'I have not discontinued composing in the same style and in the same way as at the very beginning. The difference is only that I do it better now than before; it is more concentrated, more mature.'[16]

The work of choice alongside *Gurrelieder* for those who otherwise do not care for Schoenberg's music, *Verklärte Nacht* certainly qualifies as 'great' Schoenberg. It is not, however, entirely characteristic, whether in its musical language, or, perhaps more importantly, in the relative expansiveness to which Schoenberg refers in that lecture. Let us follow the composer, then, on the next chapter of his path towards 'loneliness'.

2

Emancipating the Dissonance

The anticipated premiere of *Verklärte Nacht* did not take place, on account of the work's rejection by the Tonkünstlerverein, supposedly Vienna's platform for new music. The reason given – almost comically, yet in deadly seriousness – was the appearance of one chord that none of the society's pedantic scrutineers could find in their harmony textbooks. Small wonder that Schoenberg would, a few years later, feel compelled to write his own *Harmonielehre* (Theory of Harmony, 1911), in which, as we shall see, he would mordantly respond. For now, he promptly resigned his membership, as did Zemlinsky. Before they did, however, Schoenberg had noticed the Tonkünstlerverein's announcement of a song-cycle competition. In 1900 he therefore began work on *Gurrelieder*, setting songs by Jens Peter Jacobsen, to whom he had been introduced by Zemlinsky. It is a love story, a tragic one, but also a tale and celebration of defiance, of shaking one's fist, Job-like, to God and to the world. Jacobsen's welding together of the story of King Waldemar's love for Tove with that of the Wild Hunt appealed greatly to a composer flexing his compositional muscles, both in love with his art and already, perhaps, with an inkling that love for his particular version of that art might not be universal.

Schoenberg's first idea was of a cycle for voice and piano. Zemlinsky would recall that the songs 'were wonderfully beautiful and truly novel – however we both had the impression that, on that account, they had little prospect of winning a prize.'[1] The project thus soon outgrew its original, far from modest scale, to become the grandest of grand farewells to post-Wagner, late Romantic gargantuanism. Involving a Speaker (a reciting, 'melodramatic' role, prophetic for the future), five solo singers, massed choruses and an orchestra of a size that would have made Wagner and Strauss blanch, the work seemed destined, not for the last time in Schoenberg's career, to remain defiantly unperformable. Schoenberg had to order special manuscript paper with 48 staves, such as had never previously been requested. All that was missing from this *Gesamtkunstwerk* vision was the stage.[2] One may readily forget, given the staggering accomplishment of his orchestral writing here, that Schoenberg had never previously written a complete work calling for a full, let alone gargantuan, orchestra; indeed, the unfinished *Frühlings Tod* (Spring's Death), although conceived orchestrally, was written only in piano score with some instrumental indications. Nevertheless, among more or less digested passages from *Tristan* and *Götterdämmerung* – Schoenberg's chorus of vassals stands a little too close for comfort to its predecessor in the latter work – there continues to beat a heart of songful intimacy. In the First Part, in which we learn of and indeed experience the course taken by the love of Waldemar and Tove, developing variation again binds together the work as a whole and provides narrative thrust in tandem with words that are now actually heard, rather than a literary programme.

It seems in retrospect to gain inspiration from Schoenberg's blossoming love for Mathilde Zemlinsky. Mathilde was both Alexander's sister and a friend of Schoenberg's sister Ottilie. Or was it, perhaps, partly the case that their love was inspired and furthered by *Gurreleider*, like Wagner's 'affair' with Mathilde Wesendonck when he was at work on *Tristan und Isolde*? Financially compelled to give up work on the orchestration of *Gurrelieder*, a task that he completed only in 1911, Schoenberg held on to his real-life Tove. Instead of meeting her death at the hands of a jealous queen, Mathilde Zemlinsky fell pregnant with her

First page from the early, unfinished symphonic poem *Frühlings Tod* of 1898.

lover's child – neither *Gurrelieder*, then, nor *Verklärte Nacht*, at least not yet. The real art-meets-life drama of their marriage would come later that decade. They were married in the church of his baptism on 18 October 1901.

Soon afterwards, at Zemlinsky's suggestion, the pioneering cabaret impresario Ernst von Wolzogen offered Schoenberg the

position of *Kapellmeister* at his new, shortlived Buntes Theater
in Berlin (first in Alexanderplatz, but in an Art Nouveau hall
on Kreuzberg's Köpenickerstrasse by the time of Schoenberg's
arrival). Wolzogen had just lost the Viennese conductor Oscar
Straus from his books and wanted a replacement who might make
a similar splash. If Bismarck had divided Germany politically,
cultural connections between Vienna and Berlin, now imperial
allies, continued to strengthen. Schoenberg's Protestantism
probably did no harm either in northern Germany, in what
remained in many respects a confessionally divided society. He
was, of course, already wearily accustomed to the anti-Semitism
he would encounter there. The Schoenbergs left for Berlin in
December, and Mathilde gave birth to a daughter, Gertrude
(Trudi), in January 1902. Save for that, Schoenberg did not have
an especially happy introduction to one of the three great cities
of his life, since Mathilde was suffering additionally from ill
health. Whatever his title and whatever Wolzogen's original,
perhaps uncomprehending intention, Schoenberg rarely found the
opportunity to conduct, let alone to compose. He found himself,
then, once again mostly orchestrating other people's music,
this time with a small salary, albeit at the behest of an overtly
anti-Semitic boss: swings and roundabouts, as ever, for a Jewish
composer, converted or otherwise. Schoenberg's own delightful,
even occasionally naughty *Cabaret Songs* (one of them set to a text
by the librettist of Mozart's *Magic Flute*, Emanuel Schikaneder)
were not written for the theatre, having been composed the
previous year in Vienna. There is no evidence that those for
voice and piano were performed there. The single song for small
ensemble, 'Nachtwandler', was performed, albeit only once since
the trumpeter was unable to play his part. Schoenberg's contract
was not renewed; he left in July.

As if by magic, at least in narrative terms, Schoenberg now
came to meet Strauss in Berlin. Having shown the older, wiser

and unquestionably wealthier composer the score, such as it was, of *Gurrelieder*, Schoenberg benefited initially from copying work put his way by Strauss. Strauss continued to help thereafter, enabling the younger composer to escape such outright drudgery, recommending him both for the Liszt Scholarship in 1903 and for a small degree of conservatory teaching (the duties of which he was now able to fulfil, and which he relished). Word had reached Berlin, moreover, of the (relative) success of that first Vienna performance of *Verklärte Nacht*, which Schoenberg himself had been unable to attend. A performance was arranged for Berlin in October 1902, alongside quartets by Strauss and another Berlin resident, Ferruccio Busoni, placing Schoenberg very much in the musical limelight. Having earlier found little time or energy to compose, at Strauss's suggestion Schoenberg began work on a piece derived from Maeterlinck's *Pelléas et Mélisande*, as tragic a love tale as *Gurrelieder*. Strauss had suggested an opera, though, thinking little of the recently premiered version by one Claude Debussy. Perhaps wisely, Schoenberg decided instead to take on his mentor at his own game (or what was still his first game), and compose a symphonic poem. He would later claim not even to have known of Debussy's opera, which was premiered in 1902, a possibility not nearly so surprising as it might seem with the benefit of hindsight.

Longer than most of Strauss's essays in the genre, and again written for a very large orchestra, Schoenberg's *Pelleas und Melisande* (1903), op. 5, was not the most practical work, whether performatively or financially. Yet it marked a further step along Schoenberg's integrative path between the traditions of Brahms and Wagner (and Strauss), making its progress through interaction, even confrontation, between programmatic narrative and 'traditional' musical form. It is written in *that* key of D minor (which, incidentally or not, was always 'special' for Zemlinsky, too); Alban Berg would write a listening guide to the piece almost twenty years later, presenting it as a D minor 'symphony'. It takes

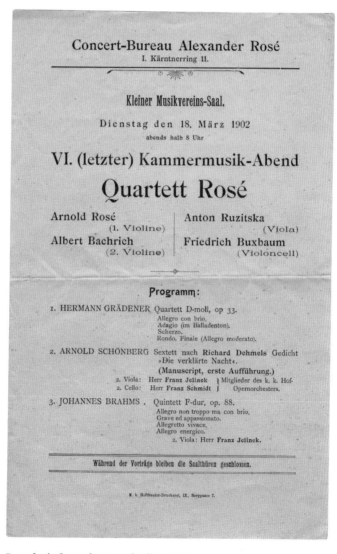

Poster for the first performance of *Verklärte Nacht*, 1902.

a bit of shoehorning – or earhorning – to hear it that way, but for listeners more accustomed to Brahms than Strauss or even Wagner, it may have both assisted comprehension and offered aesthetic justification. One may follow the progress of the work according to that of Maeterlinck's poem – that is certainly how Schoenberg presented it, even in old age – but it does not really go in for the minute visual representation of Strauss, and is less overtly sectional than *Verklärte Nacht*. There is no single 'right' way to listen; for one thing, certain performances will be more attuned to certain readings than to others. Moreover, the huge number of voices, the polyphony, of the piece looks forward already to Schoenberg's twelve-note music; the counterpoint is balanced somewhere between Brahms's more classical conception of the practice, ultimately rooted in Bach and earlier music, and the more dramatic, to some less 'correct', dramatically driven practice of Wagner and Strauss. *Pelleas* suffers as much as any of Schoenberg's later music, and perhaps even more so, from performances that fail to clarify the textures and to suggest the relative hierarchy, swiftly transforming before our ears, of several instrumental lines. Yet in the hands of a master conductor – Pierre Boulez, for instance – it emerges as the masterwork that it is. Schoenberg completed the score on 28 February 1903 and sent it to Busoni, who seems to have read the score without performing it. A personal audience would have to wait; a name, if already known, had nevertheless been enhanced.

Publishing interest in Schoenberg's music ensued, both in Berlin and Vienna. In the latter case it came from a new house, Universal Edition (established in 1901), which continues to publish much of his music to this day, although the relationship as yet amounted to little more than 'interest' and, of course, copying work. Still unable to find a permanent salaried position in Berlin, Schoenberg resolved to leave and to face those who had hissed and booed the premiere of his sextet. Traditionalist–modernist battle lines had grown still sharper as the controversial, determined Wagnerian Gustav Mahler took over the direction of the Vienna Court Opera, while remaining more or less powerless over the city's Brahmsian concert life. In September, having been unable to find Strauss in time to thank him in person, and unable also to find his summer address from the porter, Schoenberg wrote a letter 'from the bottom of my heart' to the 'Honoured Court Music Director':

> So I must bid you farewell for a long period of time . . .
> For the rest of my life, I will not forget this [your help]
> and will be eternally grateful. If I ask that you retain
> favourable memories of me, I can only trust that you will
> forget the many inconveniences I have caused you.[3]

Those words would read somewhat ironically not so many years later.

In the meantime, the Schoenbergs had returned home to Vienna via Mödling, where they stayed at David Bach's parental home and, once again, summer in Payerbach. Still smarting from his rejection by Alma Schindler, who had since become Alma Mahler, Zemlinsky took an apartment for a while in the same building in the Ninth District. Although Schoenberg and Zemlinsky's idea of an independent conservatoire, not entirely dissimilar from the contemporary Secession Movement in the visual arts, ultimately came to little, some of those university students who had attended Schoenberg's classes remained loyal to him as private students. Anton Webern was among them; the younger Berg was not, although he soon joined their number. The Holy Trinity of the Second Viennese School had come into being: Arnold the Father, Alban the Son and Anton the Holy Ghost. (Igor Stravinsky in his late, serialist phase would call the last 'a perpetual Pentecost for all who believe in music'.)[4] No music teacher, not even Nadia Boulanger or Olivier Messiaen, has exerted such influence as Schoenberg. None, moreover, would inspire such loyalty, born partly of solidarity in the face of social hostility, but also out of the enormous pains Schoenberg took on behalf of his pupils. Their relationship to him verged on, sometimes went beyond, the feudal; in return, he changed their lives and the course of musical history. Berg, for instance, and to a lesser extent Webern, came to him as gifted song composers; Schoenberg insisted that they concentrate on developing their instrumental composition. After all, he had had to learn everything the hard way, with a little help from Zemlinsky. They would be given a thoroughly traditional instruction, something he would insist on throughout his life, both in his classes and in his educational writings; they learned not primarily from his music, but from that of his revered predecessors, from Bach to Mahler.

Schoenberg, Webern and Berg, three of the five canonical pillars of classic historical early twentieth-century modernism (Stravinsky and Bela Bartók being the others), were now gathered in Vienna. The 'school' – known at the time as the School of Schoenberg – extended beyond their number, taking in musicians such as Egon Wellesz, Erwin Stein and Heinrich Jalowetz. One might even include, at a certain remove and from an earlier generation, Mahler too; he frankly owned that he did not necessarily understand Schoenberg's music, yet he proved a tireless supporter, as devoted as Schoenberg – previously sceptical and even hostile – proved to be towards Mahler's music. The turning point for Schoenberg came with the dress rehearsal on 12 December 1904 for the first Viennese performance of Mahler's Third Symphony. After that, Schoenberg wrote his first letter to Mahler, who certainly knew what it was to be treated badly by Vienna. Three years later Mahler would know even more, after being forced to relinquish his position following a campaign of anti-Semitism and anti-modernism that was virulent even by Viennese standards. The young Adolf Hitler, intriguingly, took Mahler's side in the great controversy in which, as ever, the two tendencies over Wagner performance and staging could never quite be disentangled. 'Honoured Herr Direktor,' Schoenberg wrote to Mahler, in 1904:

> In order to come close, even remotely so, to the unheard-of impression your symphony had upon me, I cannot speak to you as musician to musician, but must rather speak to you as one human being to another. For: I have seen your soul naked, stark naked. It lay before me, like a wild, mysterious landscape, with blood-curdling depths and ravines, and next, bright, comely, sunny meadows and idyllic places of repose.

Schoenberg confessed that he had not found the symphony's programme, which he had read only after the performance, remotely in correspondence with his own experience. Instead, he had felt 'the pain of one disillusioned . . . *truth*, the most relentless truth!' Signing off apologetically and perhaps unnecessarily, he owned that he could have done nothing other than rave; 'I do not have average feelings, but either – or!'[5] For what it is worth, Schoenberg's substitute 'programme' comes closer, perhaps, to my own experience of the work. In any case, Mahler, as was his wont, soon discarded his verbal scaffolding, unwilling to command such particularity of response as would be suggested, even demanded, by programmatic explanation.

Greatly touched by the response of a young composer in whom he had already taken an interest from afar, Mahler offered Schoenberg a ticket for the premiere itself, the following day.[6] Mahler would assist Schoenberg, financially and otherwise, until the former's death in 1911, and even then he worried how the younger, still prouder composer might survive without him. Alma's early dislike of what she had found to be a painfully assumed air of the *vie de Bohème* – what little she knew of his struggles – exerted little influence over her husband, even when he found himself exasperated by a certain arrogance from 'that conceited puppy', as he once described his young colleague to her. Indeed, reading between Alma's lines, there seems to have been a certain staginess to Mahler's and Schoenberg's disagreements and brief fallings out – somewhat to the embarrassment of poor Zemlinsky, who would be caught in between. Alma's testimony and judgement, though not always reliable, seems in the case of Mahler and Schoenberg to be astute. Moreover, she owned that, knowing what she later discovered concerning the difficulties and deprivations in Schoenberg's life, she would have listened more sympathetically to his 'violent' conversational 'paradoxes'.[7] It may be a cliché to speak of a father figure, but Mahler genuinely seems to have become one for Schoenberg; it is no coincidence that, when the younger man turned his hand to painting in 1907 (of which more anon), one of his first portraits was of Mahler; a little later one of his finest non-portraits would be of Mahler's funeral, the bells of which are also unforgettably evoked in the sixth of the *Six Little Piano Pieces*, op. 19.

Let us not get ahead of ourselves, though. Mahler's patronage certainly helped in the intervening years. When, in March 1904, Schoenberg, Zemlinsky and the conductor-composer Oskar Posa founded a Society of Creative Musicians (Vereinigung schaffender Tonkünstler), Mahler was persuaded – in part by a request from Webern's doctoral supervisor, the musicologist Guido Adler – to act as its honorary president and principal conductor. Intended explicitly to give voice to 'contemporary music', the society offered, during its brief lifetime, the Vienna premiere of Mahler's own *Kindertotenlieder* (Songs on the Death of Children) and Strauss's *Sinfonia domestica* (Domestic Symphony), among various works by composers of whom we now know little or nothing; such is the often harsh way of new music. In its final concert, on 25 January 1905, each of the three founding members conducted a premiere of his own: Zemlinsky his 'fantasy for orchestra', *Die Seejungfrau* (The Mermaid), Posa his five songs for baritone and orchestra; and, in the second half, Schoenberg at last his *Pelleas*. The audience did not on the whole react kindly, but the piece certainly made a splash. It may or may not be irrelevant to point out here that Schoenberg does not seem to have been a particularly good conductor. Who knows what might have been had Mahler or Zemlinsky conducted? Perhaps nothing different, for Zemlinsky declined to have his symphonic poem published. Yet although Schoenberg would necessarily continue to conduct from time to time, he recognized that his real genius, other than for composing, lay in teaching. In any case, as he recalled late in life, 'reviews were unusually violent and one of the critics suggested to put me in an asylum and keep music paper out of my reach.'[8]

Paul Stauber, critic for the *Montagspresse*, might initially seem moderate by comparison, complaining only of 'an insignificant worm-like motif', a typically anti-Semitic trope that should nevertheless have set alarm bells ringing, and 'deafening noise'. He even admitted: 'Although it is madness, it still has its methods.' (Ah, those clever Jews and their methods . . .) Not for long, though: 'It is not music at all, but an assassination of sound, a crime against nature, doubly damnable because the "composer" does not merely upset old notions but also wants to renounce the natural path of musical development.'[9] The word 'natural' – that old chestnut – was often used to suggest that there was something sick or degenerate about Schoenberg's music. Bear in mind that, although *Pelleas* is a lengthy, somewhat involved work – especially, as noted, in inadequate performance – it is still resolutely tonal. The difficulties listeners had and continue to have with Schoenberg's music are not entirely or even principally concerned with his break with tonality, or his adoption of the twelve-note method; they are at least as much a matter of density of musical argument, a superfluity of musical expression and expressiveness, rather than its caricatured absence. Notwithstanding any claims of a 'natural path of musical development', Schoenberg's path had been emphatically traditional to date.

A vitriolic opponent of Mahler too, Stauber would later play a significant role not only in print but in the audience pandemonium that greeted the first performance of the Second String Quartet in 1908. In the meantime, Schoenberg had much music to be written, a good deal of it never completed. The music that was completed and published includes three sets of songs: op. 3 (begun in Berlin, finished in Vienna), with the composition of opuses 6 and 8 following between 1903 and 1905. The first two sets are for voice and piano; op. 8 pits dramatic, unabashedly Wagnerian soprano and large orchestra against one another. In the Orchestral Songs, Wagner's influence continued to be felt, and *Götterdämmerung* again loomed large; they call, ideally, for a Brünhilde. It is surely only that and, again, the size of the orchestra that militates against these settings being heard more often, which range from folklore (*Des Knaben Wunderhorn*, or *The Boy's Magic Horn*) to Petrarch. They would have to wait until 1913 for publication and 1914 for a first performance, under Zemlinsky in Prague; even then, only three out of the six were heard. The composition of Schoenberg's official 'First' Quartet, in his 'special' key of D minor, was accomplished more or less in parallel (1904–5); here, his tightness of motivic integration, heard also in the op. 6 songs, reaches a level at least equal to that of Brahms in his own notoriously truculent First Quartet. Schoenberg's Quartet, though, is surely the more idiomatically composed and less forbidding of the two; it is easier in the construction and course of its melodic lines (those surprising, even stylized *Jugendstil* turns notwithstanding), and more at home in its skin, less rebarbative. There was also a second child to be born, after a rocky year or so partly on account of financial difficulties: Georg, in September 1906.

Earlier in 1906 Schoenberg composed his First Chamber Symphony, op. 9, one of his sunniest, most life-affirming works – and one of his very greatest, not just from his tonal period, but in the entirety of his oeuvre. We hear in this work a perfect instance of that integrative process prefigured in the First Quartet, with historical roots, as Schoenberg was well aware, that lay in such works as Schubert's *Wanderer Fantasy* and, still more, in Franz Liszt's Piano Sonata in B minor. It follows Liszt's example in the radical fusion of a traditional multi-movement sonata or symphony structure – 'sonata Allegro' first movement-scherzo-slow movement-finale – into the traditional structure of a single sonata-form movement: exposition-development-recapitulation. Put another way, it is four-in-one, and a good deal of the musical interest and tension lies in the relationship between the four and the one. As important as such formal considerations, which undoubtedly help to account for its exhilarating concision – it is one hell of a ride with a great conductor's hands on the reins – are instrumentation and harmony. For it is, prophetically, a *chamber* symphony, for fifteen solo instruments, marking a significant shift from the string-saturated or at least string-founded textures of both the Brahms symphony and the Strauss tone poem (and behind that, Wagner).

At the same time, once again, developing variation – which Schoenberg avowedly derived from Brahms – and an almost-yet-not-quite Expressionist tinge on Strauss's harmonies contribute to the historical and formal struggle. The opening horn calls signal the possibility of constructing harmonies on the interval of a fourth, as opposed to the conventional major or minor; this is present in late Liszt in his Mephistophelian guise, but perhaps more commonly associated with considerably later experiments by Bartók. In an article in the *Encyclopaedia Britannica* on harmony, the British musicologist Donald Francis Tovey, who was far from unsympathetic to all manifestations of musical modernism, would condemn such 'piling up of fourths' for having 'no origin in classical harmony'.[10] That perhaps sits a little oddly with Tovey's admiration for Paul Hindemith, but we all have our inconsistencies. Schoenberg rightly contended that, for now, it was more urgent to perform than to defend new music; theoretical justification would follow – and it did. All that, and more, in twenty minutes, means that one hears the work afresh every time, just as one would with a choice example from the 'Father of the Symphony', Joseph Haydn. The Austro-German tradition here finds new life in self-renewal – without ever veering towards the formalism of neoclassicism.

Two Ballads, published somewhat later as Schoenberg's op. 12, were composed in early 1907 to contemporary verse for a competition announced by a Berlin publishing house. Neither Schoenberg nor Zemlinsky, who also entered, won. The first song in particular fascinates, and not only on account of its subject matter. It is a setting of Heinrich Ammann's poem 'Jane Grey' and ambiguously makes its way from D minor, always a special key for Schoenberg, to a key that perhaps lies a little beyond mere major or minor without yet having become something else. Metrical contrasts and developing variation protect against the monotony that can sometimes prevail in ballad setting – and which may be perceived in a slightly later setting from 1911, as resolutely strophic as it is resolutely tonal, of the same song by the Norwegian composer Christian Sinding.

In the progressive weakening of certain tonal functions, Schoenberg later described both songs as having marked 'the transition to my second period'. Narrative drama, at least as much musical as verbal, may straightforwardly be experienced in itself, regardless of musico-historical connotation. These ballads are important and all-too-neglected contributions to a genre in which both Schubert and Robert Schumann had excelled. Two further songs, set in 1907 and 1908 and later published as Schoenberg's op. 14, edge still closer. However, even when apparently floating away from conventional tonal procedures, any suspension of traditional gravitational forces is at most temporary. There may well be other planets, but we cannot quite hear their music yet, let alone breathe their air. Even if the teleology of our story is mostly retrospective – and any good teleology is – it remains as irresistible as Schoenberg himself seems, retrospectively or otherwise, to have found it.

In 1906 Schoenberg had also begun to paint, taking lessons from his friend the art student Richard Gerstl, whom he had first met when Gerstl had requested to paint his portrait. This, it is worth reiterating, was the Vienna of the Secession Movement, and of Sigmund Freud. Berlin, too, had had its own Secession and a similarly public debate concerning official art and degeneracy, which is also likely to have made a mark on Schoenberg. Without drawing too ready lines between separate, or at least not coterminous, movements, an air of rebellion, even revolution, against artistic fathers was stronger than usual. It will of course always be present to a certain extent, at least in the Western tradition, especially since the seventeenth-century quarrel of the Ancients and Moderns had been resolved to the satisfaction of the latter. A highly public confrontation between new, 'modern' art and that of the old academies had become part of a broader public discourse since the later nineteenth century. Nowhere was that symbolized more clearly than in the Vienna Secession Building itself, a confrontational temple of art – one critic scorned it as 'the Assyrian convenience', another 'the golden cabbage' – that still comes as quite a jolt to the eye today.[11] The writer Hermann Bahr, an enthusiastic propagandist for the avant-garde, observed:

If, these days, you pass by the river Wien in the early morning . . . you can see, behind the Academy, a crowd of people standing around a new building. They are office people, workmen, women who should be on their way to work, but instead stop in amazement, unable to tear themselves away. They stare, they interrogate each other, they discuss this 'thing'. They think it strange, they have never seen anything of this kind, they do not like it, it repels them. Filled with serious reflections, they pass on their way, and then turn round yet again, cast another look backwards, do not want to depart, hesitate to hurry off about their business. And this goes on the whole day.[12]

Repel them as it might, they were not indifferent; they did not disengage. In that, they were like – indeed, they might even have been the same people as – those in Schoenberg's audiences who shouted, protested, jangled their keys. Their aesthetic, for they often certainly had one, stood closer to that of the other emperor, in Berlin: William II. In a speech of 1901, given on the Siegesallee to celebrate the completion of its double row of 'official' monuments of rulers and soldiers, he declared:

> Art should contribute to the education of the people. Even the lower classes, after their toil and hard work, should be lifted up and inspired by ideal forces. We Germans have permanently acquired these great ideals, while other peoples have more or less lost them. Only the Germans remain, and are above all others called upon to guard these great ideals, to nurture and to perpetuate them, and it is part of these ideals to enable the working and toiling classes, too, to become inspired by the beautiful, and to help them liberate themselves from the constraints of their ordinary thoughts and attitudes.
>
> But when art, as often happens today, shows us only misery, and shows it to us even uglier than misery is anyway, then art commits a sin against the German people. The supreme task of our cultural effort is to foster our ideals. If we are and want to remain a model for other nations, our entire people must share in this effort, and if culture is to fulfil its task completely, it must reach down to the lowest levels of the population. That can be done only if art holds out its hand to raise the people up, instead of descending into the gutter.[13]

The term 'gutter art' was derived from this speech and became a persistent conservative and nationalist refrain in discussion of modern German, including Austrian, art. Such anti-modernist rhetoric was also very much the stuff of Max Nordau's influential book entitled simply *Entartung* (Degeneration, 1892). The 'gutter art' of Schoenberg, Mahler and many others was viewed as 'unhealthy', 'decadent', 'degenerate', 'immoral', 'foreign' and, of course, 'Jewish'. As the notoriously anti-Semitic Christian Socialist Mayor of Vienna Karl Lueger put it, he decided who was a Jew. And if Strauss's *Salome* only just escaped William II's prohibition – the problem more its 'decadent' subject matter than its relatively 'advanced' musical material and language – the Kaiser's opera- and concert-going followers would deliver their own verdicts on successor works in no uncertain terms.

Revolutions devour their fathers, just as their sons tend to exaggerate their difference from them. Gerstl was not really a Secessionist; he was more a secessionist from Secessionism. He was seemingly more interested in contemporary music than in much other contemporary visual art, and that was why he had approached Schoenberg in the first place. The two men, in music and in painting, were tiring of the stylization of what they saw and heard around them. Gustav Klimt, for instance, had already begun his retreat from the public engagement and violent controversy seen in his commissions from the University of Vienna, and was turning instead increasingly to the world of private portraiture. Younger artists – especially those associated, as Schoenberg increasingly would be, both personally and aesthetically, with his exact contemporary the biting satirist Karl Kraus, and with the architect Adolf Loos ('Ornament is a crime!') – rejected what they saw as Romanticism lingering under another name.[14] That went, or soon would, for Richard Strauss as much as Arthur Schnitzler, Gustav Klimt as much as Stefan Zweig – and in both directions. The new establishment fathers increasingly did not care much for their angry sons either.

Gerstl and Schoenberg painted portraits too, but of a kind that it is hardly exaggerated to call Expressionist. Harsher, still less stylized than Gerstl's, Schoenberg's paintings were often self-portraits, intensely preoccupied with the subject's gaze, and were greatly admired by artists such as Wassily Kandinsky, Franz Marc and Oskar Kokoschka. Kandinsky had Schoenberg contribute to his *Blaue Reiter* almanac: both an essay, 'The Relationship [of Music] to the Text' (1912), and a facsimile edition of his Maeterlinck song *Herzgewächse* (Heart's Foliage, 1911), op. 20, for high (eventually stratospheric, fiendishly difficult at ultra-*pianissimo pppp*) coloratura soprano, harp, celesta and harmonium. There Wagner's Kundry seems to meet Melisande, approaching the range, if hardly the sensibility, of Mozart's Queen of the Night; the instrumental 'foliage' somehow seems to engage in a process of continuous refraction of darkened aural *Jugendstil* patterns. It is a painterly musical work, even by Schoenberg's standards of this time.

Moreover, Kandinsky admired Schoenberg's ability, specifically as a painter, to record what he called a 'subjective impression'. For, as Schoenberg wrote to his new friend and colleague, 'Art' – and here he makes no distinction between painting and music – 'belongs to the *unconscious*! One must express *oneself*! Express oneself *unmediated*!'[15] The distinction Kandinsky outlined, between paintings 'which are drawn perfectly true to nature, such as people or landscapes, and those which are intuitively conceived heads, which he calls "Visions"', has persisted in their discussion. The first were 'necessary finger-exercises', an interesting musical comparison and again Schoenberg's own; the second were painted 'in order to allow those stirrings of his soul, which cannot find any musical form, to come to expression'. 'Just as with his music, (inasmuch as I, a layman, may affirm), Schoenberg also in his painting renounced the superfluous,' Kandinsky continued admiringly, even going so far as to call Schoenberg's art 'the painting of essence'.[16] Here, then, was a meeting of minds, and likewise, as they would have put it, of souls. Even after 1911, when Schoenberg's painting days were for the most part behind him, that talent would be put to good use in his concepts and drafts for stage designs.

We shall hear more of Kandinsky and the Expressionist Schoenberg later. For the moment, however, we must return to Gerstl. Mathilde became his pupil too, and his model. She also became his lover – at the latest, by the time of a joint holiday at Gmunden on the Traunsee, in the summer of 1907. The Schoenbergs' marriage had already become unhappy once again, as Schoenberg was dejected by Mahler's enforced departure to conduct the New York Philharmonic and his own consequent lack of an influential supporter in what was an ever more hostile artistic environment. When he discovered the affair, Schoenberg insisted that Mathilde and the younger man (by nine years) no longer have any contact. As if locked into a dance of death, though, Gerstl found a studio in the same building as the Schoenbergs, Zemlinsky and *his* already unhappy wife, Liechtensteinstrasse 68–70, about two minutes' walk from the house on a parallel street in which Schubert had been born. Unsurprisingly – although seemingly so to Schoenberg – Mathilde started to model for Gerstl again: their encounters were not, initially, any more than that. Schoenberg valued Gerstl's companionship and instruction, and that seems to have overridden what would surely have been most husbands' misgivings.

There seems, again surprisingly, to have been a degree of normalization of relations, such that the Schoenbergs and Gerstl in 1908 again took a summer holiday in Gmunden, with Zemlinsky and his wife coming along for good measure. The drama, alas, more or less writes itself, or is dictated by some fatal unconscious. Mathilde and Gerstl had resumed their affair; Schoenberg once again discovered the fact. In a dramatic alteration of events to this apparent textbook recapitulation, the lovers fled, first to a pension in Gmunden, then the following night to another such establishment in the Viennese suburb of Nussdorf. Trudi and Georg remained with their distraught father as Mathilde, who may have been suffering from depression, initially refused to return. Eventually Webern persuaded her to come back, if only, as the cliché has it, for the sake of the children. Even after that, Mathilde would visit Gerstl at the new studio he had rented, on the very same road as the Schoenbergs: Liechtensteinstrasse 20. Webern, again, eventually persuaded her to desist. On 4 November 1908, now ostracized by Viennese artists of almost every persuasion, the 25-year-old painter burned his recent correspondence and a number of his pictures, took off his clothes and hanged himself in front of the mirror he had used to paint himself. This was the Death of an Artist.

In an extraordinary fragment of a last will and testament that Schoenberg wrote in the wake of that death, he made it clear that Gerstl's might possibly not be the only death on the dramatic agenda:

> My energy gone and my impulse to life having reached
> its end, it is very likely that I shall soon follow the path,
> find the resolution, that at long last might be the best
> coronation of human deeds . . . Whether it be my body that
> will give out or my soul – I feel no difference, but I sense
> the division . . . I deny facts. All, without exception.

The Mathilde who had done that to him was 'not my wife', for his wife could 'only be faithful'. What had happened had not happened 'to me, but to some kind of monstrosity from a woman's fantasy. It was the man she saw in me that my wife lied to and betrayed . . . This scumbag was not me. No, no, and a thousand times no.'[17] It is at first sight a strange, self-loathing dualism, perhaps more readily the concept for an artwork than a diagnosis, but its drafting seems to have helped, and perhaps – for one now so concerned with expression of the unconscious – it was not so strange after all.

The real Schoenberg, however, the one who had to live in this world, breathe the air of this planet, had lost a friend; his friendship with Zemlinsky also suffered. The Schoenbergs understandably left that building on the Liechtensteinstrasse. Almost immediately, Schoenberg began sketching the scenario for an opera, *Die glückliche Hand* (The Fortunate Hand, 1910–13), which would unquestionably draw on his experience of the Gerstl affair. That, however, lies properly in the following chapter. In the meantime, we must attend to the small matter of Schoenberg's break with tonality.

In the wake of the astonishingly complete success of the First Chamber Symphony, Schoenberg had begun work on a Second. He left it unfinished for many years, unsure where some inner, even historical, imperative of his music was taking him, and concluded it with considerable difficulty only in 1939. He reached some degree of musical peace with the composition of the treacherously difficult – to sing, that is, rather than to listen to – *a cappella* chorus (ideally *a cappella*, although he sanctioned instrumental accompaniment when necessary) *Friede auf Erden* (Peace on Earth, 1907), op. 13. Schoenberg seems to have thought of this work as embodying the peace the world so desperately needed yet would apparently never attain: the peace, one might say, that passes all understanding, fittingly enough for a setting of the angels' message to the shepherds on the hills outside Bethlehem. He then immediately resolved, apparently on the day he finished the chorus, to return to his favoured medium of the string quartet, beginning work in March 1907. Again experiencing difficulties in determining its musical course, he would not complete the Second String Quartet, op. 10, dedicated 'to my wife', until that summer holiday of 1908.

The return to a distinct four-movement structure might seem 'regressive', although only to those with the most naively teleological view of the workings of musical – or any other – history. We have an almost classical first movement in sonata form, followed by a scherzo and a set of variations on a theme.

From left to right, back row: Schoenberg's pupil Heinrich Jalowetz, Zemlinsky, Helene Berg, Mathilde, Karl Horwitz (also a Schoenberg pupil), Schoenberg; in front, the two Schoenberg children, Trudi and Georg. Photograph by Alban Berg, in front of the Schoenbergs' apartment, Hietzinger Hauptstrasse 113, *c.* 1910–11.

That would be one way to describe the first three movements, yet it would miss a great deal. Although the first movement eventually returns to where it 'should' in terms of tonality, it does not do so quite *when* it should. There is, moreover, a good deal of motivic interrelation between the movements, and continuation of that Lisztian insistence on transformation of themes into others that are on the surface highly contrasted. Kraus-like irony manifests itself in the second movement, where the second violin's singing of a line from the Viennese popular song 'Ach du lieber Augustin' is suggestive of something afoot: 'It's all over, it's all over.' The Prater was never very far away in Schoenberg's music. Is there perhaps a thought of Papageno's ineffably moving consideration of suicide, also delivered in Viennese dialect, from Mozart's *Magic Flute*? Ghosts of Vienna past are at any rate never banished. Those inclined to musical deciphering may discover – and have – the encoded names of Schoenberg, Arnold, Mathilde, Richard and Gerstl at just this point. That is hardly a coincidence, although it is perhaps more a matter of enabling the composer to construct, even to prepare for deconstruction, than a key to 'meaning'. As we have seen, the relationship between the demands of external 'programmes' and musical form (or detail) is never straightforward in Schoenberg's music.

What is 'all over', or about to be, is tonality itself, the fundamental principle guiding Western harmony for three centuries. One can hedge that with qualifications, and should. After all, it was not 'all over' for many composers; for some it never would be. Liszt, for one, had arguably gone there many years before, as in his *Bagatelle sans tonalité* (1885) for piano, fulfilling the culturally pessimistic prediction of the musical theorist François-Joseph Fétis. Even Schoenberg would return to the old hierarchies, at times, whether in order to complete works such as the Second Chamber Symphony, or to write 'occasional' pieces, testifying to the truth that, as he would tell his UCLA advanced composition class in 1940, there 'is still plenty of good music to be written in C major'.[18] He never discouraged others from writing tonally, and indeed saw no reason to do so. Moreover, he would insist that what he accomplished or, perhaps better, dramatized, here was no more or no less important than any other step in musical history. And yet . . .

First comes the surprise, unprecedented in the string quartet, although not in the symphony, of a soprano entering the fray, intoning against those instrumental variations the words of Stefan George's 'Litanei' (Litany). There is indeed something almost liturgical to the preparations for the finale, in which the same poet's 'Entrückung' (Rapture) is set.[19] Not unlike Beethoven's Ninth Symphony, the finale initially expresses its 'meaning' without words; unlike Beethoven's work, however, such meaning is not a reprise of earlier, unsatisfactory attempts at resolution. Instead, emboldened strings take their exploratory leave from conventional

Page from manuscript of the Second String Quartet, showing the soprano entry, 'I feel the air of another planet', and Schoenberg's revision (eliminating, in red, a preceding bar) to the instrumental preparation for that moment.

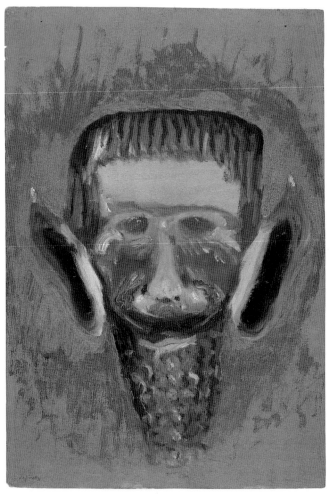

Painting of a critic, *c.* 1909–10. Severine Neff has identified elements of the physiognomy of the hostile critics Ludwig Karpath and Hans Leibstöckl. This caricature is at any rate no unambiguous study in benevolence.

tonal moorings, prefiguring and enabling the verbal explanation: 'Ich fühle luft von anderem planeten' (I feel the air of another planet). Gravity, tonal or planetary, loses its pull as Schoenberg moves towards his own Isolde-like *Verklärung*, or transfiguration: 'I lose myself in tones, circling, weaving . . . I feel I am above the last cloud.' The final 'resolution', such as it is – returning to a chord of F-sharp minor, in which key the quartet had opened – is surprising, even 'unnatural'. The tonal tables have been turned forever. The first performance, in December 1908, incited uproar that, according to Schoenberg, 'surpassed every previous and subsequent happening of this kind'; laughter erupted during the scherzo and continued throughout the third movement and much of the fourth. It nevertheless seems that the instrumental coda, floating freely into the musical ether until that problematical final chord, 'was accepted without any audience disturbance. Perhaps even my enemies and adversaries might have felt something here?'[20] Perhaps.

3

Air of Another Planet

If anything, 1909 proved a still more decisive year for Schoenberg. It is certainly to be classified as his compositional *Wunderjahr* (miracle year), akin to those of Schubert in 1815 and Schumann in 1840. The journey taken in the Second String Quartet seems to have emboldened him to trust the evidence of his inner ear, to compose, as he wished, according to the demands of his unconscious. Music poured forth in a number of works that have come to be known, rightly or wrongly, as 'freely atonal' (Schoenberg disliked the term): no longer really reliant upon the crutch of a tonal centre, but without yet straining towards the organizational demands of his later twelve-note method. If Strauss, ever eager to play the philistine all the more to treasure his art, claimed that his own ultimate desire was to compose as a cow gave its milk, Schoenberg seemed perhaps to be doing so. If so, this was a cow that never strayed – with apologies for the sub-Surrealist image – far from the Freudian couch.

New forms – hyper-Romantic in that they existed or came to being, only in a state of permanent flux, dynamically annihilated almost before that coming into being, and certainly before they could qualify as 'structures' – seemed at last to fulfil Liszt's nineteenth-century avant-gardist desire to create 'new wine for new bottles'. For, on Liszt's centenary in 1911, and clearly thinking of himself, too, Schoenberg would declare:

Liszt's importance lies in the one place where great men's importance can lie: in faith. Fanatical faith, of the kind that creates a radical distinction between normal men and those it impels. Normal men *possess* a conviction; the great man is *possessed* by a faith.[1]

Possessed, one might also add, at this time by a compulsion to compose. Resistance was futile, it seemed, and if ignorant critics and much of the public did not understand, they would eventually. It was certainly not that Schoenberg no longer cared about the attacks, but they did not prevent him from what he was frank in considering a calling, a 'mission'. Whether he were down in William II's 'gutter' or floating in the uncharted, perhaps uncharitable territory above Stefan George's 'last cloud', Schoenberg was clearly somewhere else and unable or unwilling to conceive of being otherwise.

That year brought forth the *Three Piano Pieces*, op. 11; the George song cycle *The Book of the Hanging Gardens*, op. 15; the *Five Orchestral Pieces*, op. 16; and Schoenberg's first completed opera (there are a number of earlier fragments), *Erwartung*, op. 17. The *Piano Pieces*, Schoenberg's first published solo work for an instrument that had never been 'his', retains some of its inheritance from the writing, if not really the spirit, of Brahms's late works. So too would all Schoenberg's piano music, solo or otherwise. The ghost of D minor – very much his key, as we have seen – haunts the rumbling ostinato of the second; but a ghost it is, and it is felt as such, suspended and, in the shocking violence of its successor piece, subsequently flayed alive. The second fascinated Busoni so much that he wrote a 'concert interpretation' of it, an intriguing document that nevertheless tells us more about Busoni than it does about Schoenberg; the 'interpretation' is arguably more idiomatic in purely pianistic terms, yet ultimately more pallid. In a laudable attempt, however misguided, to clarify textures that can readily sound muddy, it seems to attempt the prettification of something that should not be, cannot be, prettified. Busoni did not respond nearly so favourably to the third of the *Piano Pieces*, which Schoenberg considered the most advanced. Nevertheless, the two parties had begun one of the most illuminating correspondences in the history of twentieth-century music. Schoenberg studied intently Busoni's radical *Sketch for a New Aesthetic of Music*, which was published that year; his marginal annotations – some of them verging on essays in themselves – are not the least of our sources for understanding the development of his ideas, if, that is, one can read the script of the author, who seems to have written while breathing the air of another planet. In his piano pieces, he told Busoni, he strove

> for: complete liberation from all forms
> from all symbols
> of cohesion and
> of logic.
>> Thus:
> away with 'motivic working out'.
> Away with harmony as
> cement or building bricks.
> Harmony is *expression*
> And nothing else.
>> Then:
> Away with pathos![2]

To ask whether that be 'Romanticism' or 'modernism' is beside the point; the one flows freely from the other, even as it attempts and at least partially succeeds to liberate itself from that other.

The Book of the Hanging Gardens takes a similar transformative path to the op. 11 *Pieces*, indeed to the Second String Quartet too. In a programme note of the following year, Schoenberg wrote that in this song cycle he had 'for the first time succeeded in approaching an ideal of expression and form that I have had in mind for years'. He went on to say, pessimistically, that necessary though he considered this development, he feared that 'even those who have believed in me until now' would not want to accept that necessity.[3] The miniaturistic style, form and idea of George's fifteen poems seem especially suited to Schoenberg's desire not only to construct something greater than the sum of its parts, but to have that path burn itself out through the course of work and performance. There remains in many of the songs a strong tonal pull, but it would be exaggerated to consider them as 'tonal' as such, especially in the light of what any other composer was writing at the time (which is, of course, how the work would have been heard, if at all).

As the progress, or rather dissolution, of a love affair is constructed – more than merely narrated – through words and music, the garden 'setting' is transformed, both verbally and musically, before our ears. It is as much a character as the narrator in this reversal of the trajectory to the redemptive tale of *Verklärte Nacht*. Fragmentation and alienation are now, at least in part, our lot, whether we like it or not. The weight of the great German *Lieder* tradition, collapsing and corroding before our ears, continues to inspire. Romantic song is *aufgehoben*, to use Hegel's term: negated and yet reinstated at a higher level of mediated unity. Schubertian birds ('Vögel') sing in the piano's ambiguous 'paradise' ('Hain in diesen paradiesen'). Musical structures, related to and yet independent of word and vocal line, develop as it were in miniature and yet also with an expansiveness that is both diffident and bold, from the prior explorations of the op. 11 *Pieces*. Paradoxes, or rather dialectics, abound. There are possibilities; there is freedom. The garden and its tale – or should that be the tale and its garden? – may nevertheless turn nasty, desolate, without ever rescinding their invitation to us. We remain, as in all these works, on our guard, even as we surrender.

The *Five Orchestral Pieces* display confidence in a new manner of writing for full orchestra quite extraordinary for one with relatively little experience in writing for it at all. 'Were you to see my new orchestral pieces,' Schoenberg wrote to Busoni, 'you would clearly notice how I conspicuously fend off from the full "God-and-Übermensch-sound" of the Wagnerian orchestra.' Busoni had already declared Wagner's art to be a glorious farewell, rather than a new dawn, yet, in the light of Schoenberg's other declarations – or, as he preferred, 'confessions' – of the time, this does not seem to be a case of telling his audience what it wanted to hear. Such was never really Schoenberg's style, in any case. 'How everything,' Schoenberg continued, 'becomes more delicate, thinned down. How refracted colour-tones stand in place of what had been bright and glowing.' He could also be describing his later orchestration work on *Gurrelieder*, where the distinction, or progression, is startling: 'How my whole orchestral technique takes a path which seems to lead in quite the contrary direction to anything hitherto pursued. That is, I find, the natural reaction. We have had our fill, to the point of surfeit, of Wagner's full, smooth sonorities.' Misquoting Schiller, as set by Beethoven, he declared: 'Now let us hear other tones.'[4] As always one will hear connections with what had gone before, this distillation in intensification of Mahler's (partial) conception of the orchestra as a pool from which to draw various smaller ensembles extends beyond anything previously attempted. It also extends beyond anything Mahler, still firmly supportive, was himself able to understand.

Strauss had become quite uncomprehending too, and disparaging in private, although he commendably remained far from unsupportive in practical terms. He wrote in 1913 to the now widowed Alma Mahler that only a psychiatrist could help 'poor Schoenberg'; he would be 'better off shovelling snow' than 'scribbling on manuscript paper'. Alma, never one to miss an opportunity to stir, especially when it came to Jewish 'friends' and 'colleagues', promptly informed Schoenberg. Strauss at least conceded that one never knew what history might say, and recommended him for the Mahler Foundation grant. Unsurprisingly Schoenberg never forgave him and responded in angry fashion – hardly unwarrantedly so – when he was asked in April 1914 for a fiftieth-birthday tribute: 'He is no longer of the slightest artistic interest to me, and whatever I may once have learned from him, may God be thanked, [I had] misunderstood.' Since understanding Mahler's music, he continued, he had had no need for Strauss.[5]

A new world of *Klangfarbenmelodie*, in which a melody may be constructed upon changes in colour rather than changes in pitch – as suggested in the third of the op. 16 *Pieces* – would forever remain a closed book to Strauss, and indeed to many others. One way in, however, may be to consider it not so much as sunlight glistening on the Traunsee, which he later claimed had inspired him, as the process of looking at it, perhaps even painting it. 'Gaze' and landscape combine, aurally, in a fashion that would have satisfied Kandinsky. Or, to take a more abstract line, think of it simply, or not so simply, as 'Colours': as Schoenberg, bowing to a request by Universal Edition, agreed partly to subtitle it.[6] Alternatively, one might forget about a way in and simply find oneself walking through the door. Whatever works, works. If the ghost of D minor takes yet another bow in the bass line of the second movement, an increasing number of listeners (or score-readers, for that matter) were unable or unwilling to listen. It is possible for musical analysts to discover tonal centres elsewhere, yet for many listeners, be they as emancipated as Schoenberg's dissonances or indeed fearful of such emancipation, that perhaps misses a good deal of the point. The fifth, like the final of the *Three Piano Pieces*, sounds truly open-ended; it is a rebuke to any effort, even if only conceptual, to 'resolve', and in that respect a profound inspiration for later composers such as Boulez and for many beyond him.

Schoenberg's painting *Gaze* (*Blick*), signed and dated May 1910.

That tendency may also be perceived – one can perceive so much in this work that it is impossible to know where to start or to end – in *Erwartung* ('Expectation', not to be confused with the op. 2 song of the same name). The libretto was written by a dermatologist, Marie Pappenheim. She was later better known as a librettist and an important figure in the German sexual liberation movement.

In 1928, with Wilhelm Reich, she founded the Socialist Society for Sexual Counselling and Sexual Research; she had been born, like Samuel Schönberg, in Pressburg/Bratislava. She had already had four poems published in Karl Kraus's *Die Fackel* (The Torch), under the not-very-covert pseudonym Marie Heim. Those poems all dealt with intense emotional states, often those of women, and several from the point of view of a physician assessing a patient. She was not only interested in but very well informed concerning psychiatry, including psychoanalysis. It was long thought that Schoenberg, who came to know of her via Kraus and Zemlinsky, had presented her with her subject, but her subsequent testimony contradicts that claim. 'Write what you want,' he had told her. 'I need an opera text.' It was, after all, a genre in which he had yet to shine. Pappenheim drafted the libretto in just three weeks. She had discovered the idea for it the previous year in Bad Ischl, she told the same interviewer in 1963, in her own feelings of fear and terror during a nocturnal forest walk.[7]

Pappenheim prepared a clinical understanding of the condition of hysteria as the context for the extraordinary outpouring we hear – and feel. The original psychoanalytical patient of Freud's teacher Jean-Martin Charcot, Anna O. (or Bertha Pappenheim – with delicious ambiguity, we do not know whether she was a relative) presented *the* case study for hysteria as having been caused by a traumatic and usually sexual event. Its memory was held to have been channelled into the unconscious rather than the conscious mind, and persisted in physical form through amnesia, hallucinations and disorders of vision and speech, their connection to the event quite unknown to the patient. All that is precisely what we see and hear in *Erwartung*, certainly from Pappenheim and often from Schoenberg, not least in the light of his insistence on the primacy of the unconscious and, in particular, of sensations. A letter he wrote to Busoni just before beginning work on the score is interesting for the physiological-aesthetic light it sheds:

For a human being, it is impossible to feel but one sensation at a time. One has thousands at once . . . And this variegation, this multifariousness, this illogicality which our senses demonstrate, this illogicality presented by their interactions, set forth by a soaring wave of blood, by some sense- or nerve-reaction, this I should like to have in my music.

Music should 'be an expression of feeling, as our feeling really is, which connects us with our unconscious, not a changeling born of feelings and "conscious logic"'.[8] Hence the common description – misleading, in my view – of *Erwartung* as 'athematic'. It is more the case that motifs are, as in other works of this year, yet still more so, in a constant process of change: *werden* (becoming) as opposed to *sein* (being), to adopt in somewhat materialist fashion a traditional German Romantic concept.

At any rate, impression and reality are in constant flux, in an attempt to penetrate to the workings of the unconscious itself. This 'monodrama' (for there is but a single protagonist, an unnamed 'Woman') has its character engage in imagined dialogue – or is it simply an interior monologue? – with a missing lover as she walks through the forest, both an empirically real place and the external manifestation of the forest of her mind. Upon discovering the corpse of her lover, she asks whether another woman, a rival to whom she had lost him, has done the deed, or whether she herself is guilty. Symptoms noted by Freud's mentor Josef Breuer bear an uncanny resemblance to those depicted:

It first became noticeable that she was at a loss to find words, and this difficulty gradually increased. Later she lost her command of grammar and syntax; she no longer conjugated verbs, and eventually she used only infinitives . . . and she omitted both the definite and indefinite articles.[9]

Moreover, the Woman's hallucinations strongly resemble – most likely draw on – Anna O.'s description of 'black snakes'. String glissandi and playing *sul ponticello* (on the bridge), whistling woodwind, fateful ostinato patterns (which may or may not repeat quite as they 'should'): these and many other instrumental devices weave in and out of our verbal consciousness – and unconscious. Wagner's conception of the orchestra as Greek chorus, participant and commentator – when it came to opera, no one would ever come close to Wagner as Schoenberg's model and inspiration – takes a decidedly psychoanalytical turn.

In her reminiscence, Pappenheim continued: 'He seemed to want to compose it just as "headlong fast" as I had written it.' Schoenberg certainly did, taking only a well-nigh incredible seventeen days – including a break to contact Pappenheim by post – to compose this infinitely complex yet overwhelmingly immediate work for soprano and full orchestra. It is full in a similar sense to the op. 16 *Orchestral Pieces*, and is rarely unleashed as a whole. The prescribed orchestral forces – more or less those of a typical Mahler or Strauss orchestra (insofar as 'typical' exists) – are as follows: piccolo, three flutes, three oboes, cor anglais, four clarinets, bass clarinet, three bassoons, contrabassoon, four horns, three trumpets, four trombones, tuba, harp, celesta, glockenspiel, xylophone, timpani, percussion (cymbals, bass drum, snare drum, tam-tam, rattle, triangle), at least sixteen first and at least fourteen second violins, ten to twelve violas, ten to twelve cellos, and eight to ten double basses.

'The aim,' Schoenberg would explain in 1929, 'is to represent in *slow motion* everything that occurs during a single second of maximum spiritual excitement, stretching it out to half an hour.'[10] The single event, the Woman's stumbling over the corpse of her lover, essentially expands itself, both forwards and backwards, over time – not unlike the way Schoenberg's and other composers' later

Schoenberg's sketch for *Erwartung*, scene 2, *c.* 1911, in coloured chalk, pastel and gouache.

serialism would show itself, by contrast perhaps with tonality, of endless expansion in all directions. (Such, we might note, would also prove to be Boulez's understanding of post-Schoenberg serialism; but then he, in properly Freudian fashion, would in 1952 pen the parricidal essay 'Schoenberg est mort'.) The alterations Schoenberg made to the libretto are relatively few, but their tendency is to render it less clinical, more of an Expressionist nightmare. Pappenheim's references to wine and thus to the possibility of alcoholic influence are removed. Perhaps drawing – consciously or otherwise – on his own experience, Schoenberg also made it clearer, if still not absolutely certain, that the Woman had killed her lover. The two creators, then, seem to have acted in a number of complex, sometimes complementary, sometimes even contradictory ways, as analyst and patient. Any boundaries between mundane and visionary, perhaps even between subject and object, have collapsed.

Chronologically surrounding that work but never quite capturing its blinding uniqueness of utterance, and therefore unfairly overlooked, is its 'male' equivalent, *Die glückliche Hand*, op. 18 – usually translated as 'The Fortunate Hand', but 'The Fatal Hand' would perhaps be better. It is written for a baritone protagonist, a small chorus of a dozen solo voices, two silent actors (male and female) and, once again, a large orchestra. 'At the beginning,' Schoenberg would explain in a programme note, 'you see twelve specks of light coming from the black background: the faces of six women and six men. Or rather, *their gazes*'; that painterly preoccupation once again.[11] Schoenberg had begun initial musical sketches in the wake of the Gerstl affair, but he returned to the idea after *Erwartung*, this time acting as his own librettist, publishing the verbal text first as a purely literary work in 1911. A man loses his wife to another man; she returns, as does his happiness. She leaves him again and scorns his plea to return, and the drama and anticipated scenic realization prove despairingly cyclical, the counterpart to Schoenberg's testament.[12] The composition of this one-act opera, which is considerably shorter than *Erwartung*, nevertheless took several years, from 1910 to 1913. In a sense, normal service – although what could ever be normal with Schoenberg? – was beginning to resume. In his excellent book on the composer, Malcolm MacDonald put it thus: 'By its very nature . . . it [*Erwartung*] was an unrepeatable success. That kind of inspirational frenzy takes hold of an artist at most once or twice in a lifetime. The *conscious* impossibility of developing large-scale forms without constraints remained.'[13] That perhaps pertained still more for works without words, which will always, at least to a certain extent – Schoenberg said wildly differing things on this subject – help to shape the musical form. It is perhaps no coincidence that the composer's completed output, such as it was, over the next decade would more often than not continue to be vocal, in one sense or another.

Nevertheless, if less easily composed, *Die glückliche Hand* proved innovative, as much for Schoenberg's intense preoccupation with visual colour, especially stage lighting, as an integral part of the drama, even of its psychology. Kandinsky was experimenting with similar ideas at the same time, for instance in his 'stage composition' *Der gelbe Klang* (The Yellow Sound) of 1909. Schoenberg writes of 'the *crescendo of the light, of the storm, and of the Man's acting*'. *Klangfarbenmelodie* is, in a sense, extended to staging; perhaps it even becomes, more generally, *Klangfarbenmusik*: 'It must be evident that *gestures*, *colours*, and *light* are treated similarly here as pitches would normally be.' It is a vision, notwithstanding Schoenberg's approval of stagings in Vienna (1924) and Breslau (1928), that has failed to find many followers, although Schoenberg's son-in-law, Luigi Nono, was one of them. That may be attributed, at least in part, to the tendencies – widespread among composer-librettists – to leave too little to the performers' discretion, and to Schoenberg's decision, whatever his claims, often to have different forms of action simply mirror one another: 'Just as the gazes, rigid and fixed, are directed at the Man, so the ostinato in the music illustrates that these gazes form an ostinato on their part.'[14] Such an approach might have worked well, however, in the filmed version he longed for as early as 1913, and he considered Kandinsky, Kokoschka and Alfred Roller (Mahler's celebrated collaborator at the Court Opera) as possible designers. Whatever the truth of that,

Schoenberg's oil painting for *Die glückliche Hand*, scene 3, from 1910.

the ambition of the work as it stood remained striking. Bizarrely nightmarish Expressionism, impossible to rationalize, presenting visions such as a cat-like monster sinking its teeth into the man's neck, ought to prove attractive to directors, designers, performers and audiences alike – yet the work is rarely gifted the opportunity to be performed on stage. It is heard all too rarely in the concert hall, too.

Life went on – as Schoenberg's Piano Concerto would one day seek to point out. Somehow, he had also found time during the summer of 1909 to sketch a design for a musical notation typewriter and lodge it with the Austrian patent office. Performances of the operas had to wait, sometimes for many years. Interest from Rainer Simons, the founder of Vienna's 'other' opera company, the Volksoper, came to nothing until 1924, when *Die glückliche Hand* had its premiere there, under Zemlinsky. Unusually, Simons preferred it to *Erwartung*, the premiere of which Zemlinsky also conducted that year, in Prague. (Even after the Peace Treaties of Paris and their often calamitous rewriting of European borders,

Mitteleuropa persisted as far more than an idea; Prague, now the Czechoslovak capital, retained elements at least of its cultural relevance as a German as well as Czech city.) Earlier plans elsewhere had been thwarted, not least by the work's sheer difficulty; so much of its success lies in the performers' hands, in their ability to fuse those motivic fragments into a whole. However, the op. 11 *Piano Pieces* and *The Book of the Hanging Gardens* received first performances in a concert of Schoenberg's music in Vienna in January 1910, with extracts from *Gurrelieder* (which was still not complete; and when it was finished, its later orchestration proved radically different, being written in Schoenberg's new style).

The *Three Pieces for Chamber Orchestra*, which are fascinating perhaps in equal measure for their characteristic and uncharacteristic qualities, were composed in February 1910 but neither published nor performed during Schoenberg's lifetime. Their aphoristic quality and the radicalism of their sound are of a kind more readily associated with Webern. Lasting less than two minutes in total, they are very rarely heard now. It is almost as if Schoenberg wanted to show, if only to himself, that he could do what Webern could – and then move on to do what he actually wished to do himself. Or, alternatively, to show himself something approaching the literal musical truth of the claim he had made to Busoni – 'For a human being, it is impossible to feel but one sensation at a time. One has thousands at once' – and then, again, to move on.[15] The year 1910 also brought the publication of his *Harmonielehre*, or *Theory of Harmony*, perhaps the most celebrated harmony textbook of all, and certainly one of the most captivating reads. It is not a work for absolute beginners but nor is it abstruse. The insights it affords into the composer's mind and music, even (perhaps particularly) when speaking of his predecessors, are invaluable. He also used his gift for satire to avenge himself upon those 'theorists' who had rejected *Verklärte Nacht* on the basis of a single, allegedly non-existent chord:

Blue self-portrait by Schoenberg, signed and dated 13 February 1910.

Photograph, most likely taken by Berg, of Schoenberg at his apartment on the Hietzinger Hauptstrasse, 1911, including on the wall Schoenberg's 1910 portrait of Mahler and photographs of Mahler.

Self-portrait, walking, 1911. The painting may be understood, in one sense at least, to show Schoenberg leaving Vienna once again for Berlin.

'Inversions of ninth chords simply do not exist; hence there could be no performance either; for how can one perform something that does not exist?'[16] He proceeded to show, historically as much as theoretically, that they certainly did exist.

Schoenberg was still struggling to subsist in Vienna, despite generous assistance from Mahler and Guido Adler and an exhibition of his paintings by the bookseller Hugo Heller in October. Completion of *Gurrelieder* contributed further to the sense of that year as one of tying up loose ends, of preparation for the opening of a new chapter. Heartened by a performance of *Pelleas und Melisande* in Berlin that month that was warmly received by many – quite different from Vienna's outrage at the January concert – and having said his final farewell to Mahler in May 1911, Schoenberg elected to try his luck once again in the German capital. Webern, as was often his wont, followed his master. The welcome was not overwhelmingly warm, however. One Walter Dahms, an unlovely newspaper critic and excessively minor composer, wrote this charming public letter, which really made his name on the Berlin musical scene:

Sir!

While you were still leading your existence in Vienna, and we merely saw newspaper reports about your violations of art, you could be a matter of indifference to us. For (to be honest) what business of ours are the charlatans currently active in Vienna, the city of Haydn, Mozart and Beethoven? Vienna, where the lust for sensation is dominant, not the love of art, leaves us completely cold. Not until certain artists, lusting after sensations, tried to emerge from their obscurity by introducing your lunatic 'art' (excuse the expression!) into Berlin too, did matters become more serious. Last winter, some pianist whose name entirely escapes me played your three piano pieces, Op. 11, at the *Singakademie*. He was laughed out of court – a sign that people saw the humorous side of your attempts to bring down the final curtain on music . . . Well, we have so many jobbers and peddlers of humbug here, in all the faculties, that one more makes no difference. But now, people are taking your presence here as a cue to keep performing your 'compositions' (forgive the old-fashioned term!), and the time has come to tell you the truth . . . So, Mr Schoenberg, at some suitable opportunity, a few well-functioning house-keys, a few well-chosen missiles and a small collection (of money) to facilitate your hasty return to Vienna: with these wishes I remain . . .[17]

Poster for the world premiere of *Pierrot lunaire*, 1912.

The best response to that was to compose another masterwork, which Schoenberg promptly accomplished.

If *Erwartung*, even in its dramatic open-endedness, remains one of Schoenberg's most 'finished' works, *Pierrot lunaire*, which was both written and first performed in 1912, endures as one of his most open-ended in the apparent impossibility of 'satisfactory' performance. Several competing demands combine in what we might consider to be not only an ironic satyr-play pendant to the *Wunderjahr* of 1909, but a lodestar for the journey ahead. In March a Berlin actress, Albertine Zehme, sent Schoenberg a commission. She requested music to accompany her recitation of a text, which she enclosed: Otto Erich Hartleben's German translation of Albert Giraud's frankly bizarre verse cycle, his *Pierrot lunaire*, published in 1884.

'Melodrama' in this, rather than the more popular, sense, was new neither to Schoenberg – he had used it for the Speaker's part in *Gurrelieder* and, chorally, in *Der glückliche Hand* – nor to earlier composers; the first version of Engelbert Humperdinck's opera *Königskinder* (Royal Children) and Strauss's Tennyson setting *Enoch Arden* were two relatively recent examples, and a particularly celebrated instance on the stage was the dungeon scene in Beethoven's *Fidelio*. With *Pierrot lunaire*, though, there is not only the element of Berlin cabaret to add to the mix of time-hallowed *commedia dell'arte* and contemporary Expressionism, but Schoenberg's own, ever-controversial notion of *Sprechstimme* or *Sprechgesang* (speech-song). Much ink has been spilled on what to call it, let alone how to perform it. Strictly, Berg introduced the former term; Schoenberg – at least to begin with – used the latter. Matters are, alas, considerably more complicated than that, since Schoenberg's use changed over the course of his career. Let us leave them to one side. Whatever we choose to call it, understanding and interpreting the instruction is considerably trickier. Schoenberg calls for something between song and speech, precisely notated according to pitch, while not necessarily sounding at that pitch in practice. In his preface to the first edition, he instructs that, with notated exceptions, the melody is 'not intended for singing. The performer has the task, with good consideration of the marked pitch, to transform it into a speech melody.' One is tempted to reply: 'Yes, but . . .' It should go without saying that Schoenberg's own recording from 1940 is an important model – and indeed in many ways it is a very fine performance, but nothing can ever be the final word here. One celebrated or notorious recorded performance, by Boulez and Yvonne Minton with an instrumental ensemble including the pianist Daniel Barenboim, actually presents the work through song. According to the lights of Schoenberg and tradition, it is unquestionably wrong; and yet it works beautifully.

The element of recitation is initially the most striking one for many listeners, but there is much else of great, arguably greater, interest in *Pierrot*. The 'three times seven poems' show Schoenberg not so much retreating from the experimentalism of 1909 as moving forward to a relative classicizing of form. One should not exaggerate, though; where elements of a constructivism that goes back to Bach rear their head, as in, say, the counterpoint of 'Der Mondfleck', there remains a great deal of atonal 'freedom', not just in unfamiliar harmony but also in smaller-scale form. (The op. 19 *Six Little Piano Pieces*, in which Schoenberg is at his most aphoristic, are after all anything but classicizing: six single breaths that seem, at the time, to say all that need be said.) The 'Valse de Chopin' plays with the idea of the waltz, with reminiscences of drawing-room style, rather than reproducing it. And yet there are elements, in embryo or sometimes more than that, of the impulse to organize this dangerous post-tonal realm: an impulse or, as Schoenberg would claim, an imperative that would bear stricter fruits a decade hence. Here the number of the moment, should one seek to find it, is not twelve but seven, ironically the number of notes in the old diatonic (tonal) scale. Canon, fugato and other traditional procedures, or their echoes, abound and proliferate; however unsatisfactory the term 'athematic' might be for *Erwartung*, it would be preposterous for *Pierrot*. Developing variation never really went away; it is audible here, on the surface and in the depths, as Schoenberg magically spins his instrumental thematic thread.

The instrumental ensemble – piano, flute/piccolo, clarinets, violin/viola and cello – has proved endlessly inspiring to Schoenberg's successors, beginning perhaps with what might be considered Maurice Ravel's most radical work of all, *Trois poèmes de Stéphane Mallarmé* (which uses not quite the same forces, but very similar ones, and was unquestionably conceived as a response to Schoenberg). It would certainly come to inspire many a later new music work and ensemble; even here, it offers a seemingly endless (if far from it) variety of colouristic combinations and permutations. When, in 1967, Peter Maxwell Davies and Harrison Birtwistle founded one such group, they called it the Pierrot Players; and when, shortly afterwards, Hans Werner Henze wished to evoke a world of decadent bourgeois Expressionism in his music-theatre piece *The Tedious Way to Natascha Ungeheuer's Apartment* (1971), he too turned to the 'Pierrot ensemble'. That said, it was probably above all the element of cabaret that many in the first audiences loved, in a relatively rare popular success – 'unconditional', Webern wrote of the applause at the premiere – following no fewer than 25 rehearsals.[18] Zehme's Pierrot costume underlined the reality that this was, if not quite performance art, then certainly performers' art. The pianist was Eduard Steuermann, one of Schoenberg's most loyal pupils and the first to perform his complete oeuvre for piano; Schoenberg conducted. The work went on tour across Germany and Austria, and Schoenberg shared duties with a young Hermann Scherchen, from whom the world of New Music, indeed that of music from Bach to Nono, would hear a great deal more. With this baptism of fire, the violist Scherchen made his conducting debut.

It was at the Hamburg performance of this tour that Schoenberg first met Dehmel, who had been so significant for his earlier career, in person. A correspondence began in which Schoenberg propounded many of his increasingly syncretic, often wildly heterodox, yet always strenuously held – and preached – religious ideas. 'For a long time,' he told Dehmel in one of his letters,

I have wanted to write an oratorio with the following content: how the man of today, having passed through materialism, socialism and anarchy, and having been an atheist, has still retained a tiny remnant of the old belief (in the form of superstition), how this modern man wrestles with God (see also: Strindberg's *Jacob Wrestling*), and finally succeeds in finding God and becoming religious. Learning to pray! *Not* through action, blows of fate, still less a love-story, shall this transformation come about. Or at least these should be at most background hints, providing impetus. And above all: the mode of speech, the mode of thought, the mode of expression, should be that of modern man; the problems addressed should be those besetting us. For those who wrestle with God in the Bible also express themselves as men of their own time, speaking of their own concerns, upon their own social and intellectual level. Therefore, artistically strong though they may be, they do not lend themselves to a modern composer who observes his duty.[19]

In the wake of *Pierrot*'s success, Schoenberg had begun to dream up a plan, on such a basis, for a vast *Choral Symphony* (or oratorio) that would unite the Bible and Dehmel, Strindberg and Balzac, Rabindranath Tagore and Emanuel Swedenborg. In the context of his new style, its performing forces – at least ten, often more, of every woodwind instrument alone – would have sat rather oddly, threatening to dwarf the ambitions of Mahler and Alexander Scriabin, let alone Wagner and Strauss. What remains of that project, at least in performable terms, is the wartime fragment *Die Jakobsleiter* (Jacob's Ladder), for smaller yet still very large forces; he would write the text for it between 1915 and 1917 and compose music for it between 1917 and 1922, and again briefly in 1944. In Schoenberg's early letter to his cousin we saw his interest in the Bible as a truthful work of modernity, whatever the particular theology he might hold at any one time, and that interest would only continue to grow.

One huge, pantheistic work that did finally reach performance, though, was *Gurrelieder*, in Vienna, on 23 February 1913. It should have been – and in a sense was – one of the most glorious evenings of his life. An audience that had gathered, at least in part, to protest, to laugh, to jangle its keys, could not believe its ears, and rose to award its not-quite-prodigal son with a lengthy standing ovation. Schoenberg had been a son of Wagner all along. He was dragged unwilling from his seat and thanked the performers, led by the conductor and composer Franz Schreker. (Berg, still in Vienna, had assisted Schreker in preparing the performance.) Still

Photograph taken by Berg, following Schoenberg's Leipzig performance of *Gurrelieder* on 4 March 1914, on the Gautzsch estate of the actress Albertine Zehme (first reciter for *Pierrot lunaire*). Pictured (left to right) are Schoenberg's pupils Josef Polnauer, Eduard Steuermann, Anton Webern, and Paul Königer, Trudi Schoenberg (daughter), Marya Freund (soprano), Mathilde Schoenberg, Heinrich Jalowetz (pupil), unknown, Schoenberg, Helene Berg (Alban's wife), Emil Hertzka (publisher, Universal Edition), Edward Clark (pupil) with Georg Schoenberg on his shoulders, Albertine Zehme, Erwin Stein (pupil), unknown, Smaragda Berg (pianist, Berg's sister), and unknown (poss. Hans Nachod).

deeply affronted and wounded at his treatment by the musical establishment and audiences of Vienna, Schoenberg declined to acknowledge the Musikverein audience, keeping his back literally turned to what he now saw as the enemy.

Even if it were not a direct response, Vienna took its revenge little more than a fortnight later. In a concert conducted by Schoenberg, largely for the benefit of Webern and Berg, the protests became so loud and violent that some of the participants ended up in court. The programme of this *Skandalkonzert* was never completed; it was abandoned part of the way through two of Berg's *Altenberg-Lieder*, leaving Mahler's *Kindertotenlieder* entirely unheard, despite appeals from the podium by Berg's friend Erhard Buschbeck of the organizing Academic Society for Literature and Music in Vienna. Perhaps ironically, Schoenberg's own First Chamber Symphony and even Webern's op. 6 *Pieces for Orchestra* had been heard (sort of), as had Zemlinsky's *Maeterlinck-Lieder*. In a letter to Buschbeck outlining the ordering of the programme, Schoenberg had described Webern's work frankly as 'the bitterest pill in this concert', yet it had been swallowed.[20] The audience and many of the assembled critics had most likely always intended disruption, and were probably indifferent to quite when it took place. When, in the second of Berg's songs, the singer, Alfred Julius Boruttau, sang the words, 'Suddenly all is over', a member of the audience shouted 'Thank God!' The whole hall reacted in uproar, for and against, and soon the police intervened.

Buschbeck would be fined for assaulting a member of his audience: Oscar Straus, Schoenberg's predecessor at Berlin's Buntes Theater. Straus, now an operetta composer, testified that the punch that had floored him had been the most harmonious sound of the evening. A fellow witness, a medical doctor, testified – in a claim for the power of music that extended even beyond the wildest that Schoenberg might have made to Busoni or Kandinsky – that such music was 'enervating and injurious to the nervous system', a cause of widespread depression among the audience. Berg wrote to Schoenberg, who had dejectedly returned to Berlin, that the Musikverein ushers had attempted to evict a pupil of his, Gottfried Kassowitz, at the request of a hostile member of the audience, for having had the temerity to applaud. He continued:

Yes, that is Vienna. You were so right, dear Herr Schönberg! Your disgust toward Vienna was always right and I see – unfortunately, too late – how wrong it was of me, when

Montag, den 31. März 1913, ½8 Uhr abends
im grossen Musikvereinssaal

ORCHESTER-KONZERT

Dirigent: ARNOLD SCHÖNBERG

Orchester des Wiener Konzertvereins

Gesang: A. Boruttau, Margarete Bum, Maria Freund

1. ANTON VON WEBERN: Sechs Stücke für Orchester
   op. 4*

2. ALEXANDER VON ZEMLINSKY: Vier Orchesterlieder
   nach Gedichten von Maeterlinck
   Margarete Bum

3. ARNOLD SCHÖNBERG: Kammersymphonie op. 9 in
   einem Satz

4. ALBAN BERG: Zwei Orchesterlieder nach Ansichts-
   kartentexten von Peter Altenberg (aus einem Zyklus)
   Alfred J. Boruttau

5. GUSTAV MAHLER: Kindertotenlieder*
   Maria Freund

* Die einzelnen Teile bilden ein einheitliches Ganzes und es muss daher die
Kontinuität (auch durch Hintanhaltung von Beifallsbezeugungen u. dgl.) aufrecht
erhalten werden.

=== PREIS DES PROGRAMMES 30 HELLER ===

Poster for *Skandalkonzert*, 1913. (Webern's op. 6 is listed as op. 4; his works were
renumbered after moving to Universal Edition in 1920.)

I tried, to have you, dear Herr Schönberg, speak more mildly
of Vienna. Yes! One cannot hate this 'city of songs' enough!![21]

This 'city of songs by slain artists', as Schoenberg had called it in a
letter to Adler from Berlin the previous year, never ceased to draw
blood.[22] Schoenberg later told Scherchen he wished he had had a
revolver with him.[23]

Notoriety and indeed something rather more positive were
now spreading beyond *Mitteleuropa*. Sergei Prokofiev gave the first
performance of a Schoenberg work in Russia, offering the op. 11
Pieces in a recital in St Petersburg as early as June 1911. The twenty-
year-old *enfant terrible* met with both jeers and cheers. Stravinsky,
who would later keep his distance, found himself profoundly
impressed by *Pierrot*, which he later called 'the solar plexus as well
as the mind of early twentieth-century music'.[24] 'Stravinsky and
Diaghilev are still going on about the Austrian Schoenberg,' wrote
the painter and Ballets Russes designer Léon Bakst in 1913; 'I cannot
make head or tail [of it] . . . and even if he is a genius: who has ever
heard of the man?' Bakst had surely answered his own question
already. Sergei Diaghilev even hoped to mastermind – imagine this
follow-up to *The Rite of Spring*! – a Schoenberg–Nijinsky ballet on
the subject of Cupid and Psyche. The proposed designer, Edward
Gordon Craig, did his best to scupper that plan, favouring the
prospect of Ralph Vaughan Williams instead.[25]

Nothing resulted, in any guise, but that is not to say that
Britain showed no interest in the composer. *Five Orchestral
Pieces* was first performed, not in Vienna, not in Berlin, but in
London, in September 1912, sandwiched surprisingly between
an aria from Saint-Saëns's *Samson et Dalila* and a piano concerto
by Mendelssohn. Sir Henry Wood conducted, at one of his
Proms concerts. 'Stick to it, gentlemen,' he is said to of rallied
his orchestral troops: 'this is nothing to what you'll have to play
in twenty-five years' time.'[26] Wood then had Edward Clark,

Schoenberg's first Berlin pupil, ask Schoenberg to visit London to conduct the work, which he did in 1914. Schoenberg's performance met with a warmer, if far from unmixed, reception than Wood's had received. Schoenberg's exact contemporary Gustav Holst was in that first audience and acquired a score, and its influence is there for all to hear in *The Planets* – originally entitled *Seven Pieces for Large Orchestra*. Schoenberg proudly wrote to Zemlinsky in 1915: 'even though the fact was painstakingly hushed up in Germany and Austria, I had plenty of success abroad and gained a large following.'[27] War did not quite put a stop to that, certainly not across the Atlantic, where in 1915 Leopold Stokowski gave the first American performance of the First Chamber Symphony.

In 1913, also the year of Chicago's American premiere of the *Five Orchestral Pieces* – a 'Hallowe'en joke', snarled one critic, 'a congress of polecats', another – there had appeared the lengthiest discussion to date of Schoenberg in an American newspaper. James Gibbons Huneker, theatre and music critic and author of a book on Chopin, even included pictures of Schoenberg's paintings in an article for the *New York Times*. Under a headline that declared 'Schoenberg: Musical Anarchist Who Has Upset Europe', Huneker wrote of 'the cruelest of all composers, for he mingles with his music sharp daggers at white heat, with which he pares away tiny slices of his victim's flesh. Anon he twists his knife in the fresh wound and you receive another horrible thrill.' Huneker continued his audition for the post of sub-Poe librettist to an imaginary *Pierrot* sequel with a vindictive declaration, albeit one that seemed to be voiced more in fear that he 'might be persuaded to like this music' than in whimsy. 'If such music-making is ever to become accepted,' he declared, 'then I long for Death the Releaser.' As Sabine Feisst notes: 'Death actually released Huneker from witnessing the American *Pierrot* premiere in 1923, as he passed away in 1921.'[28]

4

'War Years' and their Aftermath

Death enveloped Europe sooner still, offering anything but a release from its agonies, aesthetic or otherwise. However, contrary to what will often be read in cultural studies of this period, nothing was certain about war until it happened, not even during the 'July Crisis' of 1914. Germany might have given a 'blank cheque' to Austria-Hungary; France might likewise have done so to Russia (something far less discussed until Christopher Clark's treatment of the origins of the First World War).[1] There was still time to pull back, even after the fateful assassination in Sarajevo; to read anything more than the vaguest presentiments of war into the art of this period is to sentimentalize, to trivialize. Neither the *Five Pieces for Orchestra* nor *The Rite of Spring*, still less the symphonies of Mahler, somehow 'foretold' the Somme.

In the meantime, at the close of 1913, Schoenberg wrote the first of his four op. 22 orchestral songs, its text Stefan George's translation of 'Seraphita', a sonnet by the London symbolist writer Ernest Dowson. The subject was an ongoing preoccupation for Schoenberg; it would soon inform his work on *Die Jakobsleiter* (Jacob's Ladder), and, after the war, be channelled into dreams of new art that incorporated talking pictures, too. 'I had dreamed,' he recalled in 1940, 'of a dramatization of Balzac's *Seraphita* [1834],' for which, enthused by its tale of elitist redemption, he had in 1912 actually composed a few bars.[2] 'None but the loftier spirits open to faith,' Balzac wrote, 'can discern Jacob's mystical stair,' an idea pleasing to Dowson, George and Schoenberg alike.[3] Alternatives, Schoenberg went on, had been

> Strindberg's *To Damascus*, or the second part of Goethe's *Faust*, or even Wagner's *Parsifal*. All of these works, by renouncing the law of 'unity of space and time', would have found the solution to realization in sound pictures. But the industry continued to satisfy only the needs and demands of the ordinary people who filled their theatres.[4]

Were they the same people who had disrupted his concerts? Probably. After war broke out, Schoenberg fitfully continued work on the op. 22 songs, each calling upon a differently constituted, often chamber-scale orchestra drawn, in an intensification of what had increasingly been Mahler's strategy, from the vast pool of the post-Wagnerian orchestra. Clarinets feature prominently – he calls for no fewer than six in 'Seraphita' – yet rarely, if ever, with the sardonicism of *Pierrot*; here a lyricism poised somewhere between recollections and reinventions of Mozart, Brahms and Wagner presages, echoes, even incites the rapt, ripe lyricism of the songs themselves. He eventually completed the third of the three Rilke settings in 1916.

Schoenberg's lack of productivity during this period is not simply to be ascribed to war, which, as did many across Europe, he initially greeted with traditional patriotism. He would soon draw closer to Karl Kraus, if never quite to that extent, in seeing the Great War for the horror that it was. Composition had been slowing down anyway, seemingly in need of new inspiration, new organizing principles, and this difficult period persisted for some while after hostilities had ceased. Those who had attacked him so mercilessly, though, had other preoccupations for now. 'I am really a little discouraged,' he wrote to Zemlinsky in October 1915; 'I should like to be left in peace just a little while longer (the only good thing the war has done for me is that I'm not being attacked by anyone).'[5]

The six-note cello ostinato (a 'hexachord') in *Jakobsleiter* offered another straw in the wind; how much more than that is open to debate. There was probably more than a little serialist revisionism in Schoenberg's claim in 1948 that he 'had contrived the plan to provide for unity – which was always my main motive: to build all the main themes of the whole oratorio from a row of six'.[6] The compositional method, moreover, was quite different from that which he would subsequently adopt. Nevertheless, he was unquestionably, as so often in his life, searching for something, for an almost mystical principle by which he might be guided, like Moses in the wilderness. It is not true to say, as sometimes one hears, that Schoenberg composed nothing more until the 1920s; it would, however, be a while before he found himself able to complete any of the sketches and torsos on which he was still working.

The single exception was the tonal *Die eiserne Brigade* (The Iron Brigade, 1916), an occasional march for piano quintet, written as a party piece – literally – during Schoenberg's military service. Is it a parody of a military march, imitation trumpet calls and all; or is it sincerely intended, as seems to be suggested by nostalgic interjections from Old Vienna's coffee houses? With Schoenberg, as indeed with Mahler and Berg, the one does not necessarily exclude the other. One may even sing along or make some animal noises, as suggested in the score:

Simple and beautiful melodies, salty rhythms, interesting harmony, sophisticated form, complicated counterpoint – the real composer writes them with the ease with which one writes a letter. 'As if he were writing a letter' – this is what my comrades in the Austrian army said, admiringly, when, in the barracks, I wrote some music for a party given by the company. That this was not a remarkably beautiful piece but only one of average craftsmanship does not make any difference, because it often takes as much time to compose a letter as to write music.

Make of that what you will; better still, try it out at a party, while recalling that 'German humour' does not always travel.

The outbreak of war had lost Schoenberg his pupils. As ever – perhaps more than ever – money was a problem. The Schoenbergs thus returned to Vienna in October 1915. Many of those initially exempted from conscription were gradually receiving the call-up, and Schoenberg's asthma was no longer considered sufficient cause for exemption. At the end of the year the call came from Budapest, since Austro-Hungarian nationality laws treated him on the basis of his father's birthplace, Pressburg/Bratislava/Pozsony. Having previously shown himself willing as a volunteer, Schoenberg had the right, which he exercised, to choose his regiment. On 15 December he entered the Hoch- und Deutschmeister-Regiment, based in Vienna, and at the beginning of the new year he was despatched for training as an officer in the Lower Austrian town of Bruck an der Leitha. Musicians from either 'side' of the Dual Monarchy campaigned for the compassionate release of one who was in anything but good health: not only Berg and Webern, but musical organizations – for once, doing the right thing – and, it seems, even Bartók in Budapest.[7]

Schoenberg's age – he was by now in his forties – had protected him from frontline service, but there was a rumour that that was about to change. Although he was (relatively) happy to perform his duties, not least on account of his long-standing, never-to-be-broken loyalty to the Habsburgs, the machinations of his peers and supporters, quite unknown to him, eventually resulted in his discharge in October 1916. He would jokingly refer to his 'war years' as the happiest in his life, since he had not had to be The Composer Arnold Schoenberg. Indeed one of the most celebrated anecdotes from that life, melancholy, even tragic, in its wry suggestion of historical necessity, results from this period. 'In the army,' he recalled in an unfinished notebook essay of 1930, 'a superior officer once said to me: "So you are this notorious Schoenberg then?"

"Beg to report, Sir, yes," I replied. "Nobody wanted to be, someone had to be, so I let it be me."[8] Even if he had wanted to, Schoenberg could hardly have absconded at the end of the Great War to Paris, to make *Les Six* 'Die Sieben' (genuine admiration from Francis Poulenc and Darius Milhaud notwithstanding). He was who he was; indeed he was who he, rightly or wrongly, felt he must be.

Would the discharged officer now have to be 'him' again? War, ironically, afforded Schoenberg cover for a little longer. He taught a little for the 'specialist' classes of the socialist educational reformer Eugenie Schwarzwald – those private classes at which he had first met Webern and a number of his pupils – and would continue to do so until 1920. Beyond that, little could be done, although he made some notes for possible books on composition. He also continued to interest himself in, even to try to influence, world affairs, drafting a fifteen-point peace plan, 'Friedenssicherung', in January 1917. Enthused by what he perceived to be the intentions of the American President, Woodrow Wilson, he wrote from Vienna to Busoni, who was now in neutral Swiss exile from his warring homes of Germany and Italy, asking him to send the plan to a newspaper for publication, albeit under a pseudonym: A. Börnscheg. It was neither the first nor the last time that he would make such a political pronouncement, although most others, on Human Rights, Zionism, his perpetual preoccupation of copyright and so forth, would be shorn of (thinly disguised) pseudonymical modesty. Schoenberg's particular concern for the fate of foreign soldiers, whether from 'larger' or 'smaller' states, speaks strongly of the impression his military service, however limited, had made on him – and indeed of the humanitarian nature of his priorities. His insistence on the supervisory role of international organizations suggests an outlook that extended beyond narrow nationalism, very much of Wilson's ilk and that of the soon-to-be League of Nations, although that would remain one of several competing tendencies in his world view.

Life remained expensive in Vienna, though, and became more so, given the wartime squeeze even on essential items of living. In April 1917 Schoenberg moved to Mödling, just outside Vienna, to an apartment on the first floor of Bernhardgasse 6.[9] It is more or less an accident that this Lower Austrian town is not a suburb of Vienna; it was incorporated after the *Anschluss*, but the founding fiction of the new Republic in 1955 – that it had had nothing to do with Nazi 'occupation' – ensured that the new twenty-fourth district, of which Mödling was part, vanished into a *Jakobsleiter*-like historical ether. While not so convenient for Viennese musical life – from which Schoenberg was, in any case, somewhat estranged – as the districts in which he had previously lived, the town was close enough, however much he complained. It had, moreover, rich musical resonances of its own; Beethoven had lived there from time to time, creating drunken havoc at the Two Ravens Inn, and composing late masterworks such as the *Hammerklavier* Sonata, the *Diabelli Variations* and the *Missa solemnis*. Schoenberg, it may be recalled, had spent a summer in Mödling in 1904, and before that he had found his first position there as a choral-society conductor. Public transport difficulties at the end of the war and during its aftermath did not help, but they would be rectified before too long; a tramline (no longer in use, having been superseded by the suburban railway) may still be seen today. Some visitors, however, would walk into Vienna: quite a journey, 14.5 kilometres (9 mi.) or so there, and of course the same distance back.

Webern, one of them, followed his teacher to Mödling in 1918, although a contretemps over his failure to attend Schoenberg's forty-fourth birthday party soured relations for a while. Berg visited on Sundays, and was finally given leave, six years after Schoenberg had extended the honour to Webern, to address Schoenberg with the familiar 'du' rather than the formal 'Sie'. (Zemlinsky, 'lieber Alex', was one of the very few to have done so all along.) Loos, Kokoschka, Marie Pappenheim, David Joseph Bach

Photograph by Berg
of Schoenberg in
uniform, 1916.

and many others also visited regularly. Schoenberg soon began
teaching once again in earnest, and his new pupils included Eduard
Steuermann; another pianist, Rudolf Serkin; the violinist Rudolf
Kolisch; the conductor Felix Greissle, who would marry Trudi in
1921, and who would do good work for Schoenberg in transcribing
his scores for piano for Universal; Hanns Eisler, the reddest of all
his pupils and one of the most underrated as a composer, whom
Schoenberg considered one of his most talented; Viktor Ullmann,
who would write his opera *Der Kaiser von Atlantis* (The Emperor
of Atlantis) – an almost unbearably moving Hitler allegory – at
Theresienstadt before dying at Auschwitz; and Josef Rufer, to
whom we shall return at the close of this chapter. The Vienna
Woods, which back on to the town, and the Romantic pastiche
Liechtenstein fortress a couple of kilometres' walk away, offered

inspiration to Webern in particular, but Schoenberg too enjoyed the countryside there, literally following in Beethoven's footsteps, often with his pupil. This was, then, not quite the exile some have claimed. Hardship would probably have been more severe in Vienna. Londoners might think of it as akin to living in Richmond rather than Bloomsbury, albeit with more dramatic scenery – and better air quality.

The year 1918 also brought the founding of the Society for Private Musical Performances. Schoenberg had for long, not unreasonably, been unhappy with the provision of New Music performances, their quality and their critical reception. From its founding concert on 23 November until its partly enforced farewell at the height of hyperinflation almost exactly three years later – the competing needs of teaching and, at last, composition also played a role – this organization, as Schoenberg would recall, allowed him to act as 'a kind of dictator'.[10] Its prospectus, which was written or at least compiled by Berg, stated its 'purpose' as being to enable 'Arnold Schoenberg' – not, be it noted, any others involved – 'to give artists and music lovers a real and exact knowledge of modern music'. 'To attain this goal,' Berg went on, three things were necessary:

1. Clear, well-rehearsed performances.
2. Frequent repetitions.
3. Performances must be removed from the corrupting influence of publicity; that is, they must not be directed towards winning of competitions and must be unaccompanied, by either applause or demonstrations of disapproval.[11]

No *Skandalkonzert II* here, then. This was to be everything Viennese 'tradition', condemned by Mahler as *Schlamperei* (sloppiness), had not been.[12] Works would be rehearsed until they were ready, sometimes receiving fifty hours, even more on occasion, of rehearsal. Critics were banished, and a sign forbade them entry at the door. Even guests, except for foreign visitors, were not allowed; one had to join. Audience members did not know what would be performed until they arrived; new works would be repeated, sometimes within a concert and often several times throughout a given season. Young performers – as ever in particular need of 'exposure', as we might now have it – were given especial attention. Schoenberg was never one to forget that musicians needed to make a living. His pupils and friends, Oskar Adler among them, naturally received many such opportunities, yet so did others. Likewise the hard yet ultimately revealing work of piano reduction – or here, arrangement for small, chamber ensemble – that Schoenberg had known during his youth could also afford opportunity. Delightful arrangements of Johann Strauss waltzes made by Schoenberg, Berg and Webern for a fundraising concert in 1921 have taken on a life of their own; so, to a lesser extent, have a good few of these arrangements, none more surprising than the equally delightful version Schoenberg made of Luigi Denza's popular Neapolitan song *Funiculì, Funiculà*. Quality in all things was held to be paramount; here, more often than not, it was also achieved.

In a self-denying ordnance that stole a march on hostile talk of the 'Vienna Schoenberg Society', not a single work of Schoenberg's own was given in the first season. A wide variety of composers was featured throughout. Music by conservative composers such as Erich Wolfgang Korngold, Franz Schmidt and even Schoenberg's (and Busoni's) arch-reactionary foe Hans Pfitzner (Schoenberg wrote a mock libretto, parodying his *Palestrina*) appeared on the programmes, as well as works by Bruckner, Mahler, Debussy, Ravel, Satie, Milhaud, Max Reger (whom Schoenberg always revered), Zemlinsky, Berg, Webern, Scriabin, Stravinsky, Bartók, Busoni, Szymanowski and others. Even Josef Matthias Hauer, who independently came up with an alternative twelve-note system – very much, it should be stressed, a 'system' in contrast to

Schoenberg's 'method' – was included. 'No school,' the prospectus declared, 'will receive preference and only the worthless shall be excluded; for the rest, all modern music – from that of Mahler and Strauss to the newest, which almost never, or at most rarely, is heard – will be performed.'[13] That, alas, included no women; in that respect, programming proved characteristic of the prejudices of a broader musical culture otherwise confronted head-on. There were, though, more than 250 different musical works performed in 113 concerts (118 if one includes 'additional', more popular events). The first concert offered Scriabin's Fourth and Seventh Piano Sonatas, Debussy songs and Alfredo Casella's arrangement of Mahler's Seventh Symphony for four hands, which appeared again less than a month later, along with the same Debussy songs. The final concert, on 5 December 1921, was devoted to *Pierrot lunaire*.

The Society's importance is not limited, however, to those concerts. Picking up the example of four additional concerts given in Prague in 1920, a smaller Prague Society was founded by Zemlinsky in 1922, with Schoenberg as its honorary president, this time opening with *Pierrot*. Still more important, a precedent had been set alongside that of the International Society for Contemporary Music (also founded in 1922) for later New Music societies, running through Boulez's Domaine musical and beyond. They might not have been run along quite the same lines, with quite the same overt sobriety of purpose, but much of their pioneering spirit may be traced back, often directly in explicit tribute, to these three years of performances in Vienna under Schoenberg's 'dictatorship'.

Not that he was always present: May 1920 brought an important visit to Amsterdam, for Willem Mengelberg's historic series of the complete Mahler symphonies. Collaboration between Schoenberg and Mengelberg soon foundered, whether on plans for an international Mahler Society, or more broadly. Yet Schoenberg attended rehearsals avidly, absorbed in the display of what a great,

willing orchestra such as Mengelberg's Concertgebouw could do
for what was still in many respects New Music. Schoenberg was
composing, too, making headway on both his *Five Piano Pieces*,
op. 23, and his *Serenade*, op. 24, on which more will be said in
the next chapter. During the harsh winter – financially as well
as meteorologically – of 1920–21, he left Mödling for the Dutch
seaside town of Zandvoort, where he was able to give some private
lessons. The young conductor Otto Klemperer visited him there, in
preparation for the bold choice of an all-Schoenberg programme
for his Berlin Philharmonic debut the following year. Although that
concert was to be of early Schoenberg, *Verklärte Nacht* and *Pelleas*,
Klemperer studied the op. 16 *Orchestral Pieces* and *Erwartung*
with the composer, subsequently owning that, however great his
personal admiration, he had never quite understood them.

In June 1921, in the wake of that Johann Strauss fundraising
concert – all three composers having taken their place in the
ensemble, and the manuscripts having been despatched for auction
– Schoenberg and his family left for Mattsee, in the Salzkammergut,
for a summer holiday. 'Holiday' was as much intended to signify a
change of scenery as an actual break, for, as we have already seen,
and just like Mahler, much of Schoenberg's compositional work
was accomplished away from Vienna – or from wherever else he
might have been living at the time. The composer's keen love of
swimming, though, could certainly be indulged – again, echoing
Mahler's practice. Alas, what should have been a happy time,
at least relatively, was disrupted by a notorious incident of anti-
Semitism, vicious even by the standards of 1920s Austria. Posters
went up declaring the town to be for Aryans only. Schoenberg was
informed by the local council that he must prove his Protestantism
to be allowed to stay. (It is, perhaps, not entirely without irony
that the Salzburg region had been the site of one of the most
notorious eighteenth-century expulsions of Protestants: now, at
least compared with the Jews, the Protestants were tolerated.)

Schoenberg's baptismal certificate was in Vienna, but in any case, he was not inclined to bow to such demands. Hurt and angry, in what turned out to be a turning point concerning the composer's Jewish identity, the Schoenbergs left Mattsee for a villa Josef Rufer had found them in the town of Traunkirchen, not far from Gmunden. In 1934, newly arrived in the United States, Schoenberg would tell Rabbi Stephen Wise that he had there been one of the very first Central European victims of an actual Jewish expulsion.

For the moment, however, Schoenberg wished to compose. One day in July of that year, Schoenberg took a walk outside Traunkirchen with Rufer, who had come to him in 1919. The young man was to prove a devoted pupil, even by the standards of Schoenberg's school, following his teacher to Berlin in 1925 and later taking upon himself a good deal of editorial work among the manuscripts Schoenberg left behind. He later made a name for himself as a musicologist, publishing an introduction to twelve-note music the year after Schoenberg's death, in 1952, and a catalogue of Schoenberg's music a few years later. However, at this remove, Rufer is most celebrated for his account of that country walk. Schoenberg turned to his pupil and made the fateful declaration: 'I have made a discovery, through which the *Vorherrschaft* [supremacy, hegemony, ascendancy, primacy: according to taste, or lack thereof] of German music will be secured for the next hundred years.'

Except that he may not have done. This famous, even notorious, declaration – wheeled out time and time again, as the composer's grandson E. Randol Schoenberg has noted, to discredit a supposedly virulent nationalism underlying Schoenberg's aesthetic ideology – seems never to have been mentioned by Rufer before 1959.[14] There is, moreover, no other source for the claim. If Schoenberg did deliver that irresistibly dramatic line, then, as his grandson argues, it may, in the wake of the Mattsee incident, even have had a touch of irony to it. Not for nothing

At the 1920 Gustav Mahler Festival, Amsterdam, May 1920: Mathilde 'Tilly' Mengelberg-Wubbe (wife of the conductor Willem Mengelberg), Alma Mahler, Schoenberg, Mathilde and violinist Alexander Schmuller in front.

were Schoenberg and Kraus close. More likely to my mind, it may have been defensive, as if to say: 'I am as German as they are, more German.' For in 1921 neither Germany nor Austria appeared to have any prospect of 'supremacy' other than of the cultural variety – if that. Schoenberg's personal, Romantic loyalty to the House of Habsburg, which had managed to keep the lid on the worst of what was to come, never wavered. But it was not, whether at this stage or later, a loyalty that was likely to be rewarded politically; hence, for many, as after the 'failed' revolutions of 1848, a renewed emphasis on art and culture. Jews, moreover, often found themselves – not unlike Muslims today – compelled to distinguish themselves in their 'patriotism'. In a published statement of that same year, Schoenberg owned: 'When I think of music, the only type that comes to my mind – whether I want it to or not – is German music.' It 'thrives even in times of hunger' – as these were; 'it will always reach for the heavens, while worldly superiority only boasts with artifice'.[15] Artistic 'dictatorship', seen in beneficent, non-nationalist mode at the Society for Private Musical Performances, had its darker side, too.

Already in 1918 Schoenberg was explicitly arguing that state funding should ensure 'the German nation's superiority in the field of music'.[16] Adolf Loos had organized a symposium to consider guidelines for the newly declared Republic of German-Austria's cultural dispensation. Responding to Loos's claim that the state must not only provide high-quality theatrical performances, mostly of new artistic work, available to all, Schoenberg insisted also on the maintenance of the great Austro-German tradition as the foundation of the repertoire. Schoenberg's proposals have been described as utopian. Perhaps they are from an extreme, neoliberal standpoint, but there is nothing especially unusual, nor unachievable, to them in principle, as present-day Germany and Austria would show. In any case, they were barely distinguishable from views that were common currency for any moderate follower of Wagner's political aesthetics, indeed of Hegel's or Schiller's, let alone Marx's.

Germany and Austria-Hungary had been defeated in war. Germany and 'German Austria' were defeated thereafter in their post-war aspiration – as much for Karl Renner's Social Democrats as for the Right – to political union, stated clearly in the second article of the draft constitution of 1918: 'German Austria is a component of the German Republic.' The 1919 Treaty of St Germain, which Renner as Chancellor had to sign, expressly forbade any such union to any Austro-Hungarian successor state. There was no reason, however, so far as Schoenberg and many others were concerned, why Germany and Austria should also be defeated culturally during the peace. Schoenberg would probably have nodded assent to Hans Sachs, in Wagner's *Die Meistersinger von Nürnberg*, explicitly dissociating a nation's cultural fortunes from political or military prowess. 'Honour your German Masters': masters of their craft, that is, not overlords. And should the

AUSSERORDENTLICHER ABEND

**Freitag, den 27. Mai 1921, 7 Uhr abends, im Festsaale
der Schwarzwald'schen Schulanstalten.**

VIER WALZER VON JOHANN STRAUSS

Bearbeitung für Kammerorchester.

Besetzung: Klavier: Eduard Steuermann, Harmonium: Alban
Berg, 1. Geige Rudolf Kolisch und Arnold Schönberg,
2. Geige: Karl Rankl, Bratsche: Othmar Steinbauer, Cello:
Anton von Webern.

SCHATZWALZER (Zigeunerbaron) Bearbeitung von Anton von Webern

WEIN, WEIB UND GESANG Op. 333, Bearbeitung von Alban Berg

ROSEN AUS DEM SÜDEN Op. 388, Bearbeitung von Arnold Schönberg

LAGUNENWALZER Op. 411, Bearbeitung von Arnold Schönberg

Nach dem Konzert: Versteigerung der Originalmanuskripte der Bearbeitungen.

Konzertflügel Steinway & Son; beigestellt von der Firma Bernhard Kohn, Wien

Zuschriften an den Sekretär Herrn Felix Greißle, V. Rainergasse Nr. 82.
Anmeldungen an den wöchentlichen Vereinsabenden jeden Montag abends 7 Uhr im Festsaale der Schwarzwald'schen Schulanstalten, I. Wallnerstr. 9 (Eingang Regierungsgasse)

Preis 7 Kronen.

Society for Private Musical Performances: special concert of waltzes by Johann Strauss,
arranged by Schoenberg, Berg and Webern, 1921.

Holy Roman Empire or its modern successors 'dissolve in mist, there would still remain to us holy German art!' Words that had spoken to Wagner's standpoint in 1860s Bavaria, torn as it was between Austria, Prussia and France, not to mention by its own particularism, would have had a not dissimilar message for 'German' artists half a century later.

As E. Randol Schoenberg allows in 1930, his grandfather unquestionably wrote words similar to those Rufer reported, albeit without that emphatic Teutonism.[17] Schoenberg wrote to a fellow member of the Circle of the Friends of the Bauhaus, no less than Albert Einstein, requesting that he put his name to a proclamation to honour Loos: to give Schoenberg's ailing aesthetic comrade's 'sick heart . . . a few sunny hours at peace'.[18] Smarting from Einstein's demurral on grounds of ignorance, Schoenberg wrote to Loos's wife, Claire, suggesting that he would reply to Einstein (it seems he did not) as follows: 'I tell you: Loos has in his field at least the same importance as I in mine. And you know perhaps; that I pride myself on having shown humanity for at least the next hundred years the way [forward] for musical creation.'[19] In the end, a declaration appeared without Einstein in the *Prager Tageblatt*, its signatories Kraus, Schoenberg, Heinrich Mann, Valery Larbaud and James Joyce.

Whatever the national hue, then, of Schoenberg's conviction – it varied – he knew very well the historical importance of his new discovery, creation, method or whatever we elect to call it. Let us now turn to that in earnest, noting – in passing and without wishing to make anything crassly psychoanalytical out of it – that Pauline Schönberg, who had moved to Berlin at about the same time as her son and had remained there when he returned, died on 12 October 1921. (At least it was not the 13th.) We know little about Pauline's death or funeral, although there is a telegram concerning the provision of flowers dated 14 October, sent by Mathilde to Ottilie, who took charge of the burial and eventually, in 1923, the tombstone.[20] There is no reason to think that Schoenberg's mother's death, clearly expected, affected his work in the profound, persistent way that Webern's music had been by that of his mother. But Schoenberg had reached that staging post, important in many people's lives, when he no longer had a living parent. The coincidence with a new musical path may be only symbolic; yet, as he would have been the first to aver, symbolism has its place.

So too does the beautiful *Weihnachtsmusik*, an occasional Christmas piece written in 1921: a seasonal fantasia on the hymn tunes *Es ist ein' Ros' entsprungen* (Lo, How a Rose E'er Blooming) and *Silent Night*, for the village church ensemble of two violins, cello, piano and harmonium. Why we have no cause to complain about its overuse during the Advent and Christmas seasons, as opposed to its almost complete absence from them, is yet another perplexing question concerning Schoenberg's work. These five minutes even offer a view in miniature of his religious syncretism: Lutheran and Roman Catholic, North German and Austrian tunes deftly, unassumingly woven together in simple, yet ingenious tonal harmony (in more than one sense). I defy you not to adore it, to hear, even to see, a pair of angels watching over the imaginary parish in question.

5

Composing with Twelve Notes Related Only to One Another

That summer of 1921 in Traunkirchen, Schoenberg began work on the Prelude and Intermezzo from the *Suite for Piano*, op. 25. This was his first work to be founded, from beginning to end, on a single twelve-note row. However, if we are to consider but a single movement from a work, the title of first fully dodecaphonic composition should go to the fifth of the *Five Piano Pieces*, op. 23. It would also be the first to be published, in 1923, albeit founded on rows of different length. (A series need not be of twelve notes, as Stravinsky would triumphantly show in his late serial works, however different their premises and aesthetic proved to be from those of Schoenberg.) Moreover, some movements from the *Serenade*, op. 24, also involve such procedures.

These three works, then, written between 1920 and 1923 (op. 25: 1921–3) may all be considered part of Schoenberg's discovery or creation of his new method, and underline the fact that it was a process, which may be traced considerably further back, whether to his own earlier work or even to that of others. It was also a process that would continue to develop until the end of his life – and, in the work of his followers, beyond. 'In this time,' he wrote in March 1923 to Emil Hertzka at Universal, 'when I have "not produced anything new for years"' (quoting yet another hostile newspaper article), the world would soon 'appreciate with astonishment how much I nevertheless have composed', once everything on which he was at work had been completed.[1] Schoenberg would return to his regular

– never exclusive – publisher for the op. 25 *Suite*, having worked with a Danish firm, Wilhelm Hansen, on its two immediate predecessors.

I do not intend here to give a full account of the new method of 'composition with twelve notes related only to one another', partly because it is misleading to consider it as a single method. I am keen not to propose too starkly a 'before and after' scenario; moreover, insistence on the method rather than the music does the latter no service and, in a book of this kind, may serve only to mystify those who are not 'in the know' already. Millions listen to Beethoven without detailed knowledge of his compositional procedures, which is not to say that such knowledge cannot deepen understanding, even love; the same can and should be true for Schoenberg. Sometimes these procedures rise closer to the surface than at other times; if one hears them, or learns to hear them, that is all to the good. They are never, however, in themselves the point of the piece; they are never the sole or even the most important key to its meaning. A Romantic *and* post-Romantic insistence on organic unity – as close, say, to Loos's abhorrence of ornament as to Beethoven's or Brahms's motivic derivations – was a goal, but not the ultimate goal; for, as Webern would put it, 'To develop everything . . . from *one* principal idea! That's the strongest unity . . . But in what form? That's where art comes in!'[2] Visions of a composer working out the combinations and permutations of a series can suggest that there is something inartistic or mechanical involved, but they were simply a starting point such as music has always required. As Wagner's Hans Sachs tells his 'pupil' Walther in *Die Meistersinger*, many have succeeded when spring sang for them, but it takes mastery to continue singing during autumn, winter and even summer.

During the summer of 1922, again in Traunkirchen, again at work on opuses 23–5, Schoenberg wrote a declaration, entitled *Art-Golem*, referring to the traditional Jewish tale of an invented clay man brought to life:

Francis Poulenc visiting Schoenberg in Mödling, June 1922. The photograph was taken outside Schoenberg's house, Bernhardgasse 6.

I conclude that if a thinker were to compose (without recourse to his imagination) an intellectually really good, *invented* piece of music which would take into account all the rules arising from a correct realization of its artistic stipulations, we should react to it with the same feeling as we might derive from such structures as are created through the purely intuitive use of the imagination. It is unlikely that such an Art/ Golem could be created; yet, were it to be possible, then no objection to its artificial, dryly cerebral origins would hold.[3]

That said, Schoenberg always insisted that he was a composer, not a twelve-note composer, that what mattered was the 'idea' of the work, not the 'style' in which it was expressed. It is not an absolute distinction; nor did he ever really claim it to be, although he came closer at some times than at others. Nevertheless, as a starting point, his words in a Berlin radio discussion from 1931 are worth citing. 'Dr [Heinrich] Strobel', he addressed Hermann Scherchen's successor as editor of the new music journal *Melos*:

You call it [the language of his earlier works] the *Tristan* style or late Romanticism; why not *Parsifal* style or *Meistersinger* style? These influenced me just as much as Brahms did. You still hear *Tristan* sounds in my music! But even if you were correct, a Chinese poet is certainly not only someone who sounds Chinese. Rather, he says something else as well![4]

He was quite happy, he said later in that discussion, still to be considered a Romantic, 'since the company in which that places me is not bad at all. If today people think the Romantics absurd, whereas earlier they listened to them enthusiastically, then all that proves is that one day they will also find anti-Romantics absurd.'[5] Let us, then, consider those three works together. We know they contain serial, not always twelve-note, writing; without drowning ourselves in the deceptively comfortable shallows of a false universalism – every language, every musical style, permits of different constructions – what else might they be saying? The best thing, of course, is to listen to or perform them. Since this is a book, however, that will not pass muster. Even if we cannot say in words 'what' they are saying, some discussion – whether contextual, descriptive or even analytical – might help.

The *Five Piano Pieces* stand to a certain extent in the tradition of Schoenberg's op. 11 and op. 19 *Pieces*. In the most obvious sense, they are designated 'pieces'. That might seem to be a point verging on the pointless, but it both places them in an essentially Romantic tradition, especially of piano literature – Schumann and Brahms immediately come to mind; so might Schubert or Liszt – and also suggests what they might *not* be. Sets of 'pieces' might share certain characteristics with genres such as the sonata or, thinking of Second Viennese School *Orchestral Pieces*, the symphony. Rarely if ever, however, are such sets straightforwardly to be equated. With the exception of the final waltz ('Walzer'), they are given not titles but tempo indications; a genre title is in any case a different thing from a 'character piece' title, such as 'Snowflakes' or 'First Love'. And yet, such practices had previously suggested a seemingly limitless freedom, born of breathing the air of another planet, could now also hint at a move towards organization prompted by consideration of that freedom and its possibilities and impossibilities.

Abstraction, of a sort, was increasingly the order of the day. This was the age of the Bauhaus; Alma Mahler (as was) had married its founder, Walter Gropius. Kandinsky went there to teach in 1921. Alma did not fail to pass up the opportunity to tell Schoenberg, mendaciously or at least mistakenly, that anti-Semitism there involved Kandinsky – it would do, apparently, since he was Russian – doing irreparable harm to their relationship (on which more below). It was also, or soon would be, the age of 'New Objectivity', *Neue Sachlichkeit*; the anti-Expressionist term was coined in 1923, the year in which all three of these Schoenberg works would be completed. Schoenberg was not necessarily partaking fully, or even consciously, in such movements. Interesting artists will rarely sign on an aesthetic dotted line, even their own; not for long, anyway. But there was a new constructivism in the air and, more to the point, on the stave. Musicians such as Klemperer and Hindemith came to seem more typical, even topical, than their apparently old-fashioned counterparts such as Schoenberg and Wilhelm Furtwängler. The latter two had yet to meet, though soon they would.

Drama, even in the (slightly) vocal *Serenade*, was held increasingly to be in the notes, not to be 'expressive' of something beyond them. Schoenberg knew he was no longer in the world of *Erwartung* and *Die glückliche Hand*; he had, as we have seen, been establishing new coordinates for quite some time. The word 'serenade' suggested not only a return to Brahms but a move beyond him to (First) Viennese Classicism. Its movements won at least their titles, often also their skeletal structure and a degree of flesh, from Mozart and Beethoven: 'March' (which ambiguously incorporates many elements of Schoenberg's old waltzes, too, recurring with seemingly inevitable symmetry in the 'Finale', to be taken at precisely the same basic tempo); 'Minuet and Trio' (the latter is repeated exactly, very much in the Classical style); and 'Theme and Variations'. Schoenberg now proudly described himself as Mozart's pupil – and the final movement of the *Suite*, the 'Gigue', comes close to explicit homage to the G major *Gigue*, KV 574, in which Mozart at *his* most neo-Baroque and most harmonically chromatic seems almost to anticipate elements of Schoenberg's serial method. A double homage to Mozart and Bach was at this time just the thing – not least as more popular, less 'German' composers were wrapping themselves in the banner of neoclassicism (which, confusing in its terminology, tended to suggest Bach as much as Mozart or Haydn). Not surprisingly, many composers were attempting at this time to find, or re-find, order from the apparent chaos – social, political and of course military – that had engulfed Europe. At any rate, overt reference to classical and Classical genres most certainly did not evoke a superfluity of new forms burning themselves out in a single outing, such as Schoenberg had celebrated in his *Wunderjahr* of 1909. If he were building and testing a new method, rather than relying on the outpouring of his unconscious, an obvious place to start was by showing, both to himself and to the world, that it worked in the old forms. 'A man such as Mozart cannot be compared to anything living or dead. Anything he did was the right thing.'[6] There were worse precedents for a cruelly – genuinely cruelly – misunderstood genius: ultimately a Romantic, whether before or after Romanticism. That crucial, often overlooked, elevation within Schoenberg's Austro-German pantheon began in earnest here.

Even in the op. 23 *Pieces*, and before the Waltz too, there is a cleanness of line, an almost self-conscious shift towards elegance of form, that at least suggests a return to the Viennese instrumental past – in order to move forwards. *Pierrot* is honoured

in the instrumentation of the *Serenade*, which is not identical yet
has a clear echo: clarinet, bass clarinet, mandolin, guitar, violin,
viola and cello. It is also honoured, or echoed, in effects – string
pizzicato, col legno and harmonics, flutter-tonguing woodwind – that
nevertheless tend to sound less heated, less bizarre, more 'classical'
than in *Pierrot. Schrammelmusik*, an invented nineteenth-century
Viennese 'folk music', is Schoenberg's too, he seems to tell us, not
least in the presence of the guitar (soon followed by Webern in
his marriage of 'folk tradition' to increasingly serial procedure
in the op. 18 *Three Songs* for soprano, E-flat clarinet and guitar).
Schoenberg had, after all, played this music when he was younger;
a photograph from 1900 seen earlier in this book pictures him
playing cello in such a quintet, with the violinist Fritz Kreisler. The
Serenade's bass soloist sings rather than 'speaks', and appears in but
a single movement, the central one of seven, a setting of a Petrarch
sonnet in translation. That is both an overtly more traditional,
indeed historical choice than, say, George or Giraud, and also
indicative of a concern for balance, of the desire to 'express'
within certain classical restraints. That movement, moreover,
as the beating Golem-like heart of a new, constructed world, is
Schoenberg's fully twelve-note piece, yet we should perhaps not
make too much of that. After all, the succeeding movements do
not represent a 'falling away'; the direction is not one-way to
dodecaphony, as it is, more or less, towards atonality in the Second
String Quartet – not quite yet, anyway. If it might be exaggerated,
at least without evidence, to hear this as a direct response to
Stravinsky's *Soldier's Tale*, there is perhaps kinship or similarity of
a sort. The experimentation Schoenberg permits himself within
such constraints is dizzying, albeit of a more 'purely musical', even
'abstract' nature than that of Stravinsky – the latter's reputation
and aesthetic ideology notwithstanding.

   Concerning the 'Theme and Variations', which comes closer
than most to his dodecaphonic *style*, and, save for the number

twelve, also to the *method* that accompanied and underlay that style, Schoenberg would describe his method as follows: 'The . . . variations use inversions and retrograde inversions, diminutions and augmentations, canons of various kinds, and rhythmic shifts to different beats – in other words, all the technical tools of the method are here, except the limitation to only twelve different notes.'[7] The theme, notably, is voiced in but a single, unaccompanied melodic clarinet line, as if to allow the listener (or performers) in, to fix it all the more firmly in the memory, almost as if it were the subject of a fugue prior to its variation. If that sounds not unlike an outline of Bach's contrapuntal procedures, there is good reason for that. Schoenberg was increasingly determined and inspired to show that he was a Great German Composer. As we have seen, he had been given a good few reasons to wear such ideology on his sleeve, but it is not simply a matter of defiance; his 'German masters', from whom this most celebrated of musical autodidacts had already learned so much, had much work to do in steadying the ship, even offering coordinates, in what remained still largely uncharted 'atonal' territory. The first variation turns the theme upside down: nothing to worry about, for Bach, even Rachmaninov, does this sort of thing regularly – and audibly. Its successor turns it the 'right' way up again, the bass clarinet then joining in in duet to voice its 'upside down' inheritance. Guitar and mandolin likewise work together on their material, similarly the trio of violin, viola and cello. Schoenberg holds one's aural hand, consciously or otherwise; there is more than one thread through this labyrinth, should one require or desire a little instruction.

Yet ultimately, there is no more or less need to know than there would be with Bach; music works in different ways, at different times, to different people. One can see the patterns on the page, hear them in the ear, and yet they are not the only thing that matters, any more than the geometry in a Persian rug or a Paul Klee painting might be.[8] The unconscious will happily do its work here, just as it would in the op. 16 *Orchestral Pieces*. Above all, so much dances in this music: in all three works and in their successors, too. It teasingly leads us on a path lying between Strauss's *Rosenkavalier* and the subsequent nostalgia for a Vienna that never was, and Weimar wit, abstraction, even cabaret. There is even in the fifth movement a 'Tanzscene', in which we flit between different ballrooms, different taverns, different *Heuriger*, even different barracks – for the music marches too. Mozart's *Don Giovanni* meets Berg's *Wozzeck*, from a slight distance that is very much 'of the age', and which yet dissolves before our ears once the dance card begins to fill up.

For Schoenberg as for many (probably most) other composers, even Strauss, the period following the First World War – in his case, until *Moses und Aron* in 1930 – showed a diminution of Wagner's direct musical influence, although arguably the impulse to escape was often another form of influence, not to be mistaken for indifference. In Schoenberg's case, none of this took the form of outright anti-Wagnerism, as it did with, say, the French composers of *Les Six* and Stravinsky, in many ways their spiritual godfather. Nevertheless, Wagner waned now for Schoenberg in proportion to the waxing of the Austro-German instrumental musical tradition, symbolized by Brahms and his predecessors. Bach became increasingly important to both Stravinsky and Schoenberg – and at this time Bach was still viewed more as an instrumental than a vocal composer. In 1922 Schoenberg orchestrated two of Bach's organ chorale preludes, *Komm Gott, Schöpfer, Heiliger Geist* (Come God, Creator, Holy Ghost), BWV 667, and *Schmücke dich, o liebe Seele* (Adorn thyself, o dear soul), BWV 654. While using equally large orchestras, the conception was very different from contemporary transcriptions by Leopold Stokowski and Ottorino Respighi; the point was not to flesh out, to create orchestral showpieces, but to recompose, albeit through orchestration alone, thus showing a deeper kinship between 'original' and 'new' composer. That Schoenberg had chosen Bach as his successor was no matter of chance, but a claim to lineage.

The Bauhaus steel frame of the op. 25 *Suite* gleams on the surface only to reveal a Bösendorfer sensibility still thinking and moving beneath. It bears the external form – and not only that – of a Baroque suite: Prelude, Gavotte, Musette, Intermezzo (less Baroque, more Brahms), Menuett and Trio, Gigue. It was, though, to a very different reimagined Bach from Stravinsky's that Schoenberg paid homage. In the former's Bach, Schoenberg believed, eighteenth-century wigs and clothes were mistaken for the spirit of the music; alleged style for idea. And had not Bach been distinctly unfashionable in his heyday, outmoded by the *style galant* of his sons, of the fêted, cosmopolitan Telemann – by Handel, too? When, a decade later, Schoenberg reworked a Handel concerto grosso into a 'Concerto for String Quartet and Orchestra', he wrote on a postcard to Berg: 'in the end it will be a very good piece and that won't be Handel's doing, if I do say so.'[9] He was, as Bach himself had done to the music of composers from Couperin to Pergolesi, making it his own – and, so he thought, legitimizing it in the royal, indeed exclusive line of Bach. Such ideology matters; it is part of the work, of its style and its idea. It matters still more both because it enabled Schoenberg once again to write and to complete musical works, and because it became an important part of his defence mechanism, in a strange new world whose aesthetics did not seem to be his and whose increasing anti-Semitism questioned his right to work, to be heard and, perhaps, even to live.

The Stravinskian slogan 'back to Bach' infuriated Schoenberg so much that he mocked his more fashionable fellow composer as a mere 'restaurateur' in an essay in 1926. He issued the charge of mere fashion more savagely still in his own text, from the previous year, to the second of *Three Satires*, op. 28:

Well, who might that be, drumming over there?
If it isn't Little Modernsky himself!
He's had his pigtails cut;

it's looking rather good!
What genuine false hair!
Like a periwig!
(Quite, as Little Modernsky represents him),
Quite the Papa Bach!

Stravinsky and the neoclassical movement, then, was aping the
style of Bach, or rather the style of a false Bach who had never
existed. Schoenberg wished to honour his Idea. Such mere fashion,
such changing of clothes, was as absurd, as trivial, as pernicious, as
petulant as the abrupt turning away from Romanticism, above all
from Wagner, of which the tenor soloist sings (with, perhaps, a hint
of his own mock Romanticism) in the opening lines of the third,
more extended *Satire*:

No longer can I remain Romantic,
I hate 'Romantic';
from tomorrow onwards,
I shall write only the purest 'Classical'!

The strong vein of Kraus in Schoenberg was not dead; indeed,
a sense of being considered slightly *démodé* arguably lent him
new life. The subtlest bite lies, however, in the music. Where
Stravinsky's music stiffens polemically, belligerently – an
observation on my part, not a negative criticism – Schoenberg's
continues to dance, as only a Viennese believes he and his work can.
He does not need to define himself as 'Romantic' or 'Classical'; the
music's path defines him as both and as neither. There is cultural
nationalism at work here, too. It probably always had been; Mattsee
had unquestionably strengthened as well as challenged it.

So did Schoenberg's raw letters to Kandinsky in 1923.[10]
Kandinsky, who had invited the composer to consider becoming
director of the music school at the Bauhaus, received from Mödling

a response such as he could never have expected. 'It cannot be,' Schoenberg wrote,

> for I have at last learned the lesson forced upon me during this year, and I shall never forget it. It is that I am not a German, not a European, indeed perhaps scarcely even a human being (at least, the Europeans prefer the worst of their race to me), but I am a Jew . . . I have heard that even a Kandinsky sees only evil in the actions of Jews and in their evil actions only the Jewishness . . . It was a dream. We are two kinds of people. Definitively!

Ominously – especially with our historical hindsight – Schoenberg says that he would have to do 'whatever is necessary to keep alive'. He would nevertheless 'like the Kandinsky I knew in the past and the Kandinsky of today' both to take their 'fair share of my cordial and respectful greetings'. From Weimar, Kandinsky responded in protest: 'I love you as an artist and a human being, or perhaps as a human being and an artist . . . Among my friends who have been tested through many years (the word "friend" has a great meaning for me, so I seldom use it) are more Jews than Russians or Germans.' He asked, not unreasonably, why Schoenberg had not written to him at once when he had heard of his purported remarks. Schoenberg's lengthy response, however unjust it may have been to Kandinsky personally, bears moving testament to the consequences of more general anti-Semitism. Any sign of it – there was, to be fair, far more than a mere sign – at the Bauhaus rendered Kandinsky complicit with those 'who are capable of disturbing the peace', a clear reference to the Mattsee trauma, 'in which I want to work'. Schoenberg could not 'walk down the street and [when] each person looks at me to see whether I'm a Jew or a Christian . . . tell each of them that I'm the one that Kandinsky and some others make an exception of, although of course that man Hitler is not of their opinion'. This, we may recall, was in 1923, long before Hitler and the Nazis were seen as especially significant politically; indeed it was a good few months before the Munich putsch, after which, while imprisoned, Hitler wrote *Mein Kampf*. Schoenberg was clearly interested and concerned to an unusual extent. Why, moreover, he went on,

> do people say that the Jews are like what
> their black-marketeers are like?
>   Do people also say that the Aryans are like their worst elements? Why is an Aryan judged by Goethe, Schopenhauer and so forth? Why don't people say the Jews are like Mahler, Altenberg, Schoenberg and many others? . . .
>   What have I to do with communism? I'm not one [a communist] and never was one! . . .
>   Wouldn't I too necessarily know something of the Elders of Zion? . . .
>   But what is anti-Semitism to lead to if not to acts of violence? . . . One thing is certain: they will not be able to exterminate those much tougher elements thanks to whose endurance Jewry has maintained itself unaided against the whole of mankind for 20 centuries . . . To survive in exile, uncorrupted and unbroken, until the hour of salvation comes! . . .
>   If you would take it on yourself to convey greetings from me to my former friend Kandinsky, I should very much wish to charge you with some of my very warmest.[11]

Thereafter, a true revival of the friendship was out of the question. Their correspondence was almost over, too. What survives is confined to a postcard from the Kandinskys on holiday in the south of France in 1928, suggesting that Schoenberg and his wife join them, and a letter of 1936 to Schoenberg, whom Kandinsky has heard is 'now a (better, "the") dictator of music in California'. It draws to a close with the following lament for a friendship and civilization, both, flawed as they might always have been, now broken irreparably:

Do you still remember, dear Mr Schoenberg, how we met –
I arrived on the steamer wearing short Lederhosen and saw
a black-and-white graphic – you were dressed completely in
white and only your face was deeply tanned. And later the
summer in Murnau? All our contemporaries from that time
sigh deeply when they remember that vanished epoch and
say: 'That was a beautiful time.' . . . How wonderfully life
pulsated then, what quick spiritual triumphs we expected.
Even today I expect them, and with the most complete certainty.
But I know that a long, long time will still be necessary.[12]

In March 1924 a Mödling neighbour, Rudolph Seiden, handed
Schoenberg a series of Zionist pamphlets. Seiden, a Zionist activist
and the inventor of tempered glass, was as early as the 1920s
involved in helping Jews to escape to Palestine from Russia and
Poland. He asked Schoenberg to write for a pamphlet, *Pro Zion!*
In a short declaration, Schoenberg stated what would remain
a fundamental belief of his later Zionism, whether focused on
Uganda, Palestine or anywhere else: that strong, unabashedly
terroristic military force would be necessary to protect a Jewish
state. It had always been so in biblical times; so would it be again,
'not through words and morality, but through victorious weapons
and a lucky confluence of interests'.[13] However much one might
wish him to have been wrong, he was not, as the history of the
State of Israel since its foundation in 1948 has shown.
    In 1923 Schoenberg had suffered a second, far greater loss than
that of Kandinsky. Mathilde, who had been ill for pretty much the
past three years, died on 22 October. Whatever her faults, Alma
Gropius was clearly one of the first to send condolences, for, in a note
dated the following day, Arnold, Gertrud (Trudi), Felix Greissle and
Georg sent thanks for her flowers and kind words. It is probably
fair to say that theirs had never, or not for a long time, been an
especially happy marriage. Mathilde – this is not to sound a note of

The Kandinskys (Wassily and Nina) and Schoenbergs (Gertrud and Arnold) on holiday in the Carinthian resort of Pörtschach, 1927.

moral disapproval – may well have pursued a number of dalliances, or at least wished to; such was not at all Schoenberg's way. There is no reason, however, to consider her death to have been in any way a relief to him, even if, in some ways, it may have been 'objectively'. Zemlinsky was too upset even to attend the funeral. A letter to him makes it clear that Schoenberg greatly missed his wife's household organizational skills, conceding also that he had never been the easiest person to live with. Schoenberg wrote a poem, 'Requiem', in her memory, with the intention (unfulfilled) of setting it to music. The presence of his daughter and her family seems to have cheered, even saved, him; according to a memoir by their son Arnold, his parents had found him 'not only smoking like a chimney, but also drinking a great deal of schnapps, as much as three litres of coffee per day, also Pantopon [opiates], and concentrated opium tablets. My mother feared he would commit suicide.'[14]

However, within a year Schoenberg had remarried. The apparent lightning speed of his relationship with Rudolf

Kolisch's sister Gertrud upset his children and Zemlinsky, whom Schoenberg seems only to have informed after the ceremony. It doubtless did not encourage the latter to examine too deeply his incomprehension of, and outright opposition to, Schoenberg's new method; it would take more than a decade, after Zemlinsky had arrived in New York in 1938 as a refugee, for their friendship to resume properly. Just a few days before young Arnold's birth, his grandfather and Gertrud were married in the Protestant church at Mödling (barely five minutes' walk from Schoenberg's apartment). Theirs seems to have been a happier union; perhaps they simply had more in common, and/or the relationship came at a better time. An improved financial situation, now that the ravages of hyperinflation were over, also helped; leisure and socializing were again, within reason, more of an option. Gertrud's gift for tennis encouraged Schoenberg, always a keen swimmer, to add the game to his sporting portfolio. Future tennis partners would, famously, include George Gershwin in Hollywood.

Towards the end of his life, Schoenberg – always fascinated by rules, analysis and invention – would come up with a form of notation to transcribe the tennis matches of his athlete son Ronald, who had more than inherited his mother's excellence at the sport. It followed in the line of 'coalition chess', designed at just the time Schoenberg was formulating his new compositional method: an expanded four-player, ten-square-by-ten-square version of the traditional game, involving superpowers and lesser powers all compelled to forge alliances, with new pieces such as aeroplanes, tanks, submarines and so forth. Beyond that should also be mentioned the inventive gaming precedent of three sets of *Jugendstil*-cum-geometrical playing cards designed during the *Wunderjahr* of 1909; designs for music stands and other furniture; even, in 1927, for a Berlin connecting public transport ticket; and, of course, a host of twelve-note slide rules still to be seen in his re-created office at the Arnold Schönberg Center in Vienna.

'To Baby Arnold' (Dem Bubi Arnold) read the dedication of the Quintet, op. 26, for flute, oboe, clarinet, horn and bassoon. Game-playing is certainly not absent from this sunny, direly neglected work, whose composition spanned the worst and best of Schoenberg's life, written as it was between 1923 and 1925. Indeed, rotations, inversions and all the rest are there for anyone to hear – it matters not a jot if one does not 'know' them as such – in a work that seems to breathe a mixture of the air of a Mozart Salzburg serenade and something yet more Alpine, more 'purified'. It is almost as if Stravinsky in his *Octet* had felt no need to assert its neoclassicism so belligerently (again, no adverse criticism intended), and had felt more self-assured in his Classical heritage. There is even a tonal centre of sorts – there often is in his apparently non-tonal music, although how much that matters is a moot point – and it 'happens' to be E-flat, emphatically so at the close. It is the tonic for both Mozart's Quintet for Piano and Wind, KV 475, and his Serenade, KV 375; it is difficult to imagine that Schoenberg was entirely unaware of the precedent and lineage, although it is a key that makes very good sense for wind instruments generally. Likewise with the suggestions – more than that, really – of the whole-tone scale generated both by the note row Schoenberg chooses and the use to which it is put. The effect is quite unlike that of Debussy (listen to the opening of his Piano *Prélude* 'Voiles' for an example), where the scale will often speak of a wondrously constructed ambiguity. Here, by contrast, with perhaps more than a nod to the use of the scale in the tonal First Chamber Symphony and 'Das Wappenschild' from the op. 8 *Orchestral Songs*, new possibilities are presented with knife-edge precision. Debussy certainly does not choose his notes arbitrarily; he rather connives to have us perceive a vagueness to them. Whatever the similarity of means, though, such is not Schoenberg's way – and certainly not here. Instead, counterpoint rules, exhilaratingly so, almost as if coalition chess

were being played before our ears. Its dazzling invention is
fun – or will be, in comprehending performance and listening.
Quite why it remains so neglected by wind ensembles, compared
with works by Hindemith, Carl Nielsen and even György Ligeti,
say, is a mystery, save for the undeserved bogeyman status of
Schoenberg himself. It merits being heard just as often as the
First Chamber Symphony, the freedom *and* organization of whose
lines, even harmonies, it often seems both to recall and to develop.
Performances of Schoenberg's work were once again becoming
more frequent across the world, with a mixture of public and
private patronage that was typical of most 'serious' composers of
the time. The *Serenade*, for instance, received its first performance
in a private house in Vienna, that of Norbert Schwarzmann, in
May 1924. Its first public performance was at the summer festival
in Donaueschingen, to which Schoenberg received a personal
invitation from Prince Max Egon Fürstenberg (a great artistic
patron and later, alas, an enthusiastic Nazi). Schoenberg – and
others – continued to conduct *Pierrot*, both to great acclaim and to
occasional dissatisfaction. Milhaud gave its Paris premiere in 1921,
as part of the Concerts Wiener series, overcoming a great deal of
anti-German (and anti-Austrian) sentiment to do so. Whether this
and the decision to perform it in Giraud's 'original' French rather
than the German translation Schoenberg had set were connected
is difficult to say; it certainly made its mark on some of Milhaud's
own works, although Paris and France in general would remain
very much in the hostile, Stravinskian camp. Boulez would recall
how difficult it had been to hear any performances of modernist
Austro-German music, even that of Mahler, during his youth.
It had been straightforwardly impossible, he said, to hear good
ones, hence his decision to perform Second Viennese School music
himself.

 Pierrot received its Italian premiere in 1924, at the Palazzo
Pitti in Florence, conducted by Schoenberg. In the audience

Schoenberg's Coalition Chess pieces and board, *c.* 1920–25.

the young Luigi Dallapiccola, then studying at the Florence Conservatory, resolved at that moment to concentrate his energy on composition. An honoured guest in the audience was Giacomo Puccini, whose late music bore the stamp of many more overtly modernist composers: Debussy, Stravinsky and, yes, Schoenberg. Listen to almost any music from that wondrous theatre of cruelty *Turandot* and affinity, if not necessarily influence, will be clear. (In some cases, Puccini's earlier music seems to have pre-empted his younger colleagues. If ever a composer, or at least his reputation, needed rescuing from his devotees, it is he.) While many in the audience laughed – not for nothing had this long been Habsburg territory – Puccini listened intently throughout, and afterwards

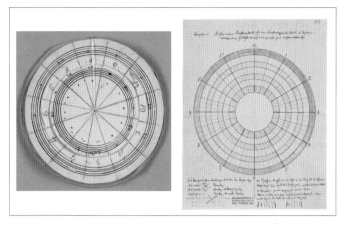

Twelve-note selection dial for the Wind Quintet, op. 26, followed on the right-hand side by Schoenberg's 1927 design for a Berlin public transport ticket to facilitate connections between buses, trams and overground trains. London's Oyster system may or may not eventually catch up.

asked Alfredo Casella, whose Corporazione della Nuove Musiche had organized the concert, to introduce him to Schoenberg; Schoenberg would subsequently relate how moved he had been by the presence of that 'great man'. The two composers talked into the early hours; alas, we have no record of what was said. A quarter of a century later Dallapiccola, now the composer of the first Italian twelve-note opera, *Il prigioniero* (The Prisoner), would write to Schoenberg:

> I had seen you in Florence at the time of the first Italian tour of *Pierrot lunaire*, but how could I, a Conservatory student, find the courage on that evening to come and shake your hand? In any case, I have never forgotten the attitude of Puccini with regard to you on that 1 April 1924, and since that evening I have considered the popular Italian composer to be of an intelligence and a humanity that I had not suspected.[15]

Schoenberg could bring out the best, as well as the worst, and all manner of in-betweens in his pupils, followers and admirers. The identity of various groups changed over time, of course, not least according to Schoenberg's current home and focus of activities. That was about to change once more, for it was again time to leave Vienna and its immediate surroundings.

First page of Schoenberg's manuscript for the Wind Quintet, op. 26.

6

Goodbye to Berlin

Berlin had changed a good deal, as had Germany 'proper', since Schoenberg had left. In 1918 the pianist and musical pedagogue Leo Kestenberg had become the senior musical representative in the Prussian Ministry of Culture. A pupil of Busoni, Kestenberg – born, like Schoenberg, an Austro-Hungarian Jew – instigated a series of reforms, informally bearing his name. Those reforms continue to shape German musical education to this day. He also made a bold series of appointments to university positions, to ensnare or to assure their beneficiaries for the Prussian and German capital, and to attempt to banish the stale conservatism of Wilhelmine Berlin once and for all. In 1920 Busoni was at last appointed to an official position. Others appointed included Wilhelm Furtwängler, Franz Schreker, Paul Hindemith, Erich Kleiber, Otto Klemperer – and Schoenberg. Busoni's Master Class in Composition for the Prussian Academy of Arts had become a crucial part of the ecology of Berlin musical life, as had Schreker's appointment to the Hochschule für Musik, since it brought many Viennese musicians to the German capital. When Busoni died, in 1924, Kestenberg was determined to ensnare Schoenberg. The following year, having obtained the approval of his minister, Carl Heinrich Becker, he did just that. Schoenberg had come close to accepting an invitation to teach at the Moscow Conservatoire, but now, at least for the moment, he dropped that plan. Following a series of delays on grounds of work and ill health, he moved back to Berlin on 10 January 1926.

Some of his Vienna pupils, such as Hans Eisler and Winfried Zillig (who would later prepare a performing edition of *Die Jakobsleiter*), joined him. Josef Rufer, who had moved there just a few months previously, became Schoenberg's assistant, teaching some of the more rudimentary classes. Roberto Gerhard, whom Schoenberg already knew from a visit to Barcelona, joined both as pupil and fellow assistant. Other new pupils attracted to Berlin from across the world included the American composer Marc Blitzstein; Nikos Skalkottas, the first Greek dodecaphonist; and Natalie Pravossudovich, Schoenberg's only Soviet pupil. A distinguished 'home', indeed Berliner, pupil was Walter Goehr: composer, conductor, far too seldom acknowledged figure in the Monteverdi revival – conductor of the first ever British performance of the Vespers, and of the first recording of *L'incoronazione di Poppea* (The Coronation of Poppea) – and father of the composer Alexander Goehr, whom we might thereby account as Schoenberg's grand-pupil. According to Gerhard, this international bunch was known to envious undergraduates at the Hochschule für Musik as *die Meistersinger von Schoenberg*.[1] Another pupil, the Swiss composer Erich Schmid, described, in a letter written to his parents shortly after having arrived in Berlin, both Schoenberg's unorthodox style and his continued concentration on the Austro-German classics:

> Schoenberg received us in a very kindly fashion and chatted for two hours in the most lively manner. Barely a word concerned music – no, about architecture, painting, and sculpture. For him, everything connects to his art. Then he also spoke about his own work. He emphasised that he understands it as having developed from tradition . . . Brahms and Beethoven are his exemplars for formal concerns, while Wagner is his starting point for harmony . . . He has a fine sense of humour and sometimes can be very sarcastic. He takes a keen interest in his students' well-being.[2]

Schoenberg used the work of those masters to point out what not to do, too. Schmid tells of his praising, to his students' surprise, the thematic invention in Max Reger's Violin Concerto, while criticizing the lack of clarity in its orchestration. Even on those relatively few occasions – longed for by his pupils – when he would discuss one of his own twelve-note works, he did not discuss the method at all. Schoenberg used the Wind Quintet, op. 26, 'to show how he integrated classical formal principles in his own style'. Just as in Vienna – and Los Angeles – he inspired fierce loyalty in his pupils, who often set out to conquer the musical world in his name. As often as not, they succeeded. Moreover, a number of musicians who were not officially his pupils were nevertheless part of his circle: for instance, two Schreker pupils, Ernst Krenek and the conductor Jascha Horenstein, a pioneering Schoenberg (and Mahler) advocate.

A great problem, perhaps the greatest problem, had not gone away. Living in Weimar Germany, even someone far less acutely aware than Schoenberg of anti-Semitism and its probable consequences would never have thought that it could. On the other hand, before the Wall Street Crash of 1929 and the ensuing Depression, there seemed little likelihood of Hitler and his party becoming a party of government. Even then, it was not over until it was over, since the Nazis never gained more than 37 per cent of the vote, and their support slipped back immediately before they seized power. (That is not to say, of course, that there were no anti-Semitic supporters of other parties.)

Schoenberg's long march back through the wilderness to Judaism and his swifter path towards Zionist commitment continued, the latter marked artistically by a spoken drama, *Der biblische Weg* (The Biblical Way) of 1926. The play is generally considered simply as an agitprop milestone on the path towards his biblical opera *Moses und Aron*, its directly contemporary concerns later subsumed into a greater theological understanding.

It depends, though, what one is looking for. As an artwork, it is of lesser, although far from negligible, interest. As a document of Schoenberg's growing insistence that the Jewish people required a state of their own, and as a document of Zionist history, it is more important. Schoenberg even sketched some set designs. It has been aptly termed, by Herbert Lindenberger, an '"unhistorical history play", a characteristically modern form which, in examples such as Hofmannsthal's *Der Turm* (The Tower) and Brecht's *Mutter Courage* (Mother Courage), employs the conventions drawn from earlier historical drama to simulate a representation of history'.[3] Great events of biblical Israel's history are present, transposed to an African New Palestine, a successful version of Theodor Herzl's Ugandan project, as a prelude to a future (although, note, a future) return to the true Promised Land. When the hero, Max Aruns, lies dying, he recognizes his hubris and addresses the Jewish God:

> Lord, thou hast smitten me. Thus I have brought it upon myself. Thus [his antagonist, David] Asseino was right, when he accused me of being presumptuous, of wanting to be Moses and Aron in one person. Thus I have betrayed the Idea . . . I am dying, but I feel that thou wilt allow the Idea to survive. And I shall die in peace, for I know that thou wilt always provide our nation with men ready to offer their lives for this concept of the one and only, eternal, invisible and unimaginable God. (*dies*).[4]

The play was never performed during Schoenberg's lifetime, after approaches to the impresario Max Reinhardt and his publisher led nowhere. To be continued, as they say.

Otherwise, especially during the earlier part of this period, life was relatively good. Schoenberg had to be in Berlin for only about half the year. He was able both to compose and to travel: sometimes for performances, sometimes on holiday and sometimes to see old acquaintances in Vienna. They would also visit him, as seen in the evocative photograph of the Schoenbergs, Kokoschka, Loos and a barman: seeming participants in a strange mixture of old-fashioned Expressionist drama and newfangled *Zeitoper*, on which more below.

There is something of the spirit, or at least the sound, of the Roaring Twenties in the *Suite*, op. 29, for piano, piccolo clarinet, clarinet, bass clarinet, violin, viola and cello, which Schoenberg began in 1924 and completed in 1926. Dance rhythms (the waltz is never far away) combine with a wind- and especially clarinet-heavy, almost swing-band sound such as one might hear in Hindemith, or in the music of Busoni's pupil Kurt Weill, whose music – or perhaps its popularity – Schoenberg loathed, claiming to find in it no positive qualities whatsoever.[5] That combination effects a somewhat rebarbative mordancy – although no more so than, say, in Stravinsky's *Soldier's Tale* – that, for many listeners, seems to have masked a declaration of marital love to 'my dear wife'. Perhaps the listener might benefit from reading a little of Kraus's satire beforehand.

A musical cipher of Gertrud's initials (a phonetic spelling of GS; 'Es', being E-flat in German notation) is, in typical Second Viennese School style, integrated into the musical texture at the opening and close of each of the four movements. More to the point, the intervals – thirds and sixths – thereby brought to the fore assist in construction and, to our ears, constructivism. Balance between competing demands seems to have proved tricky in performance, even by Schoenberg's exacting standards, and this is a sardonic and also frankly enjoyable work that is all too rarely performed, still more rarely performed well. It really needs the flexibility of *Schwung*, 'classical swing,' while at the same time maintaining a certain distance: felt and observed, one might say. Like *Così fan tutte*, it perhaps depends a little much, for a typical audience, on knowledge or at least perception of what is being stylized, even parodied; it is well worth the effort, if ultimately still more distanced, less ravishing than its agonizingly beautiful predecessor.

Oskar Kokoschka, the Schoenbergs and Adolf Loos at the Bristol Bar, Berlin, 1927.
Originally published in *Der Weltspiegel*, no. 12, 20 March 1927.

Classical proportions and indeed forms inform the Third
String Quartet, op. 30. It was commissioned by the great American
patroness Elizabeth Sprague Coolidge, to whom works by
Bartók, Webern, Frank Bridge, Benjamin Britten, Ravel, Poulenc,
Stravinsky, Prokofiev and others are owed. If one could hardly
view it as 'white music' in the sense of Stravinsky's commission,
the polemically diatonic *Apollon musagète*, there is a serenity that
brings it closer than one might initially suspect to neoclassicism.
Schoenberg, still keen to show both himself and the world that
his method worked by using it with 'old' forms, or at least close
relations, presented a sonata-form movement, followed by a theme
and variations, a scherzo and trio (its marking as intermezzo
notwithstanding), and a sonata-rondo finale – which surely
echoes Mozart's quartets for the King of Prussia in its high-lying
cello line. Not that that excluded the composer's long-standing
practice of 'developing variation'; he was simply, or not so simply,
finding inspiration and precedent in earlier music than once

he had. Increasingly, even incessantly, he heard Mozart and Beethoven in Brahms and in himself; and vice versa. The work was written in 1927. Vienna had the honour, deserved or otherwise, of the premiere that same year, in a concert of Sprague Coolidge commissions; she would also commission his Fourth (and final) String Quartet in 1936. Schoenberg would recall that, while no riot was occasioned, the Viennese understood his music no better than they had before; critics were apparently unanimous 'that I might possess a remarkable musical knowledge and technique, but did not create instinctively, that I wrote without inspiration. I was called a constructor, a musical engineer, a mathematician.'[6]

Brahms returned more forcefully to the fore in Schoenberg's *Variations for Orchestra*, op. 31, composed between 1926 and 1928 – with more than a little of Mahler's orchestral writing, even marching parody (via the *Five Orchestral Pieces*) added to the mix. In that respect it is not unlike, albeit in music of greater complexity, Webern's op. 1, the *Passacaglia*, which form Schoenberg had initially considered, and for which a compositional fragment remains. Notes from the row are split between different instruments; discerning its progress is emphatically not the thing, whether in Schoenberg's intention or our experience, although experience, conscious or otherwise, of its new-found freedoms might well be. Viennese dances, even *Schrammelmusik*, come and go – as they always did, so long as performers and listeners alike permit. Whereas with the music of Bartók, still more Janáček, excessive emphasis on 'folk' elements can sometimes obscure more fundamental qualities, here almost the opposite is true; at the very least, such traditions from the past will offer a way in for new listeners. Developing variation seems to flow more naturally than ever, at least as far as twelve-note Schoenberg is concerned, in what is after all a set of variations. The notational cipher BACH – 'B' being B-flat, and 'H' B-natural – is here enthroned, however much Schoenberg might subsequently downplay its sentimental presence, as a triumphant, or at least defiant, riposte to 'little Modernsky' and company. The orchestration in 1928 of Bach's *St Anne* Prelude and Fugue, BWV 552, in which Schoenberg 'inauthentically', and with great wit, employs a vast modern orchestra to sound both quite unlike the 'historical' Bach and yet also, on occasion, very much like him (listen to the use of reed instruments to suggest the organ), should also be understood partly in this context.

Like many variation sets from the hallowed 'three Bs' – Bach, Beethoven, Brahms – the point is not so much to listen to how the theme is varied; here, it might even take some time to appreciate that. Rather, variation form is the basis for a musical argument that one might conceivably call symphonic – especially in the line of a work such as the First Chamber Symphony – although Schoenberg himself proved more cautious. In a radio lecture given before a broadcast performance from Frankfurt in 1931, under Hans Rosbaud, the composer put it thus: 'Variations are like an album with views of some place or landscape, showing you particular aspects of it. A symphony, on the other hand, is like a panorama in which one certainly views the pictures separately: but in reality they are closely linked and merge into each other.' He nevertheless conceded that the distinction was anything but absolute, and that, in the finale, citing Beethoven's *Eroica* Symphony and Brahms's *Variations on a Theme by Haydn* as precedents, 'we . . . take our farewell of the world embodied in this work with a final bird's-eye view of our panorama – . . . that will . . . create new links between the sections, giving a total impression which . . . sums up and points to the moral.'[7]

Schoenberg broke off work on the *Variations* in order to write *Der biblische Weg* (The Biblical Way), and found it quite difficult to return to the work, although a prod from Furtwängler helped to persuade him. Furtwängler wanted to give the premiere with the Vienna Philharmonic, but Schoenberg refused, insisting that the orchestra must first make good its prior complete neglect of his music. (It is still playing catch-up, and perhaps always will be. Almost incredibly, it gave its first ever performance of the Piano Concerto as late as 2005, with Daniel Barenboim as soloist and Boulez conducting.) Instead, Furtwängler gave the premiere in Berlin, with that city's Philharmonic Orchestra, on 2 December 1928. His posthumous conservative reputation belies a sense of duty and occasional enthusiasm concerning New Music. He had already conducted not only the orchestral version of *Verklärte Nacht* and *Pelleas und Melisande*, but the *Five Orchestral Pieces* (including the premiere of its revised version in Leipzig in 1922, followed by performances in Berlin). Nevertheless, it was perhaps just as well that Schoenberg, avoiding Berlin winters as much as he could on health grounds, did not attend, remaining at Roquebrune-Cap-Martin on the French Riviera. Webern, distraught on his beloved teacher's behalf at the reception of the work, accused Furtwängler of grave irresponsibility in having scheduled only three rehearsals. In his memoirs the cellist Gregor Piatigorsky tells a similar tale, detailing several wrong entries. Furtwängler, according to Piatigorsky, had become quite lost during the performance, and indeed had spoken beforehand with great relief about the fact that the composer, who was in possession of the only other score, would be unable to attend.[8] Those in the audience unable to make head or tail of what they were hearing were not, then, necessarily at fault.

Schoenberg's post-Romantic understanding of tradition was not very distant from Furtwängler's more conservative Romanticism; it certainly proceeded from similar roots. Even a glance at the score reveals it to be conceived in terms of a mighty river's ebb and flow, such as Furtwängler would have given the music of Brahms. Schoenberg's markings stand somewhere between Mahler's always detailed provisions and a written-out version of what both he and Furtwängler believed to be implied in a Classical-Romantic score. It is rather a pity that the conductor never returned to these *Variations*, for his was just the sort of advocacy from which Schoenberg would have benefited. The performance was certainly not greeted as a success by a bewildered public, still less by critics as vicious as Schoenberg's old friends from Vienna. One even demanded that such a corrupter of musical youth be removed from his teaching position. As the political situation deteriorated, such demands would henceforth never be far away.

In the meantime, Schoenberg was preparing to surprise the world with an operatic comedy. Yes, he had a keen sense of humour, especially of sarcasm and satire, but it is fair to say that no one save Gertrud foresaw the advent of the one-act *Von heute auf morgen* (From Today to Tomorrow), op. 32, before its revelation in 1929. To a text by Max Blonda, Schoenberg had been composing the score to a modern comedy of manners, which may have been loosely based on an incident in the life of the Schrekers, and which almost certainly owed something to the concept of Strauss's *Intermezzo*, and most probably also to *Jonny spielt auf* (Jonny Strikes Up) by Schreker's pupil Ernst Krenek. The latter story of a jazz violinist had proved a great commercial success, and Schoenberg expected his new opera to do likewise. 'Max Blonda', it would emerge, was none other than Schoenberg's own fun-loving – although not in *that* sense – wife, Gertrud. The genre of *Zeitoper*, 'opera of the times', proved short-lived; the Schoenbergs both contributed to it and satirized it meta-theatrically.

With more than a nod to Schoenberg's Expressionist past, as if already to decry the dictates of fashion, the principal couple are simply a Wife and Husband, joined by a fashionable Friend and Singer. In an anticipation of the contrast between mellifluous Aron and intransigent Moses, the (operetta?) Singer's music tends to move in notably conventional fashion, by step. There is even a 'popular' song (these things are relative), replete with saxophone. Other jazzy elements, instrumental and rhythmical (syncopation in particular), suggest a merely temporal 'modernity' that Schoenberg viewed with almost as much suspicion as he did the music of Stravinsky. Ensembles both pay homage to tradition – *Così*, intentionally or otherwise, springs to mind, although *The Marriage of Figaro* is probably more likely to have been a direct inspiration – and suggest a pandemonium of thoroughly domestic proportions. Thoughts, chatter and even a degree of experience of infidelity and other modern mores lead the original couple to realize that they are much better off with each other; those sometime interlopers in a once-more-happy marriage had only ever been 'faded theatre characters'.

At the close, the couple's child asks, naively and yet with knowing irony on the part of its artistic creators, what 'modern people' are. It changes, the child is told, from one day to the next: *von heute auf morgen*. That final exchange and the opera more generally may be understood as the dramatic counterpart to Schoenberg's response to criticism such as that which he had received from the French, following the premiere in Paris in 1927 of the op. 29 *Suite*: 'A French critic thinks that I should surely by now have overcome purely intellectual counterpoint. *I* don't develop so quickly.'[9] The critic was, in Schoenberg's opinion, confusing him with mere purveyors of fashion such as Milhaud, Poulenc and Stravinsky, who must come up with a new style every season simply to stay ahead. *Von heute auf morgen* was never the hit Schoenberg, with a naivety at least equal to that of the opera's child, had anticipated. He lost a great deal of money, on the basis of that conviction, in self-publication of the score. It received but a single staging during his lifetime, in Frankfurt in 1930. (Schoenberg himself conducted a radio performance at the same time.) He had returned to opera, though, and had composed at a speed almost rivalling that of 1909.

Two piano pieces, written independently yet brought together as op. 33*a* and op. 33*b*, the *Accompaniment to a Film Scene*, op. 34, and *Six Pieces for Male Chorus*, op. 35, were all written between

1929 and 1931. The op. 33 *Pieces* are perhaps more indebted to the spirit of Brahms than any others Schoenberg had written, even in his first piano set, op. 11. Gone is any hint of dancing (or other) neoclassicism; these might, save for the harmony – and there are even hints in that – almost be entitled 'Intermezzo' in that tradition. Look at them on the page and the resemblance, albeit without a hint of imitation, is striking. Again, the trick is to make them sound, and to listen to them, as such. The choral pieces initially responded to a commission from the Deutsche Arbeiter-Sängerbund, an organization for workers' choruses from across Germany: very much part of Kestenberg's ambitions for community music, as well as a reminder of the beginnings of Schoenberg's own musical career. Berg rightly praised them in a letter to his teacher in 1931 for their navigation of what, for some, might be competing demands of compositional rigour and (relative) ease of performance. Schoenberg composed them alongside some beautiful arrangements (without opus number) of old folk songs, for *a cappella* mixed chorus and for solo voice and piano; perhaps it was that experience, or simply the need no longer to prove anything, that led him, building on tonal implications in the earlier pieces, to write a frankly tonal, non-serial piece as the last in the series, 'Verbundenheit', a moving reconciliation with his 'special' key of D minor. Its predecessor, 'Landsknechte' (Mercenaries), seems to look back in its vivid pictorialism to his war years, to the drumming and marching of *Die eiserne Brigade*, and perhaps also, with hindsight, to the horrors of the war to come and *A Survivor from Warsaw*. Schoenberg still dearly wanted to communicate to a broader public, if it would listen.

The same might be said of the miniature tone poem, or film music without film, of Schoenberg's op. 34, *Accompaniment to a Moving Picture Scene*. The style is more Expressionist than had recently been typical, but the music is dodecaphonic throughout. The composer was beginning to emerge from his self-imposed, however fruitful, Classical restraints. The philosopher Theodor Adorno, also a composition pupil of Berg, praised it, in his review of the first performance, as a 'succinct 'introduction to twelve-note technique'.[10] Schoenberg, who always distrusted Adorno's theorizing – and never esteemed him as a composer – might have retorted, as he often did when Adorno was mentioned, that he mistook method for system. Many of the 'effects' Schoenberg employs here would become stock vocabulary for later film composers, but only rarely would they display such command of self-standing musical form. It may be recalled that, even before the advent of talking pictures, Schoenberg had been interested in the possibilities of film as a medium. Klemperer, now at Berlin's modernist Kroll Opera with poor Zemlinsky as his assistant, gave an early performance there, although not the premiere, which had fallen to Rosbaud in Frankfurt. It was also Klemperer who suggested to Schoenberg that an actual film, with László Moholy-Nagy of the Bauhaus as collaborator, might be made to accompany this theoretically accompanying music. Although the plan came to naught, its possibilities greatly interested Schoenberg. Things might well have turned out differently, for music and perhaps even for film. In its three parts, in freely developing variation form, Schoenberg depicts – in one sense or another – 'Threatening Danger', 'Fear' and 'Catastrophe'. If I argued against divining presentiments of the First World War in his or anyone else's music before 1914, it is difficult here, given Schoenberg's astonishing foresight concerning National Socialism and the Jews, not to detect a sense of personal and societal foreboding. 'Danger' is 'threatened', as you might have guessed, against a backdrop of old Viennese waltzes, perhaps as much an echo of Ravel's whirling vortex in *La Valse* as of anything in Strauss. The scoring of 'Fear' and 'Catastrophe' suggests something more of contemporary Berlin, of *Neue Sachlichkeit*, even of the sounds (if hardly the styles and methods) of Hindemith and Weill. Whatever remains once tragic catastrophe, be it personal, political or just imaginary, has passed is, at very best, an uneasy, even anaesthetized calm. Even Schoenberg could – or would – see only so far ahead.

A cinematic imagination of a very different – almost Cecil B. DeMille – variety sometimes seems both to haunt and to be rejected by *Moses und Aron*. It would indeed eventually be made into a film by artists of a very different, Brechtian aesthetic: Jean-Marie Straub and Danièle Huillet.[11] Schoenberg's stage directions certainly read as if knowingly self-defeating. For instance: 'During Aron's last speech, processions of laden camels, asses, horses, as well as porters, and wagons come on stage from different directions. They bring offerings of gold, grain, wineskins, animals and the like. At many places in the foreground and background, they are unloaded and loaded once more.' Noah's Ark seems resurrected as, once again, 'processions of all manner of animals pass by'. When the opera was finally staged, in Zurich in 1957, Erwin Stein reported with apparent irony that 'there was not enough space for displaying the processions of camels, wagons and asses which are supposed to bring offerings to the idols. These tasks as well as the slaughter of cattle and the roasting of meat, which are part of the offerings, will tax the resources of any opera house.'[12]

Why mention that? It is certainly not to mock Schoenberg. Wagner's naturalism now seems at least as absurd to us, and just as unrealizable. Schoenberg, however, in this neo-Wagnerian music drama – on a different scale from his three one-act works – was writing a work about impossibility, about the reductive quality of images and those who would rely on them, about the necessity to communicate and yet the inability to do so without betraying the (divine) essence of the Idea. Written between 1927 and 1932, *Moses* started life as an oratorio text, subsequently transformed into the libretto for an opera. Notwithstanding Schoenberg's continual insistence on his intention of completing it, the work remained unfinished, the only music for the third act amounting to a few sketches. There is, however, no contradiction between that intent – in 1945 he would unsuccessfully apply for a Guggenheim Fellowship to help him finish it, *Die Jakobsleiter* and three textbooks for his students – and the potential impossibility of the task, itself finding dramatization in the work. When at work on conducting *Moses* in 1996, Boulez would succinctly point to the problem at its heart: 'Is it conceivable that one could have an artistic language capable of producing some effect? Can I convince anyone without it?'[13]

At the intellectual and dramatic heart of *Moses* lies this passage from the Bible:

> Thou shalt not make unto thee any graven image, or any likeness of any thing that is in heaven above, or that is in the earth beneath, or that is in the water under the earth: Thou shalt not bow down thyself to them, nor serve them: for I the LORD thy God am a jealous God, visiting the iniquity of the fathers upon the children unto the third and fourth generation of them that hate me. (Exodus 20:4)

In the Lutheran tradition, at least, music had tended to be considered imageless and thus exempt from that commandment. For Schoenberg, the post-Wagnerian, Lutheran-Jewish (the latter increasingly so) architect of a new *Gesamtkunstwerk*, that exemption was proving to be increasingly problematic – at least when he thought about it. Yet write the opera he did, with an array of musical representation to rival anything from those impossible stage directions. From a single twelve-note row, he derived all manner of musical expression: Moses' stern, law-giving *Sprechstimme*, laden with negative descriptions of an unimaginable, invisible, unrepresentable God; Aron's sinuously *sung*, effortlessly persuasive twelve-note *bel canto*, musico-dramatic progenitor of the idolatrous Golden Calf and the frenzied delirium of the orgy surrounding it; and, just as important, navigating unsuccessfully, tragically, between them, the music of the Children of Israel, listening to, swayed by, driven to their death by the conflict between two irreconcilable tendencies. All of Schoenberg's vast experience in orchestration and dance rhythms, as well as his proud heritage in the Passions of Bach, comes together in the fiendishly complex writing for orchestra and chorus in the Golden Calf scene.

And yet, as Adorno would comment, 'The absolute which this music sets out to make real, without any sleight of hand, it achieves as its own idea of itself: it is itself an image of something about images – the very last thing the story wanted.'[14] It ends, or rather comes to a final impasse, in the tragedy both of a broken, angry Moses and of the twin necessity and impossibility of both his and Schoenberg's tasks. The price paid for truth – and there is clearly an element of autobiography here, however wary we remain of reductionism – is that (almost) no one will or can listen. As the final words of the second act, at which point the score essentially breaks off, have it:

Unrepresentable God!
Inexpressible Idea of many meanings,
wilt thou permit this explanation?
Shall Aron, my mouth, fashion this image?
Thus, I have fashioned an image too, false,
as an image can only be!
Thus, I am defeated!
Thus, everything I believed before was madness,
and can and must not be voiced!
O word, thou word that I lack!

A lengthy violin unison builds to *fortissimo* and then subsides into silence. Music can perhaps hint at what words cannot do; whether it can go beyond them remains an open question.

Moses embraces difficulty, or rather is about difficulty. It is not, however, being 'difficult' for the sake of it. Nor is it nearly so impenetrable – or any other of those negative descriptions in which it deals – as many think, perhaps as it seems to think. It is, above all else, searing drama, which may or may not be a betrayal or failure. What it does not do, what Schoenberg never does, is pander, pretend that everything is easy. If one were, for instance, to make a very rough and ready summary of the German idealist philosophy, on which, among other things, the opera rests, it might be that the difficulty of reading, say, Kant and Hegel is in part deliberate. One might miss ready, Voltairean wit – less so when Schoenberg comes close to Kraus – but the difficulty of reading what they write drives one to think, and, especially in Hegel's case, to think differently, to think in terms of apparent contradictions, and to embrace them. Read Voltaire, by contrast – or perhaps, in a dubious musical comparison, listen to Ravel or Stravinsky – and it may seem relatively straightforward, even on a first encounter. Think about what lies beneath the surface, or even, in a red rag to Stravinsky's aesthetics, about what it 'means', and one may find oneself at a loss, needing to start again, with little assistance from that brilliant surface impression.

'Ornament is a crime', as Loos had insisted – and as Strauss, whom we might read here as Aron to Schoenberg's Moses, in the practical expression of his aestheticism so brilliantly denied. Schoenberg, insistent that everything must be there for a reason, and a good, serious reason at that, remained an heir to Wagner and Mahler, and was thus not quite so much the disciple of Loos, not quite so much the anti-Strauss, as he liked to imagine. For one thing, Schoenberg was always also involved in the communicative worlds of explanation and elucidation – radio broadcasts continued, and their scripts and in some cases the actual broadcasts survive – and that of performance, too. That is, he was necessarily engaged with the very worlds of Aronic communication that Moses, in error almost equal to that of his brother, could not and would not understand.

Edward Clark continued in his efforts to establish Schoenberg's music in Britain, bringing his teacher to London to conduct the British premiere of *Gurrelieder* in 1928 and that of *Erwartung* in 1931. Schoenberg stayed at the Strand Palace Hotel, which still stands in decidedly faded sub-grandeur today. Ill health was necessitating lengthier spells away from Berlin, for instance from October 1931 to May 1932 in Barcelona, where the Schoenbergs stayed as guests of Gerhard. There Schoenberg would strike up a firm friendship with the great cellist Pablo Casals, and there he composed, at Casals's request, a ferociously, technically difficult 'Concerto for Cello and Orchestra after the Concerto for Clavicembalo of G. M. Monn in a free arrangement by Arnold Schoenberg'. Georg Matthias Monn was an early Viennese Classical composer of the generation between Handel and Haydn; the clavicembalo is a harpsichord and this reworking slightly anticipates the zany spirit of the following year's reworking of a Handel concerto grosso. Schoenberg wrote to Casals, underlining that antipathy to Handel (in part, of course, a consequence of his worship of Bach):

> I think it is a *very* brilliant work . . . it was my main concern
> to redress the shortcomings of the Handelian style . . . Just
> as Mozart did with Handel's *Messiah*, I completely got rid of
> handfuls of sequences . . . and replaced them with real *substance*
> . . . I think that I succeeded in approximately approaching the
> style of Haydn throughout the piece. In regards to harmony,
> I sometimes go a little (sometimes more than a little) beyond
> that style. But nowhere do I go further than Brahms.[15]

Pressures of time meant that Casals never performed the piece in public, and instead Emanuel Feuermann gave the premiere in London in 1935, with Thomas Beecham (not the most obvious choice for a Schoenberg advocate, perhaps, but in many respects a consummate professional). The BBC remained a friend and advocate of Schoenberg, as indeed would Casals. In the meantime, work progressed on the second act of *Moses und Aron*, and Schoenberg conducted, too, Webern writing to Berg that he had never heard *Pelleas* so well played. On 7 May Gertrud gave birth to their first child, Dorothea Nuria; her second name, by which she has always been known, was a tribute to the patron saint of the Catalonian capital, itself soon fated to suffer 'interesting times'.

Berlin, however, required Schoenberg's services, a matter of months before Hitler's appointment as Chancellor on 30 January 1933; and so, for the last time, Schoenberg returned, remaining there against medical advice during the long, cold winter. In January and February 1933 he composed the *Three Songs*, op. 48, which owe their late opus number to having been left on one side, even seemingly forgotten – for reasons that will become clear below – until their belated publication following Schoenberg's rediscovery of them among his papers in 1948. The piano writing here is sparer, more refined even, bearing the mark, much to its benefit or at least to its specific character, of his recent writing for solo piano. Vocal lines, subject matter and general mood are varied. Metaphysics vies, or better coexists, with a closing contemporary (almost post-*Zeitoper*) shrug of the shoulder. In that final 'Mädchenlied' (Girl's Song), the irregularity of the metre – seven and five, never quite according to expectation, until suddenly four appears – seems almost a wry commentary on modern life, along the lines of *Von heute auf morgen*. Alas, its 'modern people' were becoming harder to handle, and impossible to ignore, in the world outside.

Weimar Germany in general and Berlin in particular had long been the locus of bitter cultural as well as political conflict. In 1925, just before Schoenberg's arrival in Berlin, the Prussian culture minister, Becker, had provoked a storm by dismissing the ultra-conservative – aesthetically and politically – and rabidly anti-Semitic

Schoenberg at Bajada de Briz 14 in Barcelona, *c.* 1931–2.

composer Max von Schillings from the State Opera. Its offshoot, the Kroll Opera, had courted, and certainly generated, controversy with its 'modern' stagings, none more celebrated than the 'Bolshevik' *Flying Dutchman*, in the production from 1929 by Jürgen Fehling and Klemperer (another Jewish musician). The German National Party accused the Kroll of having openly 'mocked the spirit of Richard Wagner', and demanded restitution. Hitler's support during his Vienna years for Mahler's innovations and Schoenberg's own political conservatism notwithstanding, such conflicts tended to fuse with and to proceed along predictable political lines. Schreker had already been dismissed from the Hochschule and was now also teaching at the Academy of Arts. In early February 1933 the openly Nazi composer Paul Graener, now head of the Stern Conservatory (where Schoenberg had taught three decades earlier), led a walkout from a chamber concert at the Academy involving some relatively mild dissonances, objecting – ironically, given Schoenberg's former utterances – to its performance, 'as a German artist'.[16] The next meeting of the Academy's Senate, in mid-February, strongly expressed its disapproval of such behaviour. Political and cultural situations alike, however, were fast deteriorating. The Reichstag fire came on 27 February 1933. Just two days later, enthroned since 1931 as President of the Academy, Schillings led a further discussion on issues held to have been raised by Graener's charge. The very idea offered a perfect presentiment of that mixture of comical banality and something far more repellent, even deadly, that would characterize Nazi cultural policy in the years to come. (Furnish new, German libretti for Handel's English, Old Testament oratorios; replace 'Zion' with 'coelis' in the first recording of Mozart's Requiem; and so on.) Schillings, successor to the Jewish Berlin Secessionist Max Liebermann, declared his support for the Führer's mission to 'break the Jewish grip' on musical life.

Schoenberg took this, wisely, as constructive dismissal. He angrily left the meeting, left the Academy and, two months later, barely a moment too soon, fled Berlin for good. But why then, precisely, on 17 May? That remains unclear. For a while he had remained dismissive, even angrily so, of claims voiced outside Germany concerning danger. Germany had, after all, experienced many changes of government; on the face of it there was for many, Klemperer included, no particular reason to think that the Nazis might not have faced the same fate. Then suddenly, literally overnight, everything changed. According to Gertrud's pocket diary, her brother had sent a telegram from Florence saying that a 'change of air [*Luftveränderung*]' was 'urgent'. The telegram does not seem to have survived, but that word *Luftveränderung* does, referring also to Schoenberg's asthma. It is used immediately thereafter in two letters sent from Paris's Hotel Regina: one from Schoenberg to Webern, the other from both Schoenbergs to Erika Stiedry-Wagner, noted interpreter of *Pierrot lunaire* since a celebrated performance in 1921. *Luftveränderung* had clearly been agreed on for a moment of urgency, when it came, while – given Schoenberg's state of health – also admitting of a plausible alternative explanation.

The family – Arnold, Gertrud and Nuria – as that correspondence suggests, first went to Paris. They left Ottilie and her husband to deal with most of their possessions and all their furniture; they would keep them and, two years later, send them on to California. In Paris, Schoenberg received forwarded formal notice of his dismissal from the Academy: since he was in breach of contract, his salary, supposedly guaranteed until 1935, would now endure no longer than October, but there was nothing he could do about that. There were many worse places than Paris for musical life more generally, and more particularly with respect to performance and teaching, despite the cool reception his music had received there so far. Indeed, it was in France that summer, both in Paris and further south, that Schoenberg composed the Handel String Quartet Concerto. Of greater ultimate significance, though, and still more defiant, was his re-entry, on 24 July, into the Jewish faith; Marc Chagall was among the witnesses to the ceremony.

From Paris, Schoenberg wrote to a number of Jewish musicians, the composers Joachim Stutschewsky and Ernst Toch among them, a letter in which he offered himself as leader of a nationalist movement. 'The mistake of the Jews,' he wrote, 'was always to expect help from others.' If they did not do something for themselves, however, 'it would be the end of Judaism and every single Jew if we go on sleeping'. Unless and until a better person should come to lead this movement for the idea 'of the unrepresentable God' (a clear echo of *Moses*), he himself would do so. 'I do not want to be prevented in this,' he declared, asking them to let him know their position; 'Everything for the Jews!'[17] It seems that neither Toch nor Stutschewsky responded to this alarming if undeniably prescient missive, but Schoenberg nevertheless continued to prepare outlandish plans for a United Jewish Party under his frankly dictatorial leadership. Perhaps it was as well that there was too much of Moses in him for many to listen, for his proposed brand of Zionism, quite dissociated from the Zionist movement as such, veered dangerously close, however understandably, to the authoritarianism from which he wished to rescue the Jewish people. He had a long history, and would continue to do so, of writing declarations on contemporary political topics, often connecting them with his own work in a way that few except his artistic disciples would have understood. Schoenberg's was an angry, idiosyncratic mixture of political urgency and theological reflection that was unlikely ever – to put it mildly – to attract a mass following. In any case, the precise nature of his ever-changing personal religious beliefs following his reconversion remained unclear; there was in that sense no change, nor need there have been. There was no doubt whatsoever, though, that Schoenberg now wished publicly both to identify himself and to be identified as a Jew.

7

Exile

At first, Catalonia seemed to call once again. The Schoenbergs had
enjoyed their time there, not least on account of the opportunities
to play tennis; the weather was clement (no small thing, given
Schoenberg's health); good progress had been made on *Moses*; and
Gerhard, perhaps Casals too, could be relied on to help. At the
BBC, Edward Clark continued to offer his teacher performing and
proselytizing opportunities in London. Instead, however, Schoenberg
resolved on a more dramatic move. The cellist Joseph Malkin, who
had founded a small conservatory, offered the composer a position
that would involve teaching in Boston and New York. After a little
understandable hesitation, Schoenberg signed the contract and set sail
with his family for the New World. On the same liner, the *Ile de France*,
was Artur Bodanzky, a friend from those old Café Megalomania days,
returning to his position at the Metropolitan Opera.

The assembled company disembarked at Hoboken on 31
October 1933. A young composer-conductor from Jackson,
Mississippi, Lehman Engel – later to make a name for himself on
Broadway, but at that time studying with Roger Sessions – took
it upon himself to welcome the grand old man. Engel's younger
composer friend from Jackson, Milton Babbitt, who was soon to
come to New York University to commence his journey into the
brave new world of serialism, would later recount the story. Even
if not entirely accurate – there is no evident reason to doubt its
veracity – it possesses a poetic truth of its own:

When I arrived in New York three months later Lehman
was the first musician I saw, and he told me . . . Lehman
knew no German, and Schoenberg's English was limited and
noncolloquial, so when Lehman delivered a formal greeting
and Schoenberg responded, in English, with 'Thank you,'
and Lehman further responded in American, with 'You're
welcome,' Schoenberg apparently took this to mean: 'Welcome
to this country'; his eyes teared, and he embraced Lehman.
A short time later Lehman interviewed Schoenberg at length;
the piece he then wrote began: 'Schoenberg is in America!'[1]

One of several newspaper headlines the following day read: '"Lion"
Schoenberg a Lamb at Home: Noted German Composer, Who
Likes Hisses, Quietly Resumes Career Here'.

It was, of course, a straightforward untruth to say that
Schoenberg had ever liked being hissed at; however, he had
long endured and been renowned for it. When asked, in his
first American radio broadcast, an interview for NBC, about the
Skandalkonzert of 1913 and his subsequent violent reception, he
admitted: 'Yes, my feelings are always *offended* by trouble and
misunderstanding. For I think the public could know that I have
worked with the greatest sincerity and I think I have the right
to demand the respect of the public for my work.'[2] Schoenberg's
treatment in America would be somewhat different, and he
suffered little if any such overt hostility, yet considerably greater
public indifference, at least outside certain small circles. Accounts
have often varied between Old World outrage – perhaps more than
a little rich, given Europe's own treatment of Schoenberg – at his
neglect by a more brazenly commercial society, and New World
over-emphasis on a relatively few cases of the composer having
been fêted. Babbitt probably had it about right when he continued:
'Schoenberg's further welcome to this country oscillated between
what Thomas Mann later characterized as "glorification and

neglect".' (Mann was already in Swiss exile and would later join Schoenberg and so many others in California.) There was a good deal to learn on both sides; by the same token, both at least showed willing, Schoenberg telling the *Musical Courier*: 'I am not familiar with much American music. I of course know Roger Sessions' work which greatly pleases me and some compositions by Marc Blitzstein, which are excellent. Unfortunately I was not able to attend the orchestral performance of American works in Berlin last winter. I am indeed sorry.'[3]

The first winter proved little short of horrendous, and Schoenberg's asthma and emphysema proved more debilitating even than in Berlin. He had to cancel several engagements, including his U.S. conducting debut at the invitation of Serge Koussevitzky and the Boston Symphony Orchestra, scheduled for January, and a lecture – which would have been his first on the subject – on twelve-note composition for Princeton. The latter would be given at Chicago University a little later; the Princeton date was rescheduled for a month later. Nevertheless, constant travelling in so cold a climate was doing him no good whatsoever. He still managed to meet a number of important people, domiciled or visiting, musical or otherwise. There exists a splendid photograph, for instance, of Schoenberg with Albert Einstein and Leopold Godowsky, each with his very different pose and persona, at Carnegie Hall, following a benefit concert given by Godowsky to help German Jewish children travel to Palestine. A touching note, of uncertain date, addressed to Godowsky at the Astor Hotel, reads: 'joining with all people who loves [*sic*] and appreciates you I send you my best wishes for luck and health bis hundert [until 100 years old] Schoenberg.' Schoenberg could admire, sincerely, even dearly, musicians with very different aesthetics from his own, as his time in the United States would make increasingly clear. That did not mean he made no value judgements; but who does not? Those who claim not to do so are either deluded or deluding, or perhaps just befuddled.

Malkin's conservatory was neither a large nor sustainable affair. It was decided by mutual consent not to renew Schoenberg's contract, notwithstanding the interest his presence had generated, Gershwin and Stokowski having made generous contributions to a scholarship for a young American composer to study with the great Austro-German master. The Juilliard School now seemed a distinct possibility, but for the prospect of another New York winter. In September 1934, the Schoenbergs resolved instead to move to California, leaving New York State (the Chautauqua resort, where Schoenberg had been resting) for somewhere with more clement weather and, it was hoped, financial prospects too. However implausible it may sound, Schoenberg had once again been considering a move to the USSR to help set up a music institute, at the invitation of his 'red' pupil Hanns Eisler. The Austrian conductor-composer, Fritz Stiedry (husband of Erica Stiedry Wagner), now working at the Leningrad Philarmonic, had done Schoenberg sterling service in persuading him that neither the Russian climate nor Stalinism would enhance his prospects of physical or artistic survival, even 'in the south', as Schoenberg had requested of Eisler. Following Stiedry's later emigration to the United States, he would prove an important champion of Schoenberg's music. He gave the world premiere of the finally completed Second Chamber Symphony, at Carnegie Hall in 1940. It is a strangely tragic, tonal work, quite different from the First: almost akin to a smaller-scale appendix to *Pelleas*, albeit with a dose of *Neue Sachlichkeit*.

Although it was by no means paradise for Schoenberg – where could be, in a fallen, non-dodecaphonic world? – the gamble on California seems to have paid off. The note of irony in the claim he made, in a lecture in 1935, that he had been 'driven into paradise' (later to be the title of a book on Nazi refugees in the United States) seems not necessarily to have been understood. Nevertheless, like most fellow exiles – including even Adorno, who loathed the fundamental organizational principles of the ultra-capitalist society in which he found himself – Schoenberg would remain immensely grateful for the refuge he had been offered. An approach by the MGM producer Irving Thalberg to write a score for the film *The Good Earth* did not result in collaboration, although Schoenberg did make a few sketches, one of which, somewhat surprisingly, includes some play with the theme from Elgar's *Enigma Variations*. Thalberg had heard some of Schoenberg's music – *Verklärte Nacht*, of course – and liked it; as a good businessman, he thought the lead worth following up. Schoenberg's requested fee, $50,000 (!), was not so much the problem as his insistence on absolute control of score and sound. Not a note could be altered; even the pitch of actors' voices, in a recollection of *Pierrot* and other works, was to be his domain. Perhaps it was his way of saying 'thanks but no thanks'; it is difficult to tell. Film composers, though, continued to come his way, eager to learn new tricks of the trade in 'effects' and indeed to receive a more traditional, thorough, European grounding in the fundamentals of composition.

For Schoenberg was now able to teach again. Like Hindemith at Yale, he often found himself frustrated by students' lack of a firm grounding in his beloved Austro-German classics and in much else, the educational system being quite different from anything to which he was accustomed or could previously have imagined. In that connection, he lamented, in a letter to the director of the Juilliard in 1935, 'the excessively high price of tickets for concerts and operas, and the social style in which they are set up'; the price of sheet music and study scores was likewise a problem. Here the market reigned more or less free, rendering the general level of cultural provision and knowledge poor, especially by contrast with Germany and Austria. Nevertheless, Schoenberg and his family were afforded a degree of security, if never riches, from his first appointment, in 1935, as visiting Alchin Chair at the University of Southern California (USC), and his second and final appointment,

Leopold Godowsky, Albert Einstein and Schoenberg, at a concert in honour of Einstein given by the Council of Jewish Organisations for the Settlement of German Jewish Children in Palestine, Carnegie Hall, New York, 1 April 1934.

in 1936, as Professor at the University of California at Los Angeles (UCLA), alongside private teaching, some conducting work and some royalties. The house to which they moved in Brentwood Park, West Los Angeles, from Canyon Cove, Hollywood, would be Schoenberg's home until his death; it remains the home to this day of Judge (Rudolf) Ronald – the anagram may be noted, likewise for his son, Randol – Schoenberg, born in 1937, the year the family was joined by Gertrud's mother, Henriette Kolisch. Schoenberg's third son and Gertrud's second, Lawrence, was born in 1941. Number 116 North Rockingham Avenue was and is a family home: the longest-standing, by some way, of Schoenberg's numerous addresses.

Schoenberg's teaching certainly made its mark on a generation of young composers of very different natures, ranging from the 'experimentalists' John Cage and Lou Harrison to the film composer and conductor Alfred Newman and the pianist-composer-actor-comedian Oscar Levant. Bach was the only composer chosen for analysis in advanced counterpoint classes. Schoenberg's classic composition textbooks, *Models for Beginners in Composition* (1951) and *Fundamentals of Musical Composition* (another fragment, published only after completion by pupils in 1967), grew out of his UCLA composition classes. He still never taught twelve-note or even more broadly modernist composition, continuing to insist that pupils should learn through the classics – overwhelmingly, the Austro-German classics – and wishing to guard against pupils mistaking style and method for idea. Very occasionally, as in Berlin, he would bow to student clamour and analyse his own work. However, if his pupils wrote twelve-note music, he would gladly comment on it, while happily commenting on music written in other styles too, film scores and even more popular styles included. Levant, despite having written a number of Broadway and film scores, submitted himself to relearning his craft with Schoenberg. For him, Schoenberg was quite simply 'the greatest teacher in the world', for not only did he permit 'each of his pupils to be completely himself' – occasionally herself, too – 'he insists on it.'[4] That certainly did not mean just doing whatever one wanted. Schoenberg's teaching had Levant, who had always composed at the piano, begin to think orchestrally, first by studying chamber works by Mozart, Schubert and Brahms, making him think – as Schoenberg always had – in terms of strings and then broadening his experience further.

Schoenberg seems also to have known which pupils needed encouragement, a kinder approach, and which – often, but not always, the most brilliant, the most assured – would benefit from a harder line. No teacher will ever get such things right all the time, but he seems to have done so more often than most, inspiring if not quite the same cultic practices as had been the case with Berg and Webern, then no less respect and, yes, devotion. Cage recalled:

> Schoenberg was a magnificent teacher, who always gave the impression that he was putting us in touch with musical principles. I studied counterpoint at his home and attended all his classes at USC and later at UCLA when he moved there. I also took his course in harmony, for which I had no gift . . . He told me that without a feeling for harmony I would always encounter an obstacle, a wall through which I wouldn't be able to pass. My reply was that in that case I would devote my life to beating my head against that wall – and maybe that is what I've been doing ever since. In all the time I studied with Schoenberg, he never once led me to believe that my work was distinguished in any way. He never praised my compositions, and when I commented on other students' work in class he held my comments up to ridicule. And yet I worshipped him like a god.[5]

Schoenberg's celebrated description of Cage as 'an inventor of genius' was double- or maybe triple-edged: 'Not a composer, no . . . but an inventor. A great mind.' Schoenberg had, after all, a great deal of interest in inventions himself. Cage was delighted, not offended, when he heard of Schoenberg's remark – not least because it had come about, as is less often reported, from Schoenberg having been asked whether he had yet had any interesting pupils: he had initially said no, and then, at least according to Cage, had smiled and admitted that, yes, there had been one.[6]

It was clearly a very different relationship from that of, say, Webern to Schoenberg – but then, it would be. That world had gone, its passing symbolized by the death of Berg at the close of 1935. In his letter of condolence to Helene Berg, Schoenberg initially offered to help with the completion of the score of *Lulu*, and a premature announcement was made by Universal to that effect. He changed his mind, though, put off both by the time it would take – he had an unfinished opera of his own to attend to, as well as the necessity, as he explained to Erwin Stein, of 'earning my daily bread' – and, more fundamentally, by instances of anti-Semitism he found in the libretto (Berg's own) and, so he claimed, in the score itself. 'It can hardly be expected of me,' he told Stein, 'that I should be so inspired . . . as to give the sharpest characterization to the insult, "a scoundrel because he is a Jew".' Even if, as he hoped, Berg's anti-Semitism were here to be ascribed to 'thoughtlessness', Schoenberg could no longer overlook what he might have done 'in the pre-Nazi period'.[7]

Webern was still alive. Not unlike Furtwängler, he proved vocal in his protests against the persecution of Jewish artists; he nevertheless displayed an almost incredible naivety concerning the possibilities he thought National Socialism might offer for the flourishing of Austro-German culture. That and rumours – seemingly unfounded and strenuously denied – that had reached Schoenberg of Webern's anti-Semitic remarks created, unsurprisingly, certain difficulties, which should neither be ignored nor exaggerated, in their relationship. How could people who 'yesterday were still friends suddenly have become Nazis today', Schoenberg asked Webern in a letter written on New Year's Day 1934, from Brookline, Massachusetts. How could a man such as the dramatist and novelist Gerhart Hauptmann join a party that not only had a programme that promised 'no less than the extermination of all Jews', but was actually carrying it out?[8] Hauptmann may or may not have been a proxy for Schoenberg's fears concerning his pupils, whose potential dalliances with the

Devil he hints at earlier in that letter. The old friendship would nevertheless endure until Webern's shooting and death at the hands of an occupying American soldier in 1945, after the composer had lit a cigar outside his house during curfew. (Webern's death would prove the almost perfect metaphor for the Young Turks of the post-war avant-garde, determined – in slightly contradictory fashion – both to honour Webern as, in Boulez's words, the 'threshold', and yet also to start again, at 'Year Zero', rejecting the sickness of a culture that had brought the world to Auschwitz. No matter: what aesthetic manifesto worth its salt is not at least a little confused, compromising, contradictory?) Schoenberg thus survived his two greatest and most devoted pupils. As if to underline the fact that his new life lay in America, even if this were more a matter of ill-health than of intent, he would never return to Europe.

Gershwin, Levant's friend and now Schoenberg's too, shared with Schoenberg not only a love of tennis – Gershwin's rather larger house in Beverly Hills had its own court – but a gift for painting. He was not Schoenberg's pupil in anything, although he expressed that desire more than once in one way or another. Schoenberg declined on the grounds that he could only make the younger composer a bad Schoenberg, and he was such a good Gershwin already. If Schoenberg had given up painting, Gershwin's enthusiasm continued to grow. His portrait from 1937 of his weekly, far from consistently gracious tennis partner is in its way as charming, even moving a document as the brief film footage Gershwin made of Schoenberg at home. Gershwin generously underwrote a recording made by the Kolisch Quartet (led, of course, by Schoenberg's brother-in-law) of all four of Schoenberg's numbered string quartets, in tandem with performances at UCLA, Newman having permission from his boss Samuel Goldwyn to use one of his studios for the project.

The Schoenberg–Gershwin relationship was not without friction, though. Schoenberg, always sensitive to implicit criticism, took

Gershwin's declaration that he wished to write a string quartet, 'something simple like Mozart', not only as a comment on his own music but – just as bad a thing – a misunderstanding of Mozart's. Nevertheless, Gershwin may well have brought to Schoenberg a quartet he was working on just before his death, in the hope of criticism. Moreover, according to Levant, Gershwin wanted to commission a work from Schoenberg, yet felt embarrassed to ask. On Gershwin's early death, in 1937, Schoenberg paid him fulsome tribute in a memorial broadcast that may still be heard. He concluded:

> What he has achieved was not only to the benefit of a national American music, but also a contribution to the music of the whole world. In this meaning I want to express the deepest grief for the deplorable loss to music; but may I mention that I lose also a friend whose amiable personality was very dear to me.[9]

Schoenberg continued to rank Gershwin with other estimables such as Jacques Offenbach and Johann Strauss, who may have spoken in popular tones – coinciding, as he would put it, with those of the average man in the street – yet who did so quite without condescension. He esteemed natural musicality wherever he found it; indeed, he prided himself upon it too.

Schoenberg's first American composition was a *Suite for String Orchestra*: tonal, in G major; non-serial; in the form, or at least something closer to imitation of that form than previously, of the Baroque suite – Overture-Adagio-Minuet-Gavotte-Gigue; intended, at least in part, as a primer for college orchestras, a helping hand for American students towards the strange new world of New Music. Eschewing for once the 'poison of atonality', as he described it ironically in an unpublished preface, he had begun work on it before leaving for Los Angeles, at the suggestion of a fellow autodidact, Professor Martin Bernstein of New York University, whom he had met at the Chautauqua Institution in the summer of 1934.[10]

George Gershwin painting Schoenberg's portrait, Beverly Hills, 1937.

A good deal of truculent irregularity is revealed beneath the surface as soon as one plays or listens to it, and so the string writing, if not necessarily the 'Idea', proved too difficult, or would have done had it been let loose on the unsuspecting. Instead, Schoenberg for once followed advice and presented it as a composition – which 'represents *no repudiation* of my artistic output up until this point' – for professional string ensembles. It was premiered by Klemperer, now at the Los Angeles Philharmonic, in May 1935; he would also give its first New York performance in November of that year. The *New York Times* critic Olin Downes, never slow to trumpet wrong-headed opinions on any musical subject under the sun, sneered at Schoenberg's apparent return to the air of this planet: 'Only one thing more fantastical than the thought of Arnold Schönberg in Hollywood is possible, and that thing has happened. Since arriving there about a year ago, Schönberg has composed in a melodic manner' – listen, Mr Downes, and you will hear that any 'problem' *you* might have experienced would have been owed to an apparent excess of melody in every voice – 'and in recognizable keys.' In a logically incoherent aside, presumably intended as a witticism, Downes added: 'We may now expect atonal fugues by Shirley Temple.'[11]

The *Suite* would be followed some years later, in 1943, by a work for wind-band equivalent, the *Theme and Variations*, op. 43*a*, later arranged (and first performed) for full orchestra (op. 43*b*). Schoenberg would later speak of the worthiness of yielding to an 'urge' to return to tonality from time to time, although it is noteworthy that such yielding tended to occur so manifestly only in relatively 'occasional' works, with or without opus number. That long-awaited completion of the Second Chamber Symphony was a slightly different case. So too was the lavish orchestration of Brahms's G minor Piano Quartet, op. 25, for Klemperer in 1937, as part of a Brahms series with his Los Angeles Philharmonic. I seem to be in a small minority in finding that some, at least, of the work falls a little awkwardly between two stools; Klemperer's enthusiasm was genuine, and he went so far as to proclaim that he had no need ever to hear Brahms's original again. And yet, if one of Schoenberg's aims were to resolve some of the balance problems between piano and strings, he seems to have introduced a good few more, as in his (inferior) version for full orchestra of the First Chamber Symphony. There is good orchestral fun when, in the finale, Schoenberg really lets his hair down, with xylophone, glockenspiel, brass slides and so forth, and above all in the licence he truly permits himself for Brahms's piano cadenza. On the other hand, I cannot help but wish that I could hear a little more of what is claimed for it, namely insight into the way Schoenberg heard Brahms (for obvious reasons, an enticing prospect); or that it offered a more uncompromising confrontation between old and new as in the Bach and Handel orchestrations. Yes, there are some chromatic additions to the counterpoint, but not many, and to what end? Perhaps Schoenberg was, until the finale, simply too respectful of Brahms; or maybe, like many listeners to Schoenberg's music, I await the right performance so as to eat my words.

A further variety of 'difference' is shown in the *Kol nidre* of 1938, for speaker, chorus and orchestra, commissioned by Rabbi Jacob Sonderling of the reformist Fairfax Temple in Los Angeles. Sonderling was himself a migrant from a disputed region of Silesia, and had a long-held interest in commissioning works from refugees. Schoenberg himself conducted the premiere, with Sonderling as speaker, on the eve of Yom Kippur in the somewhat surreal setting of the Cocoanut Grove Ballroom of the Ambassador Hotel, with ad hoc forces of musicians largely employed in the film industry. The location, a consequence of the large forces required, was perhaps suggestive of tension between sacred and secular, and between Schoenberg's old Mahlerian conception of tradition as sloppiness and the demands of his new conception of himself as Jew, that manifested itself also in

Lunch at Otto Klemperer's house, 12 August 1935. From left: Klemperer, José Iturbi
(who appeared in a number of Hollywood films), Richard Lert, Pierre Monteux, Henry
Svedrofsky (Klemperer's assistant at the LA Philharmonic), Pietro Cimini, Schoenberg,
Bernardino Molinari, Willem van den Burg (principal cellist and assistant conductor to
Monteux for the San Francisco Symphony Orchestra).

the composer's misgivings about the text, its associated melody
and its traditions. 'One of my principal tasks,' he wrote to the
composer Paul Dessau, had been to 'vitriolize away the cello-
sentimentality of Bruch, etc., lending this DECREE the dignity
of a law, of an "edict". I believe that I succeeded.'[12]

In between the *Suite* and the *Kol nidre*, however, Schoenberg had
shown that emigration in no sense entailed turning his back on
the 'poison of atonality', nor indeed on the twelve-note method. If
anything, his willingness on occasion to return to his first planet –
however much it might have changed in the meantime – betokened
greater self-assurance. The new world of New Music would always
be there, even in the New World. The Violin Concerto, op. 36,
and the Fourth String Quartet, op. 37, were his two twelve-note
masterpieces from this period. Schoenberg had entertained
thoughts of a violin concerto during the 1920s, and had made a few

sketches in 1922 and again in 1927. The latter was for a chamber concerto in the wake of Berg's: for violin with 'accompaniment' from piano, three clarinets (that wind-band sound again), trumpet, horn, trombone, violin, viola, cello and double bass. It was only in 1934, though, that he began work on material for this concerto, and then broke off quickly, composing the rest – as so often, at great speed – during the summer of 1936. Unlike the proposed work from 1927, moreover, it is written for full orchestra, clearly placed in and attempting to extend the grand Austro-German tradition of Mozart, Beethoven and Brahms in this particular genre. Perhaps with slight defensiveness, Schoenberg wrote to Webern in January 1936 that he had conceived of the work at the same time as Berg had of his. It is worth reminding ourselves here that it is the first of only two completed concertos of his 'own'. One might be tempted to consider the Monn and Handel reworkings from 1932–3 as

Schoenberg and Gertrud with Charlie Chaplin at Charlie Chaplin Studios, Hollywood, 1935; photograph signed by both Chaplin and Schoenberg.

preparation, but Schoenberg did not tend to work like that; he had, after all, composed *Gurrelieder* with little experience of orchestral writing and none whatsoever on that scale.

Like Liszt for the piano, albeit without personal transcendental mastery of the instrument, Schoenberg out-virtuosoed the virtuosi with a work that was declared unplayable, all of which added to its mystique – and also to the downright fear it seems to have inspired in potential performers. Schoenberg told the Los Angeles concert organizer Peter Yates that since Jascha Heifetz had declared it unplayable, there was no one alive who would be able to perform it. Schoenberg had approached Heifetz, yet another émigré, when Kolisch, over-extended with other work commitments, had regretfully declined. Moreover, the music critic José Rodriguez informed Schoenberg that 'a virtuoso' had said it would remain unplayed until violinists acquired new fourth fingers. Schoenberg, Rodriguez reported, had laughed 'like a pleased child' at that, saying: 'Yes, yes. That will be fine. The concerto is extremely difficult, just as much for the head as for the hands. I am delighted to add another *unplayable* work to the repertoire. I want the concerto to be difficult and I want the little finger to become longer. I can wait.'[13]

However, the greatest difficulty seems to have been musical rather than technical. If the concertos of Beethoven and Brahms had proved notably 'symphonic' when compared with 'easier' works in the repertoire, they nevertheless made some play of conformity to tradition, as of course did Berg's. Schoenberg seems to have rejoiced – at the very least, the score rejoices – in making mischievous play with apparently contesting demands between an extension of traditional virtuosity and the present polyphonic and motivic demands of his dodecaphonic method. Interestingly, there are a good few notes that would have to be struck out as 'wrong', were one to consider the method as a 'system'. They will always be confirmed, however, as 'correct' by a player who experiments with altering them. The fury of inspiration, to employ a Romantic category of which Schoenberg would unquestionably and unquestioningly have approved, is palpable when one consults the autograph score, corrections and all: more legible than Beethoven, say, yet evincing the white heat demanded of a successful performance. The Latvian-Canadian violinist and composer Louis Gesensway, playing in the orchestra for the first performance, was so incensed by the work's reception that he wrote to a newspaper extolling its 'utmost perfection', its lack of a single 'trite or hackneyed phrase', declaring moreover: 'The violinist is really playing "fiddle" music.'[14]

In the end the piece, dedicated to Webern, fell to Louis Krasner. Krasner, who had also commissioned and premiered Berg's concerto, learned that Schoenberg was at work on the piece when he found himself on the same ocean liner as Kolisch in 1936. He practised the part for a year before its premiere in 1940 with Stokowski and the Philadelphia Orchestra. In a relatively unusual echo of Vienna, elements in the audience resorted to 'tradition', hissing, laughing, calling out. So too, it seems, did the orchestral management, which had refused to offer the customary publicity and even the necessary funding for so unwelcome an interloper. Stokowski actually had to pay for the performing resources and Krasner's fee out of his own pocket, for which noble deed Schoenberg, who was unable to attend, praised the conductor's 'brave stand toward my work and against illiterate snobs'. Having reported that 'most critics seem to agree' the work 'sounds like an exaggerated version of the testing room at an abrasive plant,' the *Philadelphia Inquirer* continued its account of this new *Skandalkonzert*. Krasner had 'received a meed of applause from the listeners when the hissing of the music itself began':

Stokowski stepped to the front of the stage and said:
'Shall we forever make the same foolish, narrow-minded,

unsportsmanlike blunders, upon only hearing a thing
once? . . . Certainly Schoenberg is one of the greatest
musicians alive today. His music is extremely difficult to
understand. We don't ask you to like it or dislike it, but
to give it a fair chance. That's American. But to condemn
it after one hearing – that simply cannot be done.'

. . . 'if Philadelphia is to grow culturally, we
must give every kind of art a chance.'

'If Schoenberg writes any more works, and you are
willing, I would like to conduct more of them.'

A shrill feminine voice from the balcony cried: 'Funny!'

. . . None of the audience walked out during the
Concerto – but it was noted that several of the
audience didn't walk in until it was ended.[15]

The work's difficulties, of whatever nature, will speak for
themselves. As ever with Schoenberg, though, the best thing is
probably to let them do so and, however clichéd this may sound,
simply listen to the music 'as music', to let it take one where it
will. I may not have helped by talking up the difficulty, but in
a biographical study it would arguably be misleading not to do
so. In any case, tales of scandal often prove a spur to listen. The
three movements are traditional both in number and in type:
sonata form-*Andante grazioso*-marching finale. There is more than
a hint, once again, of that 'special' key, D minor. Within a more
disciplined, quasi-Classical framework, the riot of colouristic
imagination is clearly that of the same composer as the op. 16
Orchestral Pieces. Cadenza-writing offers ample opportunity for
display from the 'new' fourth finger, as elsewhere do treacherous
harmonics and double-stopping, often combining *pizzicato* and
arco (bowed) playing. If there is a better instantiation of the
lyrical slow movement in a twentieth-century concerto – a better
example of such a movement's principal theme as an heir to the

lyrical, Mozartian past – then I know of none. Needless to say, in this new understanding of the instrumental aria, there is no 'mere' ornamentation; every note counts, as it must for any fervent disciple of Loos. The work in its entirety is as clearly orientated to the blazing, fortissimo conclusion of its finale as any by Beethoven.

The Fourth Quartet, as we have seen, was granted a more civilized public baptism. 'This time,' Schoenberg wrote in his preface to the Kolisch Quartet's recording, 'it was a perfectly commonplace affair . . . The whole audience listened with respect and sincerity to the strange sounds with which they were faced and it seems a number of them were really impressed.'[16] The Quartet's traditional four movements and indeed its joy in melody attest to a degree of kinship to the Violin Concerto, as does the quasi-Romantic urgency of its goal orientation. The first movement may be understood to possess certain elements of sonata form, if less overtly than its predecessors, whether the Concerto or the Third Quartet; if one seeks, one may find, but it is questionable whether a true impression would be of something less than *sui generis* – likewise the unusual handling of the series at first, with notes repeated before they 'should' be. At the risk of sounding like a stuck record, not only was Schoenberg insistent that his was a method, not an iron-clad system, but his practice bears witness to that truth. Once again Mozart proved an important inspiration, in particular his melodic profusion and his overtly dramatic conception of form. In an interview, Schoenberg told his student the pianist Warren Langlie that Mozart had been his inspiration to be, as it were, differently inspired:

I said this time I must compose like Mozart does it, without looking at all whether I see relations or not, juxtaposing ideas. This principle I had conceived before, but this time I went very straight with this. And this is what Mozart does; in the middle of a theme he will interrupt or abandon his

THE PHILADELPHIA ORCHESTRA

Forty-first Season, 1940-1941

NINTH PROGRAM

Friday Afternoon, December 6, at Two-thirty

Saturday Evening, December 7, at Eight-thirty

LEOPOLD STOKOWSKI *Conducting*

LOUIS KRASNER, *Violinist*

MUSORGSKY-STOKOWSKI . . Night on Bare Mountain

SIBELIUS . . . . Symphony No. 7
          Adagio-Vivacissimo-Adagio
          Allegro molto moderato-Vivace
          Presto-Adagio-Largamento
          (In one continuous movement)

INTERMISSION

SCHÖNBERG . . . . . Concerto for Violin and Orchestra
      I. Poco Allegro
     II. Andante Grazioso
   III. Finale-Allegro
              (World Première)

*WAGNER . . . . Prelude and Love-Death
                      ("Tristan und Isolde")

ON FRIDAY afternoon, on account of the broadcasting of the program, the Schönberg Violin Concerto will be played in the first half of the program and the MUSORGSKY-STOKOWSKI Night on Bare Mountain, SIBELIUS Symphony No. 7 and WAGNER Prelude and Love-Death will be played in the second half. The program for Saturday will remain unchanged.

The STEINWAY is the official piano of The Philadelphia Orchestra

* Available on Victor Records

Philadelphia Orchestra programme for the premiere of the Violin Concerto, 1940.

motifs and juxtapose new thematic formulations. We have it
so clearly in the A minor [Piano Sonata, KV 310/300d]. The
characteristic for Mozart is this interruption, I would not
be sure to contend that this is a higher or a more primitive
technique. It is difficult to evaluate this aesthetically.
I think it derived from his dramatic technique.[17]

The work's temper is more Romantic than that of the Third
Quartet, but there is no contradiction there, for any true
Mozartian will tell you that the composer of *Idomeneo*, let alone
Don Giovanni, was the first true musical Romantic. So too are
elements of its overarching structure, not least its intermezzo-like
second movement. Once again, the music dances, its contrasting
dance metres suggestive perhaps of a nineteenth-century
symphonic work, even of Mahler. The harmonic language,
though, remains unquestionably of Schoenberg's own time and
practice. It does not seem far-fetched to hear a reminiscence of
the synagogue, even if it were an invented reminiscence, in the
striking opening unison theme of the *Largo* third movement; it
seems to speak in free declamation, with a truer – to Schoenberg
– note of regret, even tragedy, than he was able to offer in the *Kol
nidre*. Would Pauline's Kantor ancestors have heard it as such?
Maybe, maybe not; tradition, for Schoenberg, could never stand
still. What is meant by its increasingly Romantic development,
especially by the first violin, its inversion and gradual subsiding
through contrapuntal exercise may or may not be the right
question to ask. At any rate, there is something of that spirit of
resolution here and in the finale. Its rondo marching form has
us return several times to the main theme, which nevertheless
gathers purpose from our old friend developing variation, thus
offering both a reaffirmation and a reinvention of tradition
according to Schoenberg's, if not necessarily his critics',
understanding.

The situation continued to worsen abroad – although, as in 1914 or 1933 – nothing was quite inevitable, and not only by definition, until it happened. Nevertheless, in his *Four-point Program for Jewry* (1938) Schoenberg seemingly foresaw it all, putting many politicians and indeed members of his community to shame. Such early clear-sightedness verges on the uncanny, quite the other side of the coin from that alarming talk of political leadership. Neither should be overlooked, but this is perhaps the more interesting. He rightly recalls that he had been sounding the alarm for many years, at least since Mattsee:

500,000 Jews from Germany, 300,000 from Austria, 400,000 from Czechoslovakia, 500,000 from Hungary, 60,000 from Italy – more than one million and eight hundred thousand Jews will have to migrate in how short a time, one does not know. May God provide there will not be an additional 3,500,000 from Poland, 900,000 from Rumania, 240,000 from Lithuania and 160,000 from Latvia – almost 5,000,000; and Yugoslavia with 64,000, Bulgaria with 40,000 and Greece with 80,000 might follow at once, not to speak of other countries, which are at present less active.

Is there room in the world for almost 7,000,000 people?

Are they condemned to doom? Will they become extinct? Famished? Butchered?

Every keen and realistic observer should have known this beforehand, as I knew it almost twenty years ago. Even one who does not overrate Jewish intelligence in political affairs will admit that every Jew should have known at least that the fate of the Austrian and Hungarian Jews was sealed years ago. And can a man with foresight deny that the Jews of Rumania and Poland are in danger of a similar fate? What have our Jewish leaders, our Jewish men with foresight, done to avert this disaster? What have they done to alleviate the sufferings of the people already stricken

by this mishap? What have they done to find a place for
the first 500,000 people who must migrate or die?[18]

Where this Jewish homeland should be was always subject to
change. It is misleading to state categorically, as some have done,
that Schoenberg did not intend it to be in Palestine; there are
several occasions when he says just that. There are others, however,
when he still follows Herzl's Ugandan concept, even some when
he seems to suggest that the project is concerned with a more
metaphysical idea of a 'Promised Land' (such as that in *Moses und
Aron*). We should probably simply note his confusion, which was far
from unique, about what was an extremely thorny, complex issue –
one that has continued to be so ever since.

A good deal of old artistic Europe, and not just its Jewish
element, however defined, was now present in the United States
or very soon would be, and a high proportion was in or near Los
Angeles. Klemperer; Charlie Chaplin (another friend); Thomas
Mann and Bertolt Brecht, who both attended Schoenberg's lectures
admiringly yet could not get on with each other; Alma Mahler-
Werfel, as she now was, and her husband, Franz; Max Reinhardt;
Lion Feuchtwanger; Adorno; Stravinsky: those and many others
were gathering in what has been called, with a little exaggeration,
a 'Weimar on the Pacific'. Eisler was there too, of course; he
introduced Brecht to Schoenberg, warning him (following various,
seemingly politically inspired, fallings out with his teacher) that
he would break off all contact with Brecht should he not show due
respect. Such a warning proved quite unnecessary, as Eisler himself
recalled in 1958:

I tried desperately not to talk to Schoenberg about politics,
since nothing could be achieved by it. Besides, the man was ill
. . . my behaviour culminates in an attitude of admiration and
shyness – which I . . . you know . . . somehow put on. This is how

I wanted Schoenberg to see me; he wasn't supposed to think me arrogant or to say: 'He's a know-all'. Actually, I felt I was better off than Schoenberg. You had to make everything 'just so' for a petit bourgeois like him. Short and sweet: all of that led to my adopting an attitude of utmost respect and admiration and, as I remember, Brecht absolutely understood this.[19]

Much has been made of the lack of a true encounter between Stravinsky and Schoenberg; it is, as the reader will see, difficult indeed to resist the dramatic impulse to turn it into a story. However, it is not so surprising: many people live in the same city and attend some of the same events without formally meeting, especially when there is tension between them. They were not friends; they did not live especially close to each other; in spite of their occasionally being in the same place, it is more likely than not that it just never quite happened – which is not, of course, to claim that Stravinsky's adoption of serialism only after the death of Schoenberg was a mere coincidence.

Of course, not everyone was happy in Los Angeles, even among the German-speaking community. They had rarely been full of the joys of spring where they had come from, so why should they, modernist intellectuals, find themselves so anywhere else? By the same token, even Brecht's celebrated comparison of Los Angeles to Hell was tempered by the admission that 'even the houses in Hell are not all ugly', itself immediately qualified with the true plight of the refugee: 'But concern about being thrown into the street/ Consumes the inhabitants of the villas no less/ Than the inhabitants of the barracks.'[20] Fear, even loathing, was to be expected. Schoenberg, though, remained immensely grateful. Perhaps more to the point, he knew that there could be no going back, whether then or in the foreseeable future. He would not and did not pine. Indeed Brecht, having visited Schoenberg with Eisler, remarked on 'a seventy-year-old, rather bird-like man who has

Schoenberg's Czechoslovak passport, 1933.

great charm and is agreeably dry and sharp with it'.[21] Insofar as
Schoenberg ever could be, he was at home. The first son of Samuel
Schönberg of Pressburg – and thus citizen of an inheritor state to
Austria-Hungary, Czechoslovakia, which had itself ceased to exist
in all but name – had long been a 'citizen of the world'. To that
questionable honour he added the very real one, ever a source of
genuine pride, of American citizenship on 11 April 1941.

8

Citizenship: War and Peace

If the eight months' Phoney War until the German invasion of France and the Low Countries in May 1940 offered little clue to the later course of the Second World War, Schoenberg's first musical work as an American citizen proved equally unexpected for and unrepresentative of the final phase in his career. Its tonal qualities were by now not so unusual, but its instrument was: the organ. Responding to a commission from the New York music publisher H. W. Gray, he first started writing a twelve-note sonata, and the fragments he composed are occasionally performed. (Organists do not enjoy pianists' luxury of repertoire, at least not when it comes to 'great composers'.) Schoenberg then broke off, at least in part as a result of the publisher's wish that the work not be of too great a length, and composed instead the highly chromatic D minor (more or less) *Variations on a Recitative*, op. 40. A monument in the twentieth-century organ repertoire, this rarely performed – criminally so – work seems on the surface to take as its example less Schoenberg's own *Variations for Orchestra* than Brahms's sets of themes and variations, whether for keyboard or orchestra. There is perhaps a nod to Reger, too. However, the density of motivic integration – employing, as had the *Kol nidre*, elements of serial technique within a thoroughly tonal framework – leaves one in little doubt that this is the work of Brahms's successor, determined, consciously or otherwise, to outdo the earlier composer. In a work for this of all instruments, Bach is never far away, at least so far as Schoenberg himself was concerned.

The composer was deeply dissatisfied, however, with the printed registration suggestions offered by Carl Weinrich, the organist who gave the premiere in 1944. In a letter to the publisher he requested (unsuccessfully) that existing copies be destroyed and a new edition prepared. 'I wanted to tell you,' Schoenberg wrote,

> that Mr Weinrich's editing is written for his own great organ in Princeton, and nobody can understand it who has not about [*sic*] the same kind of organ. I don't think it is a good registration for my music . . . My music is something which one has to feel and to realize that it is different from most other compositions. By the way, I also do not like the manner in which it is registered; I hate this similar richness. I am quite sure that a registration which brings out all the dynamics – nothing more, and stops playing with colors, like a child – that such a registration will also be more suitable for the works of Bach.
>
> . . . The most urgent need would be to add something stating that people should best disregard Weinrich's registration and should not use more stops than are necessary to bring out the thematic and motival [*sic*] and melodic material.[1]

Perhaps this mighty score – to my mind, the greatest of Schoenberg's late tonal works – awaits not only an organist but an organ to do it justice. Schoenberg said it represented 'my "French and English Suites", or, if you want, my Quintet from Meistersinger, my Duet of Tristan, my Fugues of Beethoven and Mozart (who were homophonic melodic composers)'.[2]

The Japanese attacked Pearl Harbor on the morning of 7 December 1941. American support for non-interventionism had been on the wane ever since the fall of France the previous year, and this delivered the death blow. The following day Franklin Roosevelt delivered his 'day of infamy' address to both Houses of Congress, broadcast live on the wireless. Schoenberg was listening;

his student Leonard Stein attested that it made a great impression on him, and believed that it planted in the proud new citizen's head the idea of a musical response. Be that as it may, a month later the League of Composers, which had previously sponsored the American premiere (again under Stokowski) of Schoenberg's *Die glückliche Hand*, offered Schoenberg a commission on its twentieth anniversary for a 'short chamber work', which Schoenberg composed between March and June 1942. Concerned, however, that it might not be well enough performed by the commissioning forces, Schoenberg withheld it until 1944, when it received its premiere from the New York Philharmonic under its principal conductor, Artur Rodziński, with Eduard Steuermann and the baritone Mack Harrell. (Schoenberg had hoped for Orson Welles: a great musical might-have-been.) This was the *Ode to Napoleon Buonaparte (Lord Byron)*, for string quartet, piano and reciter, op. 41 – although the premiere was given in the string-orchestra version that Schoenberg had prepared the previous year.

Byron's excoriating ode, allegedly to but unmistakably against Napoleon, offered a clear contemporary parallel to Hitler. As soon as he had received the commission, Schoenberg would write:

I had at once the idea that this piece must not ignore the agitation aroused in mankind against the crimes that provoke this war. I remembered Mozart's *Marriage of Figaro*, supporting repeal of the *jus primae noctis*, Schiller's *Wilhelm Tell*, Goethe's *Egmont*, Beethoven's *Eroica* . . . I knew it was the moral duty of intelligentsia to take a stand against tyranny.[3]

This is not *Pierrot*; there is no straightforward cabaret, no sense of recitation as artfulness. The words are to be heard as words, but the mode of their expression is crucial. Schoenberg insisted to his pupil Heinrich Jalowetz, who was preparing a recording, on the necessity of a large number of 'shades, essential to express one hundred and seventy kinds of derision, sarcasm, hatred, ridicule, contempt, condemnation, etc., which I tried to portray in my music'.[4] In that vein, not only might Bonaparte become Hitler, not only might Byron's reference to the Emperor's Habsburg bride, 'proud Austria's mournful flower', evoke Schoenberg's post-*Anschluss* homeland, but Byron's 'Cincinnatus of the West . . . bequeath'd the name of Washington' might yet inspire Roosevelt, whose speech had so inspired Schoenberg at the outset.

Allusions to the *Marseillaise* and to Beethoven's Fifth Symphony – its Morse Code, 'V for Victory' connotations were especially popular at this time – nevertheless make their presence felt among 'the triumph and the vanity, the rapture of the strife – the earthquake voice of Victory', and the countervailing 'dark spirit! what must be the madness of thy memory!' This is one of the most extreme instances in his oeuvre of Schoenberg offering a post-Wagnerian conception of the artist and his role in society, of the artistic work and its angry, political standing. It is with a motivic working that owes much to Brahms and indeed to Beethoven, to style *and* idea of developing variation, that the score leads to a conclusion that both encompasses and negates tonal E-flat major. It is, moreover, no coincidence whatsoever that that is the key of the *Eroica*: Beethoven's own Napoleon work, first intended as a straightforward tribute to Bonaparte, furiously transformed into a panegyric to the memory of a great hero who had never actually existed. Schoenberg both honours and deconstructs Beethoven's humanism in the light of Hitler and Nazism. Its referential tonality clearly troubled Schoenberg, and yet it clearly mattered. He responded defensively and surely a little disingenuously in a letter to the French composer-conductor and theorist René Leibowitz (one of those who, like Adorno, treated Schoenberg's method as a system, to his frustration) in 1947: 'It is true that the *Ode* at the end sounds like E-flat. I don't know why I did it. Maybe I was wrong, but at present you cannot make me feel like this.'[5]

Meanwhile, *Verklärte Nacht*, at least, continued to gain in popularity. Bruno Walter gave enthusiastically received performances in 1944 with the New York Philharmonic, after Schoenberg refused to countenance his proposed cut to the score, rightly insistent in correspondence on the musical damage that would be wrought. Three years earlier an equally well-received ballet version – the first, it would seem, although there had been at least two earlier abortive attempts – *Pillar of Fire* by Antony Tudor, was given by the Ballet Theatre (now the American Ballet Theatre) at the New York Met. The story was not dissimilar from Richard Dehmel's original, albeit with a touch of extra spice in the central character, Hagar, bearing the child of her younger sister's lover before finding true love. Schoenberg had not been at all keen on the idea; nor had he been earlier with proposed dance versions of *Pierrot*.[6] He had telegraphed Hugo Winter of Associated Music Publishers, the American distributor for Universal: 'Must know approximately what those ballet people plan to do stop Would forbid changes but must know garanteed [*sic*] minimum earning my share.'[7] Negotiations had not been happy – they rarely are – but the inviolate nature of the musical work and, later, acceptable royalties and other conditions were agreed. Schoenberg's score and Antal Doráti's conducting drew praise in the press, although the reporting tended, naturally, to focus on Tudor's choreography. The ballet format at least ensured that the *New York Times*'s dance critic, rather than Downes, was reviewing. And Schoenberg had clearly been won over conceptually in the end, for he would conduct the San Francisco premiere of the ballet in 1945. The Met proper, alas, proved far less enthusiastic concerning Schoenberg – and has continued to do so. *Moses und Aron* would not be staged there until 1999, although the more enterprising New York City Opera staged it in 1990, just a year after James Levine finally succeeded in persuading the Met to stage *Erwartung*, in its classic pairing with Bartók's *Bluebeard's Castle*. Admittedly, Stokowski conducted

Die glückliche Hand there as early as 1930; however, as with his performance of the Violin Concerto, that was entirely to be attributed to his own zeal.

The Piano Concerto, op. 42, written for the most part during the second half of the same year, 1942, is also marked by the war, if more in a general, programmatic sort of way, which may quite readily – as in all such works from *Pelleas* onwards – be disregarded if one so wishes. It began life as a response to a commission by Oscar Levant for a small piano solo piece. During its development into a concerto, Levant withdrew, to be replaced with Henry Clay Shriver, a UCLA pupil who had occasionally attended Schoenberg's classes. Schoenberg had wanted more money than Levant's $100 for a bigger piece, and received a tenfold increase from Shriver. 'The negotiations,' which were conducted by Eisler, according to Levant in his *Memoirs of an Amnesiac*, 'had suddenly become frenzied and the familiar father figure was suffocating to me. I couldn't stand it and I sent a telegram withdrawing from the venture.'[8] Levant gave Schoenberg a cheque a few years later by way of apology. Steuermann would give the premiere in 1944 with Stokowski and the NBC Orchestra. Downes in the *New York Times* dismissed it as 'disagreeable and unconvincing', saying he preferred the Schubert *Unfinished* Symphony (also on the programme), as if that were a meaningful comparison. However, a reviewer for the *San Francisco Chronicle*, listening on the radio, found the work to be 'based entirely on the concept of music as a lyric and dramatic art . . . Schoenberg is frequently puzzling,' the reviewer, 'A. F.', disarmingly admitted, 'but he did not seem so on this occasion.'[9] Stokowski was at least spared the pandemonium of the previous concerto premiere.

Whether the programme is of any help is highly debatable. Schoenberg, speaking vaguely of war in a way that could readily be made to fit an almost infinite number of pieces of music, described the work's expressive content as follows: '1. Life was so easy;

2. Suddenly hatred broke out; 3. A grave situation was created;
4. But life goes on.' Perhaps it assisted his overall conception;
there is no more reason for us to dwell on it than Schoenberg had
found there was, all those years previously, to dwell on Mahler's
for his Third Symphony. It returns to the ideal of balance between
Schoenberg at his most Brahmsian in style – tonal implications
are at least as strong as in the *Ode*, and the sound of Schoenberg's
piano chords almost always harked back to Brahms – and a Lisztian
conception of concerto form. A single overarching movement, as in
the First Quartet or the First Chamber Symphony, combines four
sections that double up as four movements of the whole: Viennese
Ländler, scherzo of 'hatred', searching *Adagio* and another of
Schoenberg's developing rondo finales. It is perhaps a more overtly
'symphonic' work than the Violin Concerto, less belligerent in its
contest between instrumental virtuosity and serial polyphony. Life,
after all, went on.

It did in the 'real world', too, of course. Schoenberg retired in
1944, receiving the title of Emeritus Professor. The following year he
declined an honorary doctorate from UCLA on the grounds that he
had always done so from any institution. While he was very grateful
for the honour, 'it would be an insult to those who were the first to
offer me such an honour.'[10] This was the year of his application to
and rejection by the Guggenheim Foundation, ostensibly on the
grounds of age. It was quite a blow, especially given the smallness
of the pension he had earned; nothing, of course, was forthcoming
from Berlin. He also composed, in September, once the war was
over, what remains his least-known original orchestral work: the
Prelude, op. 44. (Two-and-a-half bars at the close for wordless
chorus do not in any meaningful sense render it a 'choral work'.)

It is Schoenberg's short, opening contribution to a pleasantly
bizarre project by the Hollywood musician and 'personality'
Nathaniel 'Nat' Shilkret. According to his autobiography, Shilkret
had, during a Midwest road trip, asked people 'what records they

Schoenberg with bust by Louis Zack (1937) at Rockingham Avenue piano, in *Vogue* (1945), photograph taken 1944.

would like the most, and invariably it was the Bible. This gave me the idea of starting the Bible at the beginning: Have the text read and write music to help the beauty of the text. I decided to call the record album the *Genesis Suite*.' For the six stories he selected, up to and including the Tower of Babel (Stravinsky), he recruited Schoenberg for the void before Creation (Shilkret himself), Milhaud, Alexandre Tansman, Ernst Toch and Mario Castelnuovo-Tedesco: 'I had tried to get Richard Strauss and Manuel De Falla but they were too old or too busy.' Positioning himself inevitably as an heir to Haydn and his 'Representation of Chaos' from *The Creation*, Schoenberg presents order even within Chaos, with a twelve-note series that generates a remarkable fugue, perhaps the ultimate, neo-Bachian instantiation of order. It is, perhaps, a premonition of the great Choral Symphony that never was, of which the *Jakobsleiter* fragment was to be but one section. It also netted the composer $1,500, negotiated up from $750 by the husband-and-wife team. 'Knowing that Stravinsky', who had originally been offered $500 more than Schoenberg, 'might hear . . . I came back to him and told him that both he and Schoenberg would receive the same fee. Stravinsky thanked me effusively and said it was the nicest gesture ever offered him.' The dress rehearsal for the premiere occasioned the first of two long-awaited abortive encounters between the two composers, whom Shilkret had so far managed to keep apart. Stravinsky's time with the orchestra had run well over, and the composer showed no inclination to leave, when, lo and behold,

> Arnold Schoenberg walked into the room. With his poor eyesight, Schoenberg could hardly find his place . . . [he] walked right into the same row of seats in which Stravinsky was sitting. They contacted each other. Schoenberg did not recognise his rival. However, Stravinsky looked at Schoenberg but did not greet him. A few minutes later Stravinsky left.[11]

If it did not happen that way, a musical refashioning of centuries-old dramatic variations on a theme by Elizabeth I and Mary, Queen of Scots, then it should have done.

Schoenberg was acutely aware of the compromises artists had had to make and still did, in the face of political difficulties, even danger to their lives. He showed himself commendably sympathetic to their plight, whether it were in Stalin's USSR (Shostakovich) or, perhaps still more, in the lands he knew better. He of all people knew that it was both necessary and yet impossible, to quote Max Aruns, 'to be Moses and Aron in one person'. The Austrian-born composer and critic Kurt List wrote to him in 1946, asking for his view on the case of Furtwängler (who had, after all, protested publicly to Goebbels concerning Schoenberg's treatment). Schoenberg sent him a handwritten reply, perhaps surprisingly in English, in which he defended both Furtwängler and Strauss. 'I am not a friend of Richard Strauss,' he began,

and, though I do not admire all of his work, I believe that he will remain one of the characteristic and outstanding figures in musical history. Works like *Salome*, *Elektra*, and *Intermezzo* and others will not perish. But I do not believe that he was a Nazi, just as little as W. Furtwängler. They were both . . . Nationalistic Germans . . . they consider everything German as superior . . . We know that scientists, doctors, professors, writers, poets and artists could stand the musical vulgarity of the Horst Wessel Lied and sing the horrible text with as much fire and enthusiasm as the simple man in the street. I have no information about St's and F's attitude in this respect [Furtwängler actually withstood enormous pressure from Goebbels to give the Hitler salute, never once succumbing]; but it seems to me doubtless that they at least despised the music.

Schoenberg blamed 'the intrigue of one man', the unnamed Toscanini, for Furtwängler, 'many times his superior', having been barred from the United States. He reserved especial concern, as a fellow composer, for those who would play Strauss's music and, as alleged punishment, withhold royalties; they were, straightforwardly, 'pirates'. He concluded, touchingly, as Moses, that his defence was born neither of the 'sentimental' regret that 'this old man now has lost – for the second time in his life – all his fortune', nor of the friendship he had already denied. 'I am sure that he [Strauss] does not like my music and in this respect I know no mercy: I consider such people as enemies. I speak from the standpoint of honesty.'[12] Strauss would die in 1949, almost exactly two years before Schoenberg. Webern and Berg were already gone; Bartók had died too, in exile in New York. Stravinsky would long outlive them all, but he was always different; and in any case, he was younger than Schoenberg.

Schoenberg nevertheless had five years of life and composition to go, his sometimes rapidly failing health – it had never been that good to start with – notwithstanding. On 2 August 1946, following a worsening of his asthma, deterioration in his eyesight and diagnosis of diabetes, he suffered a heart attack and nearly died, saved only by an injection to the heart. 'I have risen from a real death,' he wrote to the music critic Hans Heinz Stuckenschmidt, later the author of a major Schoenberg biography, 'and now find myself quite well.'[13] In truth, he never fully recovered; yet he was at work on one of his two final masterworks, the String Trio, op. 45, before he had even left hospital. It is a work that stands in the shadow – and inspiration – of his illness, as Mann recalled:

He told me about the new trio he had just completed, and about the experiences he had secretly woven into the composition – experiences of which the work was a kind of fruit. He had, he said, represented his illness and medical

treatment in the music, including even the male nurses
and all the other oddities of American hospitals.[14]

The Trio was written in the context of a twentieth-century revival
of interest in a punishingly difficult genre, in which Mozart was
once again the acknowledged master. Reger had written two, as
had Hindemith; Webern had composed a single, outstanding
example. Responding to a commission from Harvard University's
music department for a symposium on musical criticism in 1947,
Schoenberg's contribution stood alongside works for different
forces by Hindemith, Aaron Copland, Bohuslav Martinů and Gian
Francesco Malipiero; quite a symposium.

Schoenberg's pupil and assistant Leonard Stein went further
than Mann in relating the work to his teacher's illness, reporting
that he had

> explained the many juxtapositions of unlike material within
> the Trio as reflections of the delirium which the composer
> suffered during parts of his illness. Thus, the seemingly
> fragmentary nature of the Trio's material represents the
> experience of time and events as perceived from a semiconscious
> or highly sedated state. These unusual juxtapositions also
> represent . . . the alternate phases of 'pain and suffering'
> and 'peace and repose' that Schoenberg experienced.[15]

We may or may not choose to follow quasi-programmatic cues,
and should remind ourselves that Schoenberg had conceived the
basic outline of the work before his heart attack. Such cues may
at least offer a way in to what Michael Cherlin has described as
music that 'is full of abrupt and striking changes of texture and
affect as musical ideas are broken off, interrupted by other ideas
that are themselves interrupted'.[16] Memory plays tricks, sometimes
deliberately, mediating between youth and old age, then and

now. One way to avoid a direct comparison with Mozart was perhaps to misremember, to deal with Beethoven and a different number of instruments: just, perhaps, as Schoenberg might have misremembered, however productively, his original inspiration.

Waltz fragments from old Vienna likewise once again play a mediating role between the opposing forces of surface contrasts and unifying twelve-note technique – not unlike, say, the Violin Concerto. As in that work, yet in contrast to much of his American music, the extremity of those contrasts, however, remains. The work's character is indeed almost neo-Expressionist. Schoenberg reverts to his old, Lisztian practice of condensing four traditional sonata movements into a single-movement sonata form. Three parts are interspersed with a first and second 'Episode', violence, those alternate phases of 'pain and suffering' and 'peace and repose' both characterizing and undermining the distinct identity of different sections. The complexity of the first bar alone, replete with *tremolandi*, harmonics, syncopation, *sforzandi* and so on, sets the aural, even the visual, stage very well indeed, better than any mere identification of the series. To the question whether the Third Part be recapitulation, further development, reconciliation or dissolution, the only possible answer can be: all the above – and more.

The objection has occasionally been raised that the *Ode to Napoleon* is too hectoring: a strange objection indeed, roughly on the level of an English critic who once complained that the 'Ride of the Valkyries' was 'tasteless'.[17] A conciliatory, equable *Ode* would be as surprising, one might think, as a tasteful *Walkürenritt*. However, even those who – mistakenly, in my view – doubt its aesthetic, if not its political, value would admit the greatness of its successor piece, *A Survivor from Warsaw*, op. 46. Originally approached in April 1947 by a Russian dancer and choreographer, Corinne Chochem, with a Yiddish song and its English translation, Schoenberg had planned 'a composition of 6–9 minutes for small orchestra and chorus, perhaps also one or more soloists', to be set 'in the Warsaw Ghetto,

how the doomed Jews started singing, before gooing [*sic*] to die'.[18]
Chochem proved unable to afford Schoenberg's fee, but in early July
the composer was commissioned by the Koussevitzky Foundation
and continued work on the same project.

His own family situation would inevitably have caused reflection
on the balance, if ever there could be one, between the aesthetic
and the documentary. The Greissles (Trudi and her family) had
escaped Austria following the *Anschluss*; Zemlinsky in one of his
final acts of personal nobility and generosity had offered them
financial assistance to do so, since Schoenberg simply did not have
the funds. Georg (Görgi), always a concern to his father, remained
in Vienna throughout the Second World War, one of those rare
Jews who somehow survived transportation or worse: in his case,
shelter offered by the Weberns helped. Ottilie likewise made it
through the war in Berlin. However, other family members were
not so fortunate. Her daughter Inge Hofmann and her husband
were shot by the ss as they attempted to escape the Allied
bombing of Dresden. Heinrich, their singer brother, also escaped
transportation, on account of his marriage to a prominent Aryan,
the daughter of the mayor of Salzburg. He was nevertheless arrested
in 1941 by the Gestapo and died in decidedly murky circumstances
– injuries and injection have both been claimed – in hospital.
Schoenberg's paternal cousin Arthur and his wife, Eva, were
murdered in the 'model camp' of Theresienstadt/Terezin, where
Viktor Ullmann had been a 'guest' before going to Auschwitz.
Some have claimed that Schoenberg misunderstood or even
misrepresented the historical truth of Warsaw; such missing of the
point merits at best a shrug of the shoulders.

For 'it means at first', Schoenberg wrote, insistent both on
the particularity of his faith and on his status as a creative, not a
documentary or Hollywood artist, 'a warning to all Jews, never to
forget what has been done to us, never to forget that even people
who did not do it themselves, agreed with them and many of them

found it necessary to treat us this way . . . The main thing is, that I saw it in my imagination.'[19] The words of the piece – Schoenberg's own – were derived, he said, from accounts of survivors of the Warsaw Ghetto. It was set during a typically condensed timespan: less than a fortnight, during August. The 'survivor', according to Schoenberg's plot, has escaped from a concentration camp to the sewers of Warsaw. He recounts the indignity of prisoners' treatment, and their defiance: in the middle of their roll call, the gas chambers awaiting, they had spontaneously broken into the ancient, triumphant Hebrew song 'Shema Yisroel'.

Drawing on Expressionist ghosts of his (relative) European youth, not least the hyper-Mahlerism of the *Five Orchestral Pieces*, perhaps even recalling *Die eiserne Brigade*, Schoenberg initially perhaps runs the risk of providing a mirror image to the Nazi aestheticization of politics of which Walter Benjamin had warned before his suicide at its hand. Strings *col legno*, two-trumpet *reveille*, *accelerando* of the 'counting out' represented 'like a stampede of wild horses': might such effects return us, unconvincingly, to the world of a post-Mahlerian *Wunderhorn* song or *Pierrot*, turned sourer still? The male chorus, its theme derived from the hideous opening fanfare, militates against that. Despite the work's brevity, one should say *eventually* militates against that, for, given the intensity of the drama, it feels like an age rather than six minutes. Germany for Schoenberg was still not only Nazism: it was Bach and Mozart; it was Brahms and, yes, Wagner; it was Mahler and Schoenberg. The music begins to grope, through canonical means in restatement of musical tradition, towards a version of besmirched C major, which can never be the same again. Schoenberg constructs fragmentary, modernistic, Jewish witness out of the darkest and, to him, most personal terror. There may well still have been, as he had once told his UCLA class, plenty of good music to be written in C major.[20] *A Survivor from Warsaw* both attests to and criticizes that claim, not unlike Adorno on poetry after Auschwitz.

The premiere was given in 1948 by Kurt Frederick and the amateur Albuquerque Civic Orchestra. Frederick, born Fuchsgelb, had been not only violist in the Kolisch Quartet but choral director at Vienna's Stadttempel until the *Anschluss*. Its immediate reception was enthusiastic, even occasioning a mention in *Time*, although the discussion already included some questioning of the ethics of transforming Holocaust experience into art. Europe heard the work for the first time the following month, in December, conducted by René Leibowitz in Paris.[21] Let us then return to Vienna, albeit from afar, for the last time.

In January 1951 Hermann Scherchen wrote to Schoenberg from Zurich, informing the composer of his plan to give the Austrian premiere of *A Survivor from Warsaw* in Vienna. If only it were possible, Schoenberg replied, for Viennese performances of his music to be prohibited completely, forever: 'No one has ever treated me so badly as there.'[22] Schoenberg reluctantly conceded the following month, saying that of course he would not stand in Scherchen's way. It is to be hoped that he did not read the reviews of the April performance, although he would hardly have been surprised – save, perhaps, for one extraordinary claim that he had somehow abjured his Viennese heritage (!) under the baleful influence of American culture.[23] Variations on a theme of 'rootless cosmopolitanism' would seem potentially infinite. This episode, however, took place against the backdrop of what might seem – and has generally been taken to be – happier news, namely that Schoenberg had finally been honoured by the city of his birth.

For his seventy-fifth birthday, in 1949, he had been made a *Bürger ehrenhalber der Stadt Wien*. That has often been construed as the freedom of the city of Vienna. There is not really a direct English (or American) equivalent, but it comes closer to honorary citizen, second class. Even that was hard won, almost entirely the doing of Vienna's Cultural Minister, Viktor Matejka, a Communist survivor from Dachau. Matejka, who held that office between 1945 and 1949 – when the other parties in cosy coalition relieved the Communist Party of any further need to serve – seems to have been the sole Austrian politician during the immediate post-war period to extend any official invitation to artists in exile to return. None of them did, since the old political establishment, with which Matejka, alas, exasperatedly had to deal, declined to offer any assistance with housing. The musical establishment seemed, at best, not to hear any calls for assistance either. In the face of such obstruction, Matejka then concentrated on obtaining honours for them. He proposed Schoenberg for Freedom of the City, the status of *Ehrenbürger*, but all other parties in Vienna's municipal government opposed him; indeed, it was quite a struggle even to gain agreement from them for the second-class status Schoenberg did receive.[24] 'Here comes Majetka,' one Social Democrat councillor sneered, 'with his impossible composer.' Kokoschka, we read in Majetka's memoirs, received similar treatment.[25] It would take another 25 years for Schoenberg's ashes, along with those of Gertrud, to return to Vienna – in an honorary grave, twelve-sided, far enough away from the Zentralfriedhof's monuments to Mozart (a fake grave, if ever there were one), Beethoven, Schubert, Brahms, Johann Strauss et al., so as not to be mistaken for someone of that magnitude. With due Viennese courtesy, Schoenberg thanked the mayor for this honour in a lengthy letter. His acceptance speech at the Los Angeles Austrian Consulate spoke, however, of a Kraus-like irony. 'Seven cities,' he began, 'are recorded as claiming to be Homer's birthplace. Up to a short time ago the contrary seemed to be the case with me.'[26] Stravinsky was in the audience: once again Schoenberg did not, or could not, see him; once again Stravinsky did not move to address him. Schoenberg would at least be named Honorary President of the Israel Academy of Music, in 1951, and the acceptance of that position gave him greater pleasure – and greater hope.

So he said at the time, at least, writing in acceptance – perhaps more in hope than in actual belief – that the Jews, just as they had been chosen by God for their monotheistic mission, might yet show the world a less commercial path for music. For, the previous year, in 1950, Schoenberg had written to the editor of the Jewish magazine *Commentary*, Elliot E. Cohen, responding to the claim of a Jewish conductor, Chemjo Vinaver, who had declined to programme his *Kol nidre* on the basis that it was divorced from the tradition necessary to liturgical practice. (How many times has a third-rate choirmaster justified the ongoing performing of fourth-rate 'church music' over, say, Mozart or Brahms, let alone Schoenberg, on that basis?) In his covering letter, Schoenberg pointed first to the relative novelty of this particular tradition, which

> does not go back to the bible, or to the word of God, but only to the Spanish persecution of the Jews. It is only a few centuries old, and if a tradition can be of so recent a date, why could one not also start a new tradition today. My concept of the *Kol nidre* is at least more honorable for Jewry. There is more logic in it and it does not add to the hatred of Jews.

Moreover, in the draft letter itself, having alluded to the practice of Chinese whispers as the reality of 'tradition', Schoenberg continued: 'if only elements of the *biblical cantillation* should be used, why not also exclude all modern musical instruments and use only those of bible-time. And how about Parisian-Pitch? How about well-tempered tonality?' What had once been a dignified melody was now for Schoenberg something shop-soiled by sentimentality, yet which must still be used. Was this, then, yet another impossible task, albeit on a smaller scale than *Moses*? It was Schoenberg's first completed work in English, and was certainly intended to speak to a larger community than had often, sadly, been the case – to *his* community. The text had after all been addressed to Spanish Jews, returning to their faith following forced conversion: not quite his experience, but not entirely opposed to it, either. But his ambivalence was perhaps best summarized in the final point made in his letter; his new people was in some respects no better disposed to him than his old people: 'It is curious that Jews are always the last ones to accept my achievements, whether in Israel or in the rest of the world. They perform everything: Debussy, Ravel, Hindemith, Stravinsky, Shostakovich, Bartók, etc. – but not me! In spite of my contributions, they are my greatest enemies!'[27] Always keen to safeguard his intellectual property, he added in his own hand a claim of copyright to the typed letter. In many ways, then, whether in respect of Vienna or of Israel, it was a matter of *plus ça change, plus c'est la même chose.*

Another of Schoenberg's final reckonings with past and present took place in a drama that had begun slightly earlier, 'also starring', as it were, Mann and Adorno. Mann's fictional composer, Adrian Leverkühn, in *Doctor Faustus* was clearly inspired by Schoenberg – or rather, his method of composition was clearly inspired by Schoenberg's. Indeed, it was his, albeit of a rather more Adornian variety. Adorno had acted as Mann's unofficial musical adviser; Mann signed Adorno's copy with a dedication to his 'privy counsellor' and had him appear in different guises, whether visually or verbally allusive, throughout the book. Schoenberg frankly admitted that he 'never could bear' Adorno, and almost always referred to him by his father's name, 'Wiesengrund', rather than the maternal 'Adorno' he had long since adopted.[28] Schoenberg especially disliked Adorno's description of his 'method' as a 'system', and told Rufer that while Wiesengrund 'naturally knows all about twelve-tone music, . . . he has no idea of the creative process.'[29] Adorno was a composer of whom Schoenberg clearly thought very little at all, and a recommendation he had to write offers a perfect example of the lukewarm reference we have all read (or perhaps even written): 'Mr Wiesengrund is a composer, who has been played internationally. He is also a philosopher and an important theorist (musicologist) and has published interesting essays.'[30] Schoenberg was particularly concerned about the consequences of Adorno's *Philosophy of New Music*, a celebrated, indeed notorious defence of Schoenberg against Stravinsky: 'The book will give many of my enemies a handle, especially because it is so scientifically done.'[31] He was not necessarily wrong on that score. Both books increased Schoenberg's personal revulsion to Berg's sometime pupil, who would remain, whatever one might think of him otherwise, a tireless supporter for the rest of his life and work. Schoenberg's parting gift was to deny Adorno access to his papers after his death.

Not unreasonably, Schoenberg took warmly neither to the twin pilfering and misunderstanding, nor – and for this, Mann was unquestionably responsible – to the composer with whom he was being associated contracting syphilis, thereafter making a pact with the Devil in order to achieve genius. Mann never actually thought highly of or even understood Schoenberg's music; nevertheless, in January 1948 he sent Schoenberg a copy inscribed: 'To the only one.' Although Schoenberg could no longer read for himself, he would have sections read to him, by Gertrud and his amanuensis, Richard Hoffmann. Alma Mahler-Werfel filled in some of the gaps – as only she could. Schoenberg wrote a piece of bitter satire and sent it to Mann, a 'Text from the Third Millennium', in which an encyclopaedia article credits Mann as the inventor of twelve-note music. If there were something on which Schoenberg would never fail to go on the attack, it was the slightest inkling of a threat to his intellectual property. A very public debate, stoked gleefully by Alma, was conducted in letters pages and elsewhere, nearing an uneasy ceasefire when Mann agreed to insert an acknowledgement of Schoenberg's copyright, still to be seen in all copies of the novel. Schoenberg remained troubled, though. Lion Feuchtwanger's wife reported that one day, while reaching for a grapefruit in a Brentwood Park supermarket, she had seen Schoenberg at the opposite end of the aisle. He had shouted – in

German, which was probably just as well – 'Lies, Frau Marta, lies! You have to know, I never had syphilis!' Schoenberg and Mann, at least, were finally reconciled in 1950, after Mann wrote him another letter of friendship and apology, which Schoenberg took to be genuine. He clearly believed Adorno, the non-artist, to be the greater villain, even suggesting that he would have been only too happy to have invented a special, fictional compositional system for Mann to have used instead of Wiesengrund's half-digested 'twelve-tone goulash'.

There remains one 'major' non-goulash work to discuss. In March 1949 Schoenberg composed his *Phantasy*, op. 47, 'for violin and piano accompaniment', at the request of Kolisch's friend the violinist Adolph Koldofsky, whose ensemble had given the premiere of the String Trio. The *Phantasy* partly takes up the challenge of the Violin Concerto, albeit in a different, self-imposed way. In place of having to contend with competing demands of concerto 'style' and twelve-note polyphony, Schoenberg, as is implied in the title, first wrote the violin part, then added – filling in the dodecaphonic gaps – the piano part. No one will hear it that way: art and an excellent performance conceal art, although the stated hierarchy between violin and piano remains to a certain extent. Haunted still by old Vienna, by waltzes owing more to Brahms than Johann Strauss – they always had, really – Schoenberg's new neo-Expressionism speaks once again, as if the violin were the protagonist in an instrumental sequel – or perhaps prelude – to *Erwartung*. The ending offers a startling surprise, which I shall not spoil in advance. Koldolfsky and Leonard Stein gave the first performance later that year, on 13 September, Schoenberg's birthday, at a party following his acceptance of Vienna's 'honour'.

In addition – on reflection, we should, like Beethoven's late *Bagatelles*, consider these to be in many ways as important as 'bigger' works – Schoenberg also composed a number of choral pieces. It might be tempting to consider them as a final return

Schoenberg's children, Lawrence, Ronald and Nuria, watch their father 'tune' a tennis racket at the Santa Monica tennis courts, 1948.

Final manuscript page of the incomplete *Modern Psalm*, op. 50*c*.

to his choral-society roots; yet, had his final pieces been songs, or works for piano or for string quartet, we should doubtless speak accordingly. In 1948 he composed a successor set, op. 49, to his earlier *a cappella* German folksong arrangements. His op. 50, unfinished – it almost had to be – offers two *a cappella* works (*Dreimal Tausend Jahre*, or Thrice a Thousand Years, and a setting of Psalm 130) and the torso of a *Modern Psalm* for chorus and orchestra, the words Schoenberg's own. Op. 50*a* was written in 1949 for a limited edition of the Swedish magazine *Prisma*; it is Schoenberg's completed tribute to the new State of Israel, founded a year previously, symbolized here as 'God's return'. In the Hebrew-language op. 50*b*, the familiar Latin *De profundis* words are sung, spoken, whispered, even shouted. It is as if, for one last time, he is returning to the Burning Bush with which *Moses* had opened, perhaps also to the upward 'seeking' of another incompletable work, *Die Jakobsleiter*. Both those works and op. 50*c* are twelve-note compositions. The last, the *Modern Psalm*, which was projected as the first in a series for which Schoenberg wrote all the texts, returns to the idea of speaker to, or against, chorus and orchestra. The composer seems here to be enjoying his ever-personal combination of canon, Expressionism and their purgation. Perhaps in some way, though, he sensed that this work too was incapable of completion, if only poetically. At any rate, having broken off, not unlike Moses, at his setting of the words 'And yet, I pray', he seems to have shown no intention, for the last year or so of his life, of ever returning to the score.

That may, of course, have been straightforwardly attributable to ill health. The final photograph we have of Schoenberg, again from 1950, is well-nigh unbearable to behold, his head shrunken like a bird's, the skull more alarmingly prominent than any in his paintings. On 2 July 1951 Scherchen gave the premiere of the Golden Calf scene from *Moses und Aron* at Darmstadt. Schoenberg had written to him just three days earlier, telling him that he looked forward to a performance of the whole of the second act. For the moment, this would do. As proud as ever, both of his works' progress and of his children's achievements at school and in sport, he had known for at least a fortnight that his time was up. According to Gertrud in a later account to Ottilie, who was still in Berlin, he had exchanged fear of death for resignation in its shadow, even welcoming its advent. On 14 July she sent Ottilie a telegram in English: 'Our beloved Arnold passed away 11.45 p.m. Friday 13 Trude and family.' In that later account, dated 4 August, Gertrud told of him having taken to his bed, too ill to spend more than a few minutes at a time with his children, yet loving to hear of them. He was also happily speaking of his youth, especially his Uncle Fritz. 'Up until the end,' Gertrud wrote, 'if he were weak, he was in spirit young. He could until his final day curse his enemies and cared about his friends up to the very end.' And then, 'on [Friday] 13th (he and I both greatly feared that)', Schoenberg had insisted

that I take in a sitter for the night. He was a German doctor, who did not have permission to practise here. I was very tired, and yet woke every hour and we had the light on. Arnold slept fitfully, but he slept. At about a quarter to midnight, I saw the clock and said to myself: just another quarter of an hour, and the worst is over. Then the doctor called me. His throat rattled twice, his heart gave out a strong beat, and that was everything. However, I could scarcely believe it for some time afterward. His face was so relaxed and peaceful as if he were asleep. No convulsion, no death struggle. I had always prayed for this end. Only not to suffer!

Gertrud would give lectures at home and abroad in the years to come. She made notes for them, and seems to have intended to write a biography. From those notes, we learn of Schoenberg's last words, in an account that, like the multiple openings with which the first chapter began, may or may not be quite reconcilable. Memory, as the *String Trio* had shown, is a strange, seductive, yet often productive thing:

The last known photograph of Schoenberg, *c.* 1950–51.

It is difficult to deal with the end. However, this is what I alone know and it must be told. Sch. died on 13 July 1951. On our clock 10 minutes before twelve. I had already looked at the clock and noted with relief: and so, now the 13th is almost over. There was no death struggle. He woke from his sleep as induced by injection and said one word: *HARMONIE*![32]

The word could be seen 'in space', she said, unsure whether it were the fruits of medication. Perhaps, at long last, Schoenberg had seen that other planet, whose air he had felt now for the best part of half a century. We continue to feel it, to breathe it – and, as he feared, to reject it.

References

Introduction

1 Pierre Boulez, 'Éventuellement', in *Relevés d'apprenti*, ed. Paule
Thévenin (Paris, 1966), p. 149.
2 Richard Wagner, *Oper und Drama*, ed. Klaus Kropfinger (Stuttgart,
1994), p. 215.
3 To the reader who may protest that Schoenberg was Austrian: identity,
as we shall see, was far more complicated than that.
4 I am grateful to Erik Levi for drawing my attention to this.
5 Arnold Schoenberg, 'Franz Liszt's Work and Being', in *Style and Idea:
Selected Writings of Arnold Schoenberg*, ed. Leonard Stein, trans. Leo
Black, revised edn (London, 1984), p. 442. Where, as here, I have used
existing editions and translations of Schoenberg's writings and letters,
this will be noted. Quotations will otherwise have been taken directly
from originals and/or copies in the Arnold Schönberg Center, Vienna.

1 Birth and Transfiguration

1 For consistency, I shall use Schoenberg throughout Arnold's life, as
has generally been the convention in English-language writing. Both
forms, Schönberg and Schoenberg, are justified, since the German ö is
often rendered as *oe*, in German and other languages. However, after
1934, when Schoenberg legally Anglicized the name to 'Schoenberg'
in the United States, it would, strictly speaking, be incorrect to use
'Schönberg'.
2 One early biographer, Schoenberg's pupil Dika Newlin, claims that
Pauline was a piano teacher, but there is no evidence to support that

claim, and strong reason to think she was not. Newlin proved to be a fascinating figure in her own right: musicologist, composer and, late in life, punk rock performance artist.

3   Arnold Schoenberg, 'Program Notes for the Juilliard String Quartet Performance of the Four String Quartets', in *Schoenberg's Program Notes and Musical Analyses*, ed. J. Daniel Jenkins (New York, 2016), p. 356.

4   Arnold Schoenberg, 'My Evolution', in *Style and Idea: Selected Writings of Arnold Schoenberg*, ed. Leonard Stein, trans. Leo Black, revd edn (London, 1984), p. 80.

5   Schoenberg, 'Program Notes', p. 357.

6   Ibid., p. 359.

7   Hans Nachod, 'A Cousin's Memories', in 'Involuntary Pilgrimage of Arnold Schönberg. From Vienna to California: A Symposium', *The Listener*, 1194 (17 January 1952), p. 107.

8   Arthur Kahane, *Tagebuch des Dramaturgen* (Berlin, 1928), p. 157.

9   Schoenberg, 'My Attitude Toward Politics,' in *Style and Idea*, p. 505.

10 Letter to Malvina Goldschmied, 25 May 1891, *A Schoenberg Reader: Documents of a Life*, ed. Joseph Auner (New Haven, CT, and London, 2003), p. 15.

11 Nicolas Slonimsky, *The Listener's Companion: The Great Composers and Their Works* (New York, 2003), p. 235.

12 Letter of 13 December 1912, in *Schoenberg Reader*, p. 119.

13 Schoenberg, 'Liner Notes for the Capitol Records Release of *Verklärte Nacht*', in *Schoenberg's Program Notes*, p. 124.

14 Alexander Zemlinsky, 'Jugenderinerungen', in *Arnold Schönberg zum 60: Geburtstag, 13 September 1934* (Vienna, 1934), p. 34.

15 Schoenberg, 'Program Notes', p. 129.

16 Schoenberg, 'How One Becomes Lonely', in *Style and Idea*, p. 30.

2   Emancipating the Dissonance

1   Alexander Zemlinsky, 'Jugenderinerungen', in *Arnold Schönberg zum 60: Geburtstag, 13 September 1934* (Vienna, 1934), p. 35.

2   The Dutch National Opera recently put that omission right, to considerable acclaim, in a staging by Pierre Audi in 2014.

3   Letter of 10 September 1903, Arnold Schönberg Center.

4   Igor Stravinsky and Robert Craft, *Memories and Commentaries* (Berkeley and Los Angeles, CA, 1981), p. 105.

5   Letter of 12 December 1904, Arnold Schönberg Center.

6   We can readily forget how excellent the postal system was, which permitted several daily deliveries even between cities and between countries, let alone within Vienna.

7   Alma Mahler, *Gustav Mahler: Memories and Letters*, ed. Donald Mitchell and Knud Martner, trans. Basil Crighton, revd edn (London, 1973), p. 78.

8   Arnold Schoenberg, 'Liner Notes for the Capitol Records Release of *Pelleas und Melisande*', in *Schoenberg's Program Notes and Musical Analyses*, ed. J. Daniel Jenkins (New York, 2016), p. 147.

9   Review in *Montagspresse*, Feuilleton, 30 January 1905.

10 Donald Francis Tovey, 'Harmony', in *Musical Articles from the Encyclopedia Britannica*, ed. Hubert J. Foss (London, 1944), pp. 69–70.

11 Quoted in Ian Latham, *Joseph Maria Olbrich* (New York, 1980), p. 32.

12 Quoted in Peter Vergo, *Art in Vienna, 1898–1918: Klimt, Kokoschka, Schiele and their Contemporaries* (London, 1975), p. 35.

13 Quoted in Peter Paret, *The Berlin Secession* (Cambridge, 1980), pp. 26–7.

14 Adolf Loos, 'Ornament und Verbrechen,' in *Sämtliche Schriften*, ed. Franz Glück, 2 vols (Vienna and Munich, 1962), vol. I, pp. 276–88.

15 Letter of 24 January 1911, Arnold Schönberg Center.

16 Wassily Kandinsky, 'Die Bilder', in *Arnold Schönberg: Mit Beiträgen von Alban Berg et al* (Munich, 1912), pp. 59, 64.

17 Schoenberg, 'Testaments-Entwurf ', Arnold Schönberg Center.

18 Dika Newlin, 'Secret Tonality in Schoenberg's Piano Concerto', *Perspectives of New Music*, XIII/1 (Autumn/Winter 1974), p. 137.

19 George was nothing if not the cultic priest. However, whatever the parallels one might draw between his 'Circle' and Schoenberg's, the former's homoeroticism was quite alien to the latter.

20 Schoenberg, 'Program Notes to and Audio Commentary for the Kolisch Quartet Recording of the Four String Quartets,' in *Schoenberg's Program Notes*, ed. J. Daniel Jenkins (Oxford and New York, 2016), p. 351.

3 Air of Another Planet

1 Arnold Schoenberg, 'Franz Liszt's Work and Being,' in *Style and Idea: Selected Writings of Arnold Schoenberg*, ed. Leonard Stein, trans. Leo Black, revd edn (London, 1984), p. 442.

2 Letter of *c*. 18 August 1909, in *A Schoenberg Reader: Documents of a Life*, ed. Joseph Auner (New Haven, CT, and London, 2003), p. 70.

3 Schoenberg, 'Program Notes for the Society for Art and Culture', in *Schoenberg's Program Notes*, ed. J. Daniel Jenkins (Oxford and New York, 2016), pp. 184–5.

4 Letter to Busoni, 24 August 1909, Arnold Schönberg Center.

5 Letter to Richard Specht, 22 April 1914, Arnold Schönberg Center.

6 The second part of the subtitle refers to that alleged initial inspiration: 'Summer Morning on the Lake'.

7 Bryan Simms, *The Atonal Music of Arnold Schoenberg, 1908–1923* (Oxford and New York, 2000), pp. 90–91.

8 Letter of 13(?) August 1909, Arnold Schönberg Center.

9 Josef Breuer, 'Case 1: Fräulein Anna O', in Josef Breuer and Sigmund Freud, *The Standard Edition of the Complete Psychological Works of Sigmund Freud*, vol. II: *Studies on Hysteria*, ed. and trans. James Strachey et al. (London, 1955), p. 55.

10 Schoenberg, 'New Music: My Music', in *Style and Idea*, p. 105.

11 Schoenberg, 'Breslau Lecture on Die glückliche Hand', in *Schoenberg's Program Notes*, p. 207.

12 Contrary to what many Anglophone writers – working from the same mistranslation, perhaps, or even from one another – have claimed, the woman does not throw a rock at the man; still less does she hurl several such 'boulders', as that rabid Schoenbergophobe Richard Taruskin claimed in 'The Poietic Fallacy', *Musical Times*, CXLV/1886 (Spring 2004), p. 31. What a misogynist, that Schoenberg! As a modernist, he would be . . . The German stage directions are clear: the rock falls, having dislodged itself.

13 Malcolm MacDonald, *Schoenberg*, 2nd edn (Oxford, 2008), p. 131.

14 Schoenberg, 'Breslau Lecture', p. 208.

15 Letter of 13(?) August 1909, Arnold Schönberg Center.

16 Schoenberg, *Harmonielehre* (Vienna, 1986), p. 417.

17 Review in *Das kleine Journal*, 26 February 1912. I have used here the

translation in Willi Reich, *Schoenberg: A Critical Biography*, trans. Leo
Black (London, 1971), p. 63.

18 Letter to Berg, 19 October 1912, reproduced online at *Anton Webern
Gesamtausgabe*, www.salsah.org/webern, accessed 21 October 2018.

19 Letter of 13 December 1912, in Schoenberg, *Briefe*, ed. Erwin Stein
(Mainz, 1958), p. 31.

20 Letter of 20 March 1913, Arnold Schönberg Center.

21 Letter of 4 April 1913, in *The Berg–Schoenberg Correspondence: Selected
Letters*, ed. Juliane Brand, Christopher Hailey and Donald Harris
(Basingstoke, 1987), p. 170 (translation slightly modified).

22 Letter to Guido Adler, 20 August 1912, Arnold Schönberg Center.

23 Hermann Scherchen, 'Mein Erstes Leben (1891–1950)', in *Werke und
Briefe*, vol. I, ed. Joachim Lucchesi (Berlin, 1991), p. 169.

24 Igor Stravinsky and Robert Craft, *Dialogues* (Berkeley and Los Angeles,
CA, 1982), p. 105.

25 Sjeng Scheijen, *Diaghilev: A Life*, trans. Jane Hedley-Prôle and S. J.
Leinbach (Oxford, 2009), pp. 259–60.

26 Arthur Jacobs, 'Sir Henry J[oseph] Wood', *Grove Music Online*,
www.oxfordmusiconline.com/grovemusic, accessed 21 October 2018.

27 Letter of 9 October 1915, in *Arnold Schoenberg Letters*, ed. Erwin Stein,
trans. Eithne Wilkins and Ernst Kaiser (London and Boston, MA, 1964),
p. 53.

28 Sabine Feisst, *Schoenberg's New World: The American Years* (Oxford and
New York, 2011), p. 17.

4 'War Years' and their Aftermath

1 Christopher Clark, *Sleepwalkers: How Europe Went to War in 1914*
(London, 2012).

2 Arnold Schoenberg, 'Art and the Moving Pictures', in *Style and Idea:
Selected Writings of Arnold Schoenberg*, ed. Leonard Stein, trans. Leo
Black, revd edn (London, 1984), p. 154.

3 Honoré de Balzac, *Séraphîta*, trans. Clara Bell (Sawtry, Cambridgeshire
and New York, 1989), p. 123.

4 Schoenberg, 'Art and the Moving Pictures', p. 154.

5 Letter of 9 October 1915, in *Arnold Schoenberg Letters*, ed. Erwin Stein,

    trans. Eithne Wilkins and Ernst Kaiser (London and Boston, MA, 1964), p. 53.

6   Schoenberg, 'Composition with Twelve Tones (2)', in *Style and Idea*, p. 247.

7   It is unclear what Bartók, himself rejected for military service, was able to do; his help was enlisted, but neither Schoenberg nor Bartók scholars – nor, it seems, anyone else – have been able to establish anything further.

8   Schoenberg, 'New Music: My Music', in *Style and Idea*, p. 104.

9   One can visit the little museum there today. Two smaller apartments are available on the ground floor for visiting scholars; I have been fortunate enough to stay there once, on a scholarship.

10 Schoenberg, 'A Four-point Program for Jewry' from 1940, Arnold Schönberg Center.

11 Schoenberg, 'Prospectus of the Society for Private Performances', in *A Schoenberg Reader: Documents of a Life*, ed. Joseph Auner (New Haven, CT, and London, 2003), p. 151.

12 See Henry-Louis Grange, *Gustav Mahler*, vol. III: *Vienna: Triumph and Disillusion (1904–1907)* (Oxford, 1999), pp. 4–5.

13 Ibid., p. 153 (translation slightly modified).

14 E. Randol Schoenberg, 'The Most Famous Thing He Never Said', *Journal of the Arnold Schönberg Center*, V (2003), pp. 27–30.

15 Schoenberg, 'When I think of music . . .', in *Schoenberg Reader*, p. 160.

16 Schoenberg, excerpts from '"Guide-lines for a Ministry of Art" edited by Adolf Loos', in *Style and Idea*, p. 369.

17 E. Randol Schoenberg, 'The Most Famous Thing He Never Said', p. 30.

18 Letter of 1 November 1930, Arnold Schönberg Center.

19 Letter of 17 November 1930, Arnold Schönberg Center.

20 Pauline had been living with her daughter and son-in-law at Hauptstrasse 155, Schöneberg – to be confused with neither Schönberg nor Schoenberg. The house would later, in a slightly odd coincidence, be David Bowie's Berlin address. It also lies directly in front of the small street on which I began writing this book.

5 Composing with Twelve Notes Related Only to One Another

1 Letter of 13 March 1923, Arnold Schönberg Center.

2 Anton Webern, *The Path to the New Music*, ed. Willi Reich, trans. Leo Black (London, 1963), p. 35.

3 Arnold Schoenberg, 'Art Golem', in *A Schoenberg Reader: Documents of a Life*, ed. Joseph Auner (New Haven, CT, and London, 2003), p. 163.

4 Schoenberg, 'Discussion over Radio Berlin with Preussner and Strobel', in *Schoenberg's Program Notes*, ed. J. Daniel Jenkins (Oxford and New York, 2016), p. 55.

5 Ibid, p. 64.

6 Warren Langlie's notes from study with Schoenberg, quoted in Matthias Schmidt, *Schoenberg und Mozart: Aspekte einer Rezeptionsgeschichte* (Vienna, 2004), p. 15.

7 Schoenberg, 'My Evolution', in *Style and Idea: Selected Writings*, ed. Leonard Stein, trans. Leo Black (London, 1984), p. 91.

8 Affinities between Webern and Klee have often been remarked on, not least by Boulez, a keen interpreter and collector.

9 August 1933, in *The Berg–Schoenberg Correspondence: Selected Letters*, ed. Juliane Brand, Christopher Hailey and Donald Harris (Basingstoke, 1987), p. 444.

10 This exchange may be read as a whole in translation in Jelena Hahl-Koch, ed., *Arnold Schoenberg, Wassily Kandinsky: Letters, Pictures and Documents*, trans. John C. Crawford (London and Boston, MA, 1984), pp. 76–82.

11 Letter of 4 May 1923, in *Letters*, pp. 89–93.

12 Letter of 1 July 1936, Arnold Schönberg Center.

13 Quoted in Klara Moricz, *Jewish Identities: Nationalism, Racism, and Utopianism in Twentieth-century Music* (Berkeley and Los Angeles, CA, 2008), p. 230.

14 Arnold Greissle-Schönberg, *Arnold Schönberg und sein Wiener Kreis: Erinnerungen seines Enkels* (Vienna, Cologne and Weimar, 1998), p. 17.

15 Letter of 9 September 1949, quoted in Raymond Fearn, *The Music of Luigi Dallapiccola* (Rochester, Kent, and Woodbridge, Suffolk, 2003), p. 6.

6 Goodbye to Berlin

1 Roberto Gerhard, 'Schoenberg Reminscences', *Perspectives of New Music*, XIII/2 (Spring–Summer 1975), p. 59.

2 Quoted in Chris Walton, 'Erich Schmid in Schoenberg's Composition Masterclass', *Tempo*, 218 (2001), p. 16. Translation slightly modified.

3 Herbert Lindenberger, 'Arnold Schoenberg's "Der Biblische Weg" and "Moses und Aron": On the Transactions of Aesthetics and Politics', *Modern Judaism*, IX/1 (February 1989), p. 58.

4 Author's own translation from Schoenberg's original German typescript, Arnold Schönberg Center.

5 According to Virgil Thomson's autobiography, quoted in David Drew, 'Der Weg der Verheissung: Weill at the Crossroads', *Tempo*, 208 (April 1999), p. 35. Set against that remark, which should perhaps be viewed in the context of Weill's American popularity, one should recall that Weill had once wished to study with Schoenberg. Schoenberg had looked kindly upon the prospect, and he had recommended the pre-*Threepenny Opera* Weill for membership of the Prussian Academy of Arts in 1927.

6 Schoenberg, 'Program Notes to and Audio Commentary for the Kolisch Quartet Recording of the Four String Quartets', in *Schoenberg's Program Notes*, ed. J. Daniel Jenkins (Oxford and New York, 2016), p. 352.

7 Joseph Auner, ed., *A Schoenberg Reader: Documents of a Life* (New Haven, CT, and London, 2003), pp. 229–30.

8 Gregor Piatigorsky, *Cellist* (New York, 1965), pp. 76–7.

9 Schoenberg, 'The Tempo of Development', in *A Schoenberg Reader*, p. 210.

10 *Die Musik*, XXII/10 (July 1930), p. 775.

11 So was *Von heute auf morgen*. Straub-Huillet, as they were collectively known, also made an 'introduction' to the *Accompaniment to a Film Scene*.

12 Erwin Stein, 'Moses und Aron', *Opera*, VIII/8 (August 1957), pp. 485–6.

13 'Boulez on Schoenberg's "Moses und Aron": An Interview with Wolfgang Schaufler', trans. Stewart Spencer, in booklet accompanying Deutsche Grammophon CD 449 174-2, p. 14.

14 Theodor Adorno, 'Sacred Fragment: Schoenberg's "Moses und

Aron"', in *Quasi una Fantasia: Essays on Modern Music*, trans. Rodney Livingstone (London and New York, 1998), p. 229.

15 Letter of 20 February 1933, in *Schoenberg's Program Notes*, p. 334.

16 Arturo Toscanini, as resolutely anti-modernist a musician as he was anti-fascist in politics, was one of a number of prominent musicians who had earlier performed Graeber's music, a fact that once more counsels us against too ready association of artistic and political 'Right' and 'Left'.

17 'Letter on the Jewish Question', in H. H. Stuckenschmidt, *Schoenberg: His Life, World and Work*, trans. Humphrey Searle (London, 1959), pp. 541–2.

7 Exile

1 Milton Babbitt, '"My Vienna Triangle at Washington Square": Revised and Dilated', in *The Collected Essays of Milton Babbitt*, ed. Steven Peles et al. (Princeton, NJ, 2003), pp. 466–7.

2 Interview with William Lundell, 19 November 1933, in *Schoenberg's Program Notes and Analyses*, ed. J. Daniel Jenkins (Oxford and New York, 2016), p. 70.

3 Babbitt, 'My Vienna Triangle at Washington Square', pp. 466–7.

4 Quoted in Sabine Feisst, *Schoenberg's New World: The American Years* (Oxford and New York, 2011), p. 229.

5 Richard Kostelanetz, *Conversing with Cage*, 2nd edn (New York and London, 2003), p. 5.

6 For a summary of Cage's various versions of this story, see Michael Hicks, 'John Cage's Studies with Schoenberg,' *American Music*, 8 (1990), pp. 133–5.

7 Letter of *c.* 11 March 1936, translated in George Perle, *The Operas of Alban Berg*, vol. II: *Lulu* (Berkeley and Los Angeles, CA, 1985), pp. 283–4.

8 Letter of 1 January 1934, Arnold Schönberg Center.

9 The address 'On Gershwin's Death' may be found on the website of the Arnold Schönberg Center, www.schoenberg.at, accessed 21 October 2018.

10 Arnold Schoenberg, 'Draft of a Foreword to the Suite for String Orchestra for College Orchestra Composed by Arnold Schoenberg', *Schoenberg's Program Notes*, p. 338.

11 Olin Downes, 'New Suite by Arnold Schoenberg,' *New York Times*, 13 October 1935.

12 Letter of 22 November 1941, Arnold Schönberg Center.

13 Merle Armitage, ed., *Schoenberg* (Westport, CT, 1977), p. 149.

14 'Schoenberg Violin Concerto Finds a Champion', *Evening Bulletin – Philadelphia*, 11 December 1940.

15 Linton Martin, 'Music Hissers Given a Rebuke by Stokowski', *Philadelphia Inquirer*, 8 December 1940.

16 Schoenberg, 'Program Notes to and Audio Commentary for the Kolisch Quartet Recording of the Four String Quartets', in *Schoenberg's Program Notes*, p. 353.

17 Quoted in Matthias Schmidt, *Schoenberg und Mozart: Aspekte einer Rezeptionsgeschichte* (Vienna, 2004), p. 167, n. 75.

18 Schoenberg, 'A Four-point Program for Jewry' from 1940, Arnold Schönberg Center.

19 Hanns Eisler, *Brecht, Music and Culture: Hanns Eisler in Conversation with Hans Bunge*, ed. and trans. Sabine Berendse and Paul Clements (London and New York, 2014), p. 7.

20 Bertold Brecht, 'Nachdenkend über die Hölle', in *Poetry and Prose*, ed. Reinhold Grimm (New York and London, 2006), pp. 100, 102.

21 Eisler, *Brecht, Music and Culture*, p. 26.

8 Citizenship: War and Peace

1 Letter to Donald W. Gray, 19 April 1950, in *Schoenberg's Program Notes and Analyses*, ed. J. Daniel Jenkins (Oxford and New York, 2016), pp. 409–10.

2 Letter to René Leibowitz, 4 July 1947, Arnold Schönberg Center.

3 Arnold Schoenberg, 'How I came to compose the "Ode to Napoleon"', in *Schoenberg's Program Notes*, pp. 411–12.

4 Letter of 8 September 1943, Arnold Schönberg Center.

5 Letter of 4 July 1947, Arnold Schönberg Center.

6 Schoenberg had, in the meantime, made that work's first recording in 1940, conducting Los Angeles musicians and Erika Stiedry-Wagner.

7 Telegram of 2 October 1941, Arnold Schönberg Center.

8 Oscar Levant, *The Memoirs of an Amnesiac* (New York, 1965), p. 137.

9 'Busch, Serkin Triumph at Opera House', *San Francisco Chronicle*, 7 February 1944.

10 Letter to Robert Gordon Sproul, 14 May 1945, Arnold Schönberg Center.

11 Nathaniel Shilkret, *Sixty Years in the Music Business*, ed. Neil Shell and Barbara Shilkret (Lanham, MD, 2005), pp. 196–8.

12 Schoenberg, 'On Strauss and Furtwängler', in *A Schoenberg Reader: Documents of a Life*, ed. Joseph Auner (New Haven, CT, and London, 2003), pp. 316–17.

13 Letter of 21 May 1947, Arnold Schönberg Center.

14 Thomas Mann, *The Story of a Novel: The Genesis of Doctor Faustus*, trans. Richard Winston and Clara Winston (New York, 1961), p. 217.

15 As told to Walter Bailey, recounted in the latter's *Programmatic Elements in the Works of Schoenberg* (Ann Arbor, MI, 1984), pp. 151–2.

16 Michael Cherlin, 'Memory and Rhetorical Trope in Schoenberg's String Trio', *Journal of the American Musicological Society*, LI/3 (Autumn 1998), p. 559.

17 Quoted in Deryck Cooke, *I Saw the World End: A Study of Wagner's 'Ring'* (Oxford, 1979), p. 343.

18 Letter of 20 April 1947, Arnold Schönberg Center.

19 Letter to Kurt List, 1 November 1948, Arnold Schönberg Center.

20 Dika Newlin, 'Secret Tonality in Schoenberg's Piano Concerto', *Perspectives of New Music*, XIII/1 (Autumn/Winter 1974), p. 137.

21 Joy H. Calico has written a fascinating study of the work's progress throughout Europe, highly recommended to those curious about later Schoenberg reception: *Arnold Schoenberg's 'A Survivor from Warsaw' in Postwar Europe* (Berkeley and Los Angeles, CA, and London, 2014).

22 Letter of 29 January 1951, Arnold Schönberg Center.

23 Calico, *Survivor from Warsaw*, pp. 61–2.

24 I am grateful to Sebastian Smallshaw for initially elucidating to me the ins and outs of this grubby affair.

25 Viktor Matejka, *Widerstand ist alles: Notizen eines Unorthodoxen* (Vienna, 1993), pp. 189–202.

26 Letter of 23 October 1949, in *Style and Idea: Selected Writings of Arnold Schoenberg*, ed. Leonard Stein, trans. Leo Black, revd edn (London, 1984), pp. 29–30.

27 Draft letter to Elliot E. Cohen, 28 January 1950, in *Schoenberg's Program Notes*, ed. Jenkins, pp. 402–3.
28 Letter to Hans Heinz Stuckenschmidt, 5 December 1949, Arnold Schönberg Center.
29 Letter to Josef Rufer, 5 December 1949, Arnold Schönberg Center.
30 Letter to Robert Emmett Stuart, in *A Schoenberg Reader*, p. 285.
31 Letter to Josef Rufer, 5 December 1949, in H. H. Stuckenschmidt, *Schoenberg: His Life, World and Work*, trans. Humphrey Searle (London, 1959), p. 508.
32 Material yet to be catalogued, courtesy of the Arnold Schönberg Center Archive.

Select Bibliography

I have tended to favour English versions of original sources for this list, although I have generally worked from the originals and have always consulted them. I have also favoured books over articles, although there are a good number of collected volumes of essays here too, from which, for reasons of space alone, I have not listed individual contributions nor have I included everything cited in the footnotes. The Bibliography is anything but exhaustive, neither of what I have read, nor of what there is to read. It is intended, however, to offer the reader a variety of options for further reading, with something of a bias towards English-language literature. The extraordinary Schoenbergian treasure trove that is the website of the Arnold Schönberg Center should be the first port of call for primary sources, followed by archival enquiry to the Center, should a sketch, manuscript, letter, essay or picture not prove available online. The Center's annual *Journal* also offers an excellent conspectus of recent scholarship, only a little of which is listed here.

Adorno, Theodor W., *Quasi una Fantasia: Essays on Modern Music*,
    trans. Rodney Livingstone (London and New York, 1998)
——, *Essays on Music* (Berkeley and Los Angeles, CA, and London, 2002)
——, *Philosophy of New Music*, trans., ed. and with an introduction by
    Robert Hullor-Kentor (Minneapolis, MN, 2006)
Armitage, Merle, ed., *Schoenberg* (Westport, CT, 1977)
Arnold Schönberg zum fünfzigsten Geburtstage, Musikblätter des Anbruch
    (Vienna, 1924)
Arnold Schönberg zum 60. Geburtstag (Vienna, 1934)
Auner, Joseph, *A Schoenberg Reader: Documents of a Life* (New Haven, CT,
    and London, 2003)
Babbitt, Milton, *The Collected Essays of Milton Babbitt*, ed. Steven Peles et al.
    (Princeton, NJ, 2003)

Bailey, Kathryn, 'Formal Organization and Structural Imagery in Schoenberg's *Pierrot lunaire*', *Studies in Music from the University of Western Ontario*, II (1977), pp. 93–107

——, *The Life of Webern* (Cambridge, 1998)

Bailey, Walter B., 'Oscar Levant and the Program for Schoenberg's Piano Concerto', *Journal of the Arnold Schönberg Institute*, VI/1 (1982), pp. 56–79

——, *Programmatic Elements in the Works of Schoenberg* (Ann Arbor, MI, 1984)

——, *The Arnold Schoenberg Companion* (Westport, CT, and London, 1998)

Beaumont, Antony, *Zemlinsky* (London, 2000)

——, ed., *Ferruccio Busoni: Selected Letters* (London, 1986)

Berg, Alban, *Arnold Schönberg: Pelleas und Melisande, op. 5: Kurze thematische Analyse* (Vienna, 1920)

——, et al., *Arnold Schönberg in höchster Verehrung von Schülern und Freunden* (Munich, 1912)

Berry, Mark, *After Wagner: Histories of Modernist Music Drama from 'Parsifal' to Nono* (Woodbridge, Suffolk, and Rochester, NY, 2014)

——, 'Representing a Representation of the Unrepresentable: Staging – and Filming – *Moses und Aron*', *Journal of the Arnold Schönberg Center*, XIII (October 2016), pp. 49–66

Boulez, Pierre, 'Schoenberg Is Dead', *The Score*, VI (1952), pp. 18–22

——, *Relevés d'apprenti*, ed. Paule Thévenin (Paris, 1966)

——, *Orientations: Collected Writings*, ed. Jean-Jacques Nattiez, trans. Martin Cooper (London, 1986)

Brand, Juliane, Christopher Hailey and Donald Harris, *The Berg–Schoenberg Correspondence* (Basingstoke, 1987)

——, and Christopher Hailey, *Constructive Dissonance: Arnold Schoenberg and the Transformations of Twentieth-century Culture* (Berkeley and Los Angeles, CA, 1997)

Brinkmann, Reinhold, and Christoph Wolff, eds, *Driven into Paradise: The Musical Migration from Nazi Germany to the United States* (Berkeley and Los Angeles, CA, 1999)

Brown, Julie, *Schoenberg and Redemption* (Cambridge, 2014)

Bujić, Bojan, *Arnold Schoenberg* (London and New York, 2011)

Busch, Regina, 'On the Horizontal and Vertical Presentation of Musical Ideas and Musical Space', *Tempo*, 154 (September 1985), pp. 2–10

Calico, Joy H., *Arnold Schoenberg's 'A Survivor from Warsaw' in Postwar Europe* (Berkeley and Los Angeles, CA, and London, 2014)

Cherlin, Michael, 'Memory and Rhetorical Trope in Schoenberg's String
    Trio', *Journal of the American Musicological Society*, LI/3 (Autumn 1998),
    pp. 559–602
——, 'Dialectical Opposition in Schoenberg's Music and Thought', *Music
    Theory Spectrum*, XXII/2 (2000), pp. 157–76
——, *Schoenberg's Musical Imagination* (Cambridge, 2007)
Christensen, Jean, and Jesper Christensen, *From Arnold Schoenberg's Library
    Legacy: A Catalog of Neglected Items* (Detroit, MI, 1998)
Clark, Christopher, *Sleepwalkers: How Europe Went to War in 1914* (London, 2012)
Coffer, Raymond, 'Richard Gerstl and Arnold Schönberg: A Reassessment
    of their Relationship (1906–1908) and its Impact on their Artistic
    Works', PhD thesis, Institute of Germanic and Romance Studies,
    University of London, 2011
Cook, Nicholas, *The Schenker Project: Culture, Race, and Music Theory*
    (Oxford and New York, 2007)
Covach, John, 'The Sources of Schoenberg's "Aesthetic Theology"',
    19th-century Music, XIX/3 (Spring 1996), pp. 252–62
Cross, Charlotte M., and Russell A. Berman, eds, *Political and Religious
    Ideas in the Works of Arnold Schoenberg* (New York and London, 2000)
——, and Russell A. Berman, eds, *Schoenberg and Words: The Modernist
    Years* (New York and London, 2000)
Dahlhaus, Carl, *Schoenberg and the New Music*, trans. Derrick Puffett and
    Alfred Clayton (Cambridge, 1987)
Dunsby, Jonathan, *Schoenberg: Pierrot Lunaire* (Cambridge, 1992)
Eisler, Hanns, *Brecht, Music and Culture: Hanns Eisler in Conversation
    with Hans Bunge*, ed. and trans. Sabine Berendse and Paul Clements
    (London and New York, 2014)
Ertelt, Thomas, et al., eds, *Briefwechsel der Wiener Schule*, 6 vols (various, 1995–)
Feisst, Sabine, 'Arnold Schoenberg and the Cinematic Art', *Musical
    Quarterly*, LXXXIII/1 (March 1999), pp. 93–113
——, *Schoenberg's New World: The American Years* (Oxford and New York, 2011)
Forte, Allen, *The Structure of Atonal Music* (New Haven, CT, 1973)
——, 'Schoenberg's Creative Evolution: The Path to Atonality', *Musical
    Quarterly*, LXXXIII/1 (1999), pp. 93–113
Franklin, Peter, *The Idea of Music: Schoenberg and Others* (Basingstoke, 1985)
Frisch, Walter, *The Early Works of Arnold Schoenberg, 1893–1908* (Berkeley,
    Los Angeles and London, 1993)

——, ed., *Schoenberg and his World* (Princeton, NJ, 1999)

Gerhard, Roberto, 'Schoenberg Reminiscences', *Perspectives of New Music*, XIII/2 (Spring–Summer 1975), pp. 57–65

Goehr, Alexander, 'Schoenberg's *Gedanke* Manuscript', *Journal of the Arnold Schoenberg Institute*, II/1 (1977), pp. 4–25

——, *Finding the Key: Selected Writings of Alexander Goehr*, ed. Derrick Puffett (London, 1998)

Greissle-Schönberg, Arnold, *Arnold Schönberg und sein Wiener Kreis: Erinnerungen seines Enkels* (Vienna, 1998)

Gruber, Gerold, ed., *Arnold Schönberg: Interpretationen seiner Werke*, 2 vols (Laaber, Germany, 2002)

Hahl-Koch, Jelena, ed., *Arnold Schoenberg, Wassily Kandinsky: Letters, Pictures and Documents*, trans. John C. Crawford (London and Boston, MA, 1984)

Haimo, Ethan, *Schoenberg's Serial Odyssey: The Evolution of his Twelve-tone Method, 1914–1928* (Oxford, 1990)

——, *Schoenberg's Transformation of Musical Language* (Cambridge, 2006)

——, ed., *Schoenberg's Early Correspondence*, trans. Sabine Feisst (Oxford and New York, 2016)

Hamao, Fusako, 'On the Origin of the Twelve-tone Method: Schoenberg's Sketches for the Unfinished Symphony', *Current Musicology*, 42 (Autumn 1986), pp. 32–45

——, 'The Origin and Development of Schoenberg's Twelve-tone Method', PhD diss., Yale University, 1988

Harvey, Jonathan, 'Schönberg: Man or Woman?', *Music and Letters*, LVI/3–4 (July 1975), pp. 371–85

Heneghan, Aine, 'Tradition as Muse: Schoenberg's Musical Morphology and Nascent Dodecaphony', PhD diss., Trinity College, Dublin, 2006

Herrmann, Matthias, *Arnold Schönberg in Dresden* (Dresden, 2001)

Heyworth, Peter, *Otto Klemperer: His Life and Times*, 2 vols (Cambridge, 1996)

Hicks, Michael, 'John Cage's Studies with Schoenberg', *American Music*, VIII/2 (1990), pp. 125–40

Hilmar, Ernst, ed., *Arnold Schönberg, Gedenkausstellung 1974* (Vienna, 1974)

Hindinger, Barbara, and Ester Saletta, eds, *Der musikalisch modellierte Mann: Interkulturelle und interdisziplinäre Männlichkeitsstudien zur Oper und Literatur des 19. und frühen 20. Jahrhunderts* (Vienna, 2012)

Jalowetz, Heinrich, 'On the Spontaneity of Schoenberg's Music', *Musical Quarterly*, XXX/4 (October 1944), pp. 385–408

Jenkins, J. Daniel, ed., *Schoenberg's Program Notes and Analyses* (Oxford and New York, 2016)

Johnson, Julian, *Webern and the Transformation of Nature* (Cambridge, 1999)

Kahane, Arthur, *Tagebuch des Dramaturgen* (Berlin, 1928)

Kandinsky, Wassily, 'The Paintings of Schoenberg', *Journal of the Arnold Schoenberg Institute*, II/3 (June 1978), pp. 181–4

——, *The Complete Writings on Art*, ed. Kenneth C. Lindsay and Peter Vergo (Boston, MA, 1982)

——, and Franz Marc, eds, *Der blaue Reiter* (Munich, 1912)

Karnes, Kevin C., *A Kingdom Not of this World: Wagner, the Arts, and Utopian Visions in Fin-de-siècle Vienna* (New York, 2013)

Kohlbauer-Fritz, Gabriele, and Weibke Krohn, *Beste aller Frauen: Weibliche Dimensionen im Judentum* (Vienna, 2007)

Kolleritsch, Otto, ed., *Alexander Zemlinsky: Tradition im Umkreis der Wiener Schule* (Graz, 1976)

Kostelanetz, Richard, *Conversing with Cage*, 2nd edn (New York and London, 2003)

Krasner, Louis, 'A Performance History of Schoenberg's Violin Concerto, op. 36', *Journal of the Arnold Schoenberg Institute*, II/2 (February 1978), pp. 84–98

Kurth, Richard, 'Suspended Tonalities in Schönberg's Twelve-tone Compositions', *Journal of the Arnold Schönberg Center*, 3 (2001), pp. 239–65

La Grange, Henry-Louis de, *Gustav Mahler*, 4 vols (Oxford, 1973–2008)

Langlie, Warren, 'Arnold Schoenberg as a Teacher', PhD diss., University of California, Los Angeles, 1960

Leibowitz, René, *Schoenberg and his School: The Contemporary Stage of the Language of Music*, trans. Dika Newlin (New York, 1975)

Levant, Oscar, *The Memoirs of an Amnesiac* (New York, 1965)

Levi, Erik, *Music in the Third Reich* (Basingstoke and London, 1996)

Lewin, David, '*Moses und Aron*: Some General Remarks, and Analytic Notes for Act I, Scene I', *Perspectives of New Music*, VI (1967), pp. 1–17

Lindenberger, Herbert, 'Arnold Schoenberg's "Der Biblische Weg" and "Moses und Aron": On the Transactions of Aesthetics and Politics', *Modern Judaism*, IX/1 (February 1989), pp. 55–70

Lloyd, Jill, and Ingrid Pfeiffer, in collaboration with Raymond Coffer, *Richard Gerstl* (Frankfurt and New York, 2017)

MacDonald, Malcolm, *Schoenberg*, 2nd edn (Oxford, 2008)

McGrath, William J., *Dionysian Art and Populist Politics in Austria* (New Haven, CT, 1974)

Maegaard, Jan, *Studien zur Entwicklung des dodekaphonen Satzes bei Arnold Schönberg*, 3 vols (Copenhagen, 1972)

Mahler, Alma, *Gustav Mahler: Memories and Letters*, ed. Donald Mitchell and Knud Martner, trans. Basil Crighton, revd edn (London, 1973)

Mann, Thomas, *The Story of a Novel: The Genesis of Doctor Faustus*, trans. Richard Winston and Clara Winston (New York, 1961)

——, *Dr Faustus: The Life of the German Composer as Told by a Friend*, trans. John E. Woods (New York, 1999)

Matejka, Viktor, *Widerstand ist alles: Notizen eines Unorthodoxen* (Vienna, 1993)

Metzger, Heinz-Klaus, and Rainer Riehn, eds, *Musik-Konzepte Sonderband: Arnold Schönberg* (Munich, 1980)

——, and Rainer Riehn, eds, *Musik-Konzepte: Arnold Schönbergs 'Berliner Schule'* (Munich, 2002)

Meyer, Christian, ed., *Arnold Schönberg: Spiele, Konstruktionen, Bricolagen* (Vienna, 2004)

——, and Therese Muxeneder, eds, *Arnold Schönberg: Catalogue raisonné* (Vienna, 2005)

Milstein, Silvina, *Arnold Schoenberg: Notes, Sets, Forms* (Cambridge, 1992)

Muxeneder, Therese, ed., *Arnold Schönberg und Jung-Wien* (Vienna, 2018)

Nachod, Hans, 'The Very First Performance of Schoenberg's *Gurrelieder*', *Music Survey*, 3 (Summer 1950), pp. 38–40

Neff, Severine, ed., *Arnold Schoenberg: The Second String Quartet in F-sharp minor, op. 10: Authoritative Score, Background and Analysis, Commentary* (New York, 2005)

Neighbour, Oliver, Paul Griffiths and Richard Perle, *The New Grove Second Viennese School* (London, 1983)

Newlin, Dika, *Schoenberg Remembered: Diaries and Recollections, 1938–76* (New York, 1980)

Paret, Peter, *The Berlin Secession* (Cambridge, 1980)

Pauli, Hansjörg, and Dagmar Wünsche, eds, *Hermann Scherchen, Musiker, 1891–1966* (Berlin, 1986)

Payne, Antony, *Schoenberg* (London, 1968)

Perle, George, *Serial Composition and Atonality: An Introduction to the Music of Schoenberg, Berg, and Webern*, 6th edn (Berkeley, CA, 1991)

Piatigorsky, Gregor, *Cellist* (New York, 1965)

Reich, Willi, *Schoenberg: A Critical Biography*, trans. Leo Black (London, 1971)

Ringer, Alexander, *Arnold Schoenberg: The Composer as Jew* (Oxford, 1990)

Rosen, Charles, *Arnold Schoenberg* (New York, 1975)

Ross, Alex, *The Rest is Noise: Listening to the Twentieth Century* (London, 2008)

Rufer, Joseph, *Das Werk Arnold Schönbergs* (Kassel, 1959)

Samson, Jim, 'Schoenberg's "Atonal" Music', *Tempo*, 109 (June 1974), pp. 16–25

——, *Music in Transition: A Study of Tonal Expansion and Atonality, 1900–1920* (Oxford, 1995)

Scheijen, Sjeng, *Diaghilev: A Life*, trans. Jane Hedley-Prôle and S. J. Leinbach (Oxford, 2009)

Schmidt, Matthias, *Schoenberg und Mozart: Aspekte einer Rezeptionsgeschichte* (Vienna, 2004)

Schoenberg, Arnold, *Models for Beginners in Composition*, ed. Gordon Root (1951)

——, *Briefe*, ed. Erwin Stein (Mainz, 1958)

——, *Exercises in Counterpoint*, ed. Leonard Stein (London, 1963)

——, *Letters*, ed. Erwin Stein, trans. Eithne Wilkins and Ernst Kaiser (London, 1964)

——, *Structural Functions of Harmony*, ed. Humphrey Searle and Leonard Stein (London, 1969)

——, *Fundamentals of Musical Composition*, ed. Gerald Strang with the collaboration of Leonard Stein (London, 1970)

——, *Berliner Tagenbuch*, ed. Josef Rufer (Frankfurt, 1974)

——, *Style and Idea*, ed. Leonard Stein, trans. Leo Black, revd edn (London, 1984)

——, *Harmonielehre*, trans. Roy E. Carter (London, 1978)

——, *Theory of Harmony*, trans. Roy E. Carter (London, 1978)

——, 'The Biblical Way', trans. Moshe Lazar, *Journal of the Arnold Schönberg Institute*, XVII/1–2 (1994), pp. 162–330

——, *Coherence, Counterpoint, Instrumentation, Instruction in Form*, ed. Severine Neff, trans. Charlotte M. Cross and Severine Neff (Lincoln, NE, 1994)

——, *Zusammenhang, Kontrapunkt, Instrumentation, Formenlehre: Coherence, Counterpoint, Instrumentation, Instruction in Form*, ed. Severine Neff, trans. Charlotte M. Cross and Severine Neff (Lincoln, NE, and London, 1994)

——, *The Musical Idea and the Logic, Technique, and Art of its Presentation*, ed. and trans. Patricia Carpenter and Severine Neff (New York, 1995)

——, *Stile herrschen, Gedanken siegen: Ausgewählte Schriften*, ed. Anna Maria Morazzoni (Mainz, 2007)

——, and Thomas Mann, 'Der "Eigentliche": Die Dissonanzen zwischen Arnold Schönberg und Thomas Mann', *Der Monat*, 6 (1949), pp. 76–8

Schoenberg, E. Randol, 'Arnold Schoenberg and Albert Einstein: Their Relationship and Views on Zionism', *Journal of the Arnold Schoenberg Institute*, X/2 (1987), pp. 134–91

——, 'The Most Famous Thing He Never Said', *Journal of the Arnold Schönberg Center*, V (2003), pp. 27–30

Schoenberg-Nono, Nuria, *Arnold Schönberg, 1874–1951: Lebensgeschichte in Begegnungen* (Klagenfurt, 1992)

——, ed., *Arnold Schoenberg: Self-portrait* (Pacific Palisades, CA, 1988)

Schorske, Carl E., *Fin-de-siècle Vienna: Politics and Culture* (New York, 1979)

Shaw, Jennifer, 'Schoenberg's Choral Symphony, *Die Jakobsleiter*, and Other Wartime Fragments', PhD diss., State University of New York at Stony Brook, 2002

——, and Joseph Auner, *The Cambridge Companion to Schoenberg* (Cambridge and New York, 2010)

Shawn, Allen, *Arnold Schoenberg's Journey* (New York, 2002)

Shilkret, Nathaniel, *Sixty Years in the Music Business*, ed. Neil Shell and Barbara Shilkret (Lanham, MD, 2005)

Silverman, Lisa, *Becoming Austrians: Jews and Culture Between the World Wars* (Oxford and New York, 2012)

Simms, Bryan A., *The Atonal Music of Arnold Schoenberg, 1908–1923* (Oxford and New York, 2000)

——, ed., *Pro Mundo – Pro Domo: The Writings of Alban Berg* (Oxford and New York, 2014)

Stein, Erwin, 'Moses und Aron', *Opera*, VIII/8 (August 1957), pp. 485–9

——, *Arnold Schoenberg/Wassily Kandinsky: Letters, Pictures and Documents* (London, 1984)

Stephan, Rudolf, 'Der musikalische Gedanke bei Schönberg', *Österreichische Musik Zeitschrift*, XXXVII/10 (1982), pp. 530–40

——, ed., *Bericht über den 1. Kongress der Internationlane Schönberg-Gesellschaft, Wien: 4–9 Juni, 1974* (Vienna, 1978)

Steuermann, Clara, 'From the Archives: Schoenberg's Library Catalog', *Journal of the Arnold Schoenberg Institute*, III/2 (1979), pp. 203–18

Stevens, Halsey, 'A Conversation with Schoenberg about Painting', *Journal of the Arnold Schoenberg Institute*, II/3 (1978), pp. 178–80

Straus, Joseph N., *Twelve-tone Music in America* (Cambridge, 2009)

Stuckenschmidt, Hans Heinz, *Arnold Schoenberg*, trans. Edith Temple Roberts and Humphrey Searle (London, 1959)

——, *Schoenberg: His Life, World and Work*, trans. Humphrey Searle (London, 1977)

Taruskin, Richard, 'The Poietic Fallacy', *Musical Times*, CXLV/1886 (Spring 2004), pp. 7–34

Tippett, Michael, et al., 'Involuntary Pilgrimage of Arnold Schönberg. From Vienna to California: A Symposium', *The Listener*, 1194 (17 January 1952), pp. 106–7.

Tomlinson, Gary, *Metaphysical Song: An Essay on Opera* (Princeton, NJ, 1999)

Tresize, Simon, 'Schoenberg's *Gurrelieder*', PhD diss., University of Oxford, 1987

Veitl, Karin, 'Aspekte des Tanzes in der Musik Arnold Schönbergs: Bewegungsdramaturgie und musikalische Konzeption in der *Verklärten Nacht* und in *Moses und Aron*', PhD diss., University of Vienna, 1992

Vergo, Peter, *Art in Vienna, 1898–1918: Klimt, Kokoschka, Schiele and their Contemporaries* (London, 1975)

Walton, Chris, 'Erich Schmid in Schoenberg's Composition Masterclass', *Tempo*, 218 (2001), pp. 15–19

Watkins, Holly, 'Schoenberg's Interior Designs', *Journal of the American Musicological Society*, LXI/1 (Spring 2008), pp. 123–206

Webern, Anton, *The Path to the New Music*, ed. Willi Reich, trans. Leo Black (London, 1963)

Wellesz, Egon, *Arnold Schoenberg: The Formative Years* (London and New York, 1971)

White, Pamela C., *Schoenberg and the God-idea: The Opera 'Moses und Aron'* (Ann Arbor, MI, 1985)

Whittall, Arnold, *Schoenberg Chamber Music* (London, 1972)

——, 'Schoenberg and the "True Tradition": Theme and Form in the String Trio', *Musical Times*, CXV/1579 (1974), pp. 739–43

——, *The Cambridge Introduction to Serialism* (Cambridge, 2008)

Wickes, Lewis, 'Schoenberg, *Erwartung*, and the Reception of Psychoanalysis in Musical Circles in Vienna until 1910/11', *Studies in Music*, XXIII (1989), pp. 88–106

Wörner, Karl Heinrich, *Schoenberg's 'Moses and Aaron'*, trans. Paul Hamburger (London, 1963)

Wright, James K., and Alan M. Gillmor, *Schoenberg's Chamber Music, Schoenberg's World* (Hillsdale, NY, 2009)

Youens, Susan, 'Excavating an Allegory: The Texts of *Pierrot lunaire*', *Journal of the Arnold Schoenberg Institute*, VIII/2 (1984), pp. 95–115

Zillig, Winfried, 'Notes on Arnold Schoenberg's Unfinished Oratorio "Die Jakobsleiter"', *The Score*, XXV (June 1959), pp. 7–18

Select Discography

The first of Schoenberg's works to be recorded was the op. 11 *Three Piano Pieces*, on a piano roll by Walter Gieseking in 1922. *Verklärte Nacht* followed on phonograph in 1924–5, by the Spencer Dyke String Quartet. Since then, everything has been recorded, some works – usually the most predictable ones – many times. There is, however, no complete recorded edition comparable, say, to the editions we have for Bach or Mozart; nor is there likely to be. I am not sure that it would even be desirable, save as a handy way to store items on the shelf: a desire not entirely to be sneezed at, and yet . . .

One collection, far from comprehensive yet certainly wide-ranging, is the series of recordings made by Pierre Boulez for Sony, most recently reissued as an eleven-CD set. (There seems to me little point here in giving catalogue numbers, since they tend very quickly to be outdated; so much is in any case increasingly available for downloading.) Boulez had recorded some works earlier, for instance with his ensemble Domaine musical, and would also return to some of it, often with fascinatingly different results, for Erato (Warner Classics) and for Deutsche Grammophon (DG). Yet, with the very important exceptions of the Piano and Violin concertos and *Herzgewächse*, there is nothing new in the later recordings; nor is there, so far as I am aware, anything recorded earlier that is not also to be found in the Sony set. As a 'starter pack', and with its obvious exclusion of certain solo and chamber repertoire, as well as the non-orchestral songs, it would be impossible to match, let alone to beat. I heartily recommend the interpretations, too: none a last word, of course, yet every one thoughtful, convincing and indeed provocative in its way.

Many gaps would be filled, in a positive rather than negative sense, by the five-LP London Sinfonietta set of works for chamber ensemble (Decca, 1974), which has remained, bafflingly, without full reissue on CD. Should it reappear, or should you be able to listen to it in its original guise, do snap it up. Likewise by the 'Complete Songs' on Capriccio, by various artists, with Urs Liska at the piano. What I shall offer below is at least one recommendation for every work with opus number, and for the most important works without. (Neither *Gurrelieder* nor *Moses und Aron*, for instance, has a number, yet a discography omitting them would simply be absurd.) * denotes a work's appearance on the Boulez set; ** in the London Sinfonietta set; and *** in the Complete Songs. Where, as on the Decca set, only single movements from a work appear, I have not marked them with asterisks.

Works with opus numbers

1 *Two Songs****: Dietrich Fischer-Dieskau and Aribert Reimann (EMI) is a firm recommendation, although here, as elsewhere, the Capriccio set has much to offer.

2 *Four Songs****: The first recording of one of these songs (op. 2 no. 1) was made by Martha Mödl and Otto Franze in 1948 (Melodram); there is also a memorable recording by Fischer-Dieskau and Reimann (see op. 1). For all four, try Lucia Popp and Geoffrey Parsons (BBC Legends).

3 *Six Songs****: Various songs have been recorded separately, often with distinction. For all six, however, the best bet would be either the Capriccio set or an older, 'complete' set by Glenn Gould and various singers (Sony).

4 *Verklärte Nacht** **: The (augmented) Hollywood String Quartet (1950, EMI/Testament) remains a gramophone classic. For something completely different, try the Domaine musical (augmented Parrenin Quartet) under Boulez's supervision (most recently on DG).
   Version for string orchestra*: Even though the sextet version is to my mind infinitely preferable, this version (strictly, these versions: 1917 and 1943) will never go away. For a chamber orchestra, try Heinz Holliger and the Chamber Orchestra of Europe (Teldec); or Alisa Weilerstein and the Trondheim Soloists (Pentatone) for full, massed strings – and why not? – the Berlin Philharmonic and Herbert von Karajan (DG).

5 *Pelleas und Melisande**: The last of Boulez's three commercially recorded versions, with the Gustav Mahler Youth Orchestra (DG), offers a near-ideal blend of orchestral clarity, heft and drama.

6   *Eight Songs****: Susanne Lange and Tove Lønskov (Kontrapunkt) are well worth hearing as an alternative to the Capriccio set.

7   *String Quartet no. 1 in D minor*: As with the other numbered quartets, the Kolisch Quartet recording (1936, Music and Arts) is self-recommending. The Pražak (Praga) and Arditti (Naïve) Quartets offer more recent complementary standpoints.

8   *Six Songs*: It is difficult to beat the Vienna Philharmonic in Schoenberg when it puts its mind to this music. Anja Silja and Christoph von Dohnányi (Decca) make the most convincing case I have heard for these woefully neglected songs.

9   *Chamber Symphony no. 1 in E major** **: Fast, furious, uncompromising: Boulez's early Domaine musical performance takes no prisoners (DG). For something less abrasive and no less intelligent, the Birmingham Contemporary Music Group and Simon Rattle (EMI) may be warmly recommended.

10 *String Quartet no. 2 in F-sharp minor*: Clemence Gifford joined the Kolisch Quartet for its first recording on New Year's Eve, 1936 (Music and Arts). Margaret Price and the LaSalle Quartet (DG) offer a fascinating blend of tendencies Wagnerian and (post-)Brahmsian. The Arditti Quartet and Dawn Upshaw (Naïve) perhaps breathe more openly and without regret the 'air of another planet'.

11 *Three Piano Pieces*: Maurizio Pollini, in his classic recording of the 'complete' (that is, those with opus numbers) piano works (DG), and Daniel Barenboim (Teldec) both have much to offer. Barenboim also offers Busoni's 'concert version' of op. 11 no. 2.

12 *Two Ballads****: Try Sarah Connolly (no. 1) and Roderick Williams (no. 2) with Iain Burnside at the piano (Black Box).

13 *Friede auf Erden**: As an alternative to Boulez's recording with the BBC Singers (from the Sony set), Stefan Parkman and the Danish National Radio Chamber Choir (Chandos) has much to be recommended.

14 *Two Songs****: Fischer-Dieskau and Reimann (EMI) only offer, alas, the first of the two songs. Lange and Lønskov (see op. 6) are well worth hearing, too.

15 *Das Buch der hängenden Gärten****: No single performance of such a work can be definitive, but if one could, Christian Gerhaher's might be it (with Gerold Huber; Sony).

16 *Five Orchestral Pieces**: Hans Rosbaud's mono recording with the Southwest German Radio Symphony Orchestra Baden-Baden (Wergo) shows its age only a little in terms of sound. Should stereo be a priority, Boulez (the Sony set) or the Cleveland Orchestra/Dohnányi (Decca) will not disappoint.

17 *Erwartung**: Silja, the Vienna Philharmonic and Dohnányi (Decca) come as close as any to encompassing the manifold musico-dramatic demands of Schoenberg's monodrama. Phyllis Bryn-Julson with the City of Birmingham Symphony Orchestra and Rattle (EMI) offers a fine alternative.

18 *Die glückliche Hand**: Siegmund Nimsgern with Boulez and BBC forces (Sony) is an estimable choice.

19 *Six Little Piano Pieces**: Pollini (DG) and Mitsuko Uchida (Decca) both offer rewarding interpretations. So, unsurprisingly, does Eduard Steuermann, Schoenberg's own pupil (Soundmark).

20 *Herzgewächse***: Christine Schäfer, the Ensemble Intercontemporain and Boulez (DG) aim for the stratosphere in more than mere pitch – and reach it.

21 *Pierrot lunaire** ***: Schoenberg's own recording from 1940, readily available online, is as close to mandatory listening as any recording can be. No performance of this of all works can begin to encompass all possibilities, though. Forced to choose just one other, I should choose Boulez's third (DG), with the Ensemble Intercontemporain and Schäfer, although all his versions – the notorious 'sung' *Pierrot* included (Yvonne Minton; Sony) – have much to be said in their favour.

22 *Four Orchestral Songs**: Minton, the BBC Symphony Orchestra and Boulez on the Sony set remains highly recommendable; a fine alternative is Silja with the Philharmonia and Robert Craft (Koch).

23 *Five Piano Pieces*: Pollini, once again, would be my firm first recommendation (DG). Steuermann (Soundmark) and, recently, Pino Napolitano (Odradek) offer different, equally valid standpoints.

24 *Serenade** ***: Boulez's Sony recording (Ensemble Intercontemporain) remains outstanding, as does his earlier, fiercer Domaine musical version (DG). The aforementioned London Sinfonietta version is at present available as a download (Decca).

25 *Suite*: Should Pollini's gleaming Bauhaus version (DG) fail to satisfy, or you simply feel in need of a change, try Peter Serkin (Arcana).

26 *Wind Quintet***: The London Sinfonietta performance under David Atherton (Decca) seems to me a clear first choice here.

27 *Four Pieces for Chorus**: Boulez and the BBC Singers will do very nicely here (Sony).

28 *Three Satires**: Boulez and the BBC Singers will likewise do nicely here (Sony).

29 *Suite** **: For an alternative, still more biting, to his Sony recording, try Boulez with the Domaine musical (DG). Atherton and the London Sinfonietta (Decca) is excellent, too; as, in perhaps slightly more relaxed style, are the Wiener Concert-Verein and Martin Sieghart (Orfeo).

30 *String Quartet no. 3*: The Kolisch (Music and Arts) recording demands to be heard. More recently, the Pražák (Praga) and Leipzig (MDG Gold) quartets have taken their place among a number of excellent alternatives.

31 *Variations for Orchestra**: How fascinating it would be if a recording of Wilhelm Furtwängler's Berlin premiere were to have survived – although I suspect that, sadly, it might disappoint in practice. In lieu of that, pioneering recordings by Rosbaud (Southwest German Radio Symphony Orchestra; Music and Arts) and Hermann Scherchen (Bavarian Radio; Tahra) offer fascinating, almost 'historic' standpoints. Barenboim and the West–Eastern Divan Orchestra, however, speak more clearly and more passionately to me than any other recording – or performance – I have heard (C major on DVD, Decca audio download).

32 *Von heute auf morgen*: This, sadly, was the Schoenberg opera that Boulez never recorded (unless somewhere there exists a record of his performances at the Châtelet). Michael Gielen's Frankfurt Radio Symphony recording (CPO) is outstanding; it is difficult to imagine it being eclipsed any time soon.

33 *Two Piano Pieces*: Pollini (DG) and Serkin (Arcana) are both firm recommendations.

34 *Begleitmusik zu einer Lichtspielszene**: Boulez's Sony recording is excellent indeed; he may also be heard – and seen – to excellent effect with the same orchestra, the BBC Symphony, on DVD (Medici Arts). Holliger and the Chamber Orchestra of Europe (Teldec) prove equally outstanding.

35 *Six Pieces for Male Chorus*[*]: Boulez and the BBC Singers (Sony) will
    not disappoint. There seems little reason to hunt for an alternative;
    however, the Südfunk-Cor Stuttgart and Rupert Huber (Arte Nova) will
    do very well, should you wish.

36 *Violin Concerto*: Zvi Zeitlin with Rafael Kubelík and the Bavarian
    Radio Symphony Orchestra (DG) would be my first choice: warm and
    comprehending in equal measure. Piere Amoyal, Boulez, and the LSO
    (Erato) have been oddly underrated. A fine recent alternative is offered
    by Hilary Hahn, the Swedish Radio Symphony Orchestra and Esa-
    Pekka Salonen (also DG).

37 *String Quartet no. 4*: As with the earlier quartets, the self-selecting
    Kolisch (Music and Arts) and modern Pražák (Praga) receive my
    wholehearted recommendation.

38 *Chamber Symphony no. 2*[*]: Holliger and the Chamber Orchestra
    of Europe (Teldec) present a fine blend of textural clarity and
    post-Expressionist drama; so, on a larger scale, do Gielen and his
    Südwestfunk forces (Philips) and, perhaps best of all, Maderna and the
    Saarland Radio Orchestra (usually readily to be found on YouTube).

39 *Kol nidre*[*]: Boulez's BBC recording (Sony) has its virtues, but Gielen and
    the Southwest German Radio Symphony Orchestra Baden-Baden and
    Freiburg (Hänssler) seem to speak of greater belief in this often strange
    work.

40 *Variations on a recitative*: Kevin Bowyer presents Schoenberg's
    only completed work for organ in a fine recital alongside works by
    Hindemith and Ernst Pepping (Nimbus).

41 *Ode to Napoleon Buonaparte*[*][***]: Boulez's later recording, with David
    Pittman-Jennings and the Ensemble Intercontemporain (DG), is my
    clear first choice; musical and dramatic demands barely need to be
    balanced, since they were never separate in the first place.

42 *Piano Concerto*: Boulez recorded this work three times, and all versions
    (Serkin/LSO/Erato; Uchida/Cleveland/Decca; Barenboim/Vienna/
    Peral, download only) have much to recommend them. If forced to
    choose, I should probably opt for Uchida. For a non-Boulez recording,
    Pollini with the Berlin Philharmonic and Claudio Abbado (DG) will
    delight many of those musicians' admirers, among whom I certainly
    count myself.

43 *Theme and Variations*: For the original wind-band version (43*a*), try the Royal Norwegian Navy Band and Ingar Bergby (2L); for the orchestral version (43*b*), John Mauceri and the Deutsches Symphonie-Orchester Berlin (Decca).

44 *Prelude to Genesis*: A Naxos disc (Berlin Radio Symphony Orchestra/ Gerard Schwarz) offers this composite work in its entirety. Bruno Maderna (Stradivarius) may be listened to with great interest for Schoenberg's Prelude alone.

45 *String Trio*: Members of the Arditti (Auvidis) and Pražák (Praga) quartets may both be highly recommended, the former (broadly) more brazenly modernistic, the latter more 'traditional', although such descriptions are of limited use in such wide-ranging interpretations.

46 *A Survivor from Warsaw**: Boulez's Sony BBC recording is very fine; an equally fine alternative, perhaps slightly more 'Romantic' in hue, comes from Abbado and the Vienna Philharmonic (DG).

47 *Phantasy, for violin and piano***: The venerable – not quite the first – recording, live from Darmstadt, by Rudolf Kolisch and Steuermann (Col Legno) is obviously not to be missed. My own first choice, however, would be Vlastimil Holek and Sachiko Kayahara (Praga), warm and incisive in equal, dialectical measure. A fine, still more recent alternative comes from Carolin Widmann and Simon Lepper (ECM).

48 *Three Songs****: It is a pity that Fischer-Dieskau and Reimann (EMI) recorded only the first two of these songs. Lange and Lønskov (Kontrapunkt) offer all three in typically thoughtful interpretations.

49 *Three Folksongs**: Boulez and the BBC Singers (Sony) do very well here. If, for whatever reason, you would like an alternative, try the Südfunk-Chor Stuttgart and Huber (Arte Nova).

50 *(Unfinished) Choral Works**: Boulez and the BBC Singers (Sony) once again will do very well. For the two completed works, op. 50*a* and op. 50*b*, a fine alternative is offered by Accentus and Laurence Equilbey (Naïve).

'Major' works without opus numbers

String Quartet in D major: The Pražak Quartet (Praga) give a warm yet
incisive performance on a splendid set cited above for other chamber
works.

Gurrelieder* ***: The asterisks refer to an early, piano-only setting of some
of Jens Peter Jacobsen's texts. It is of great interest, but no one will
be satisfied with it alone. Boulez's Sony recording is outstanding;
so is Abbado's with the Vienna Philharmonic (DG), my alternative
recommendation.

Brettl-Lieder (Cabaret Songs): Jessye Norman and James Levine show
themselves alert to both the fun and the sensuality of these songs.

Three Pieces for Chamber Orchestra*: Boulez and the Ensemble
Intercontemporain, part of the Sony set, will do very well here.

Die Jakobsleiter*: Gielen and the Southwest German Radio Symphony
Orchestra Baden-Baden and Freiburg (Hänssler) offer a splendid
alternative to Boulez and BBC forces (Sony).

Die eiserne Brigade**: Should you be unable to find the London Sinfonietta
set – there was briefly a CD reissue (Decca) and a download version was
available at the time of writing – the Schönberg Ensemble (Philips)
offers a good alternative.

Song of the Wood-Dove from Gurrelieder, arranged for chamber ensemble***:
No need to look any further than Norman, the Ensemble
Intercontemporain and Boulez (Sony).

Weihnachtsmusik**: In addition to the London Sinfonietta recording, the
Arditti Quartet and friends (Naïve) may be highly recommended.
Should you be able to find it, a *BBC Music Magazine* recording from the
Taverner Consort & Players and Andrew Parrott is quite special indeed.

Moses und Aron*: There is much to be said for Boulez's first recording, but
his second (DG), with the Concertgebouw Orchestra, made after live,
staged performances in Amsterdam and Salzburg, eclipses it. Gielen's
Austrian radio recording (Philips) is at least as fine, and may be heard
either simply as audio, or as the soundtrack to the celebrated Straub-
Huillet film (if you can find it). On DVD, Reto Nickler's production
from the Vienna State Opera, conducted by Daniele Gatti (Arthaus), is
a clear first choice, with interesting commentary from participants as
'extras'.

Cello Concerto after Monn's D major Keyboard Concerto: Try Heinrich Schiff with the Southwest German Radio Symphony Orchestra Baden-Baden and Freiburg and Gielen (Wergo).

Concerto for String Quartet and Orchestra after Handel's Concerto Grosso in B-flat Major, op. 6 no. 7: There is, obviously, much of interest in the recording by the Kolisch Quartet with the Los Angeles Philharmonic and Otto Klemperer in 1938 (Archiphon). However, a clearer sense of the work will probably be gleaned from the American String Quartet, the New York Chamber Symphony and Schwarz (Apex).

Suite for String Orchestra in G major: The Berlin Radio Symphony Orchestra and Mauceri (Decca) give a very good account, but the same orchestra with Scherchen (EMI), almost forty years earlier, perhaps offer something more special.

'Major' transcriptions

Bach, St Anne Prelude and Fugue: It is a pity that Boulez, who conducted this transcription, never recorded it. Salonen and the Los Angeles Philharmonic (Sony) are excellent.

Bach, Chorale Preludes: Try the Philharmonia and Craft (Koch) in these two pieces.

Brahms, Piano Quartet in G minor, op. 25: The Berlin Philharmonic and Rattle (Warner) seem far more at home here than in their recordings of the 'actual' Brahms symphonies.

Mahler – Das Lied von der Erde, with Webern, completed by Rainer Riehn: Mark Wigglesworth's RCA recording with the Premiere Ensemble, Jean Rigby and Robert Tear is my first choice.

Johann Strauss Waltzes (along with those of Berg and Webern): The Boston Symphony Chamber Players (DG) offer a splendid collection, with pieces by Stravinsky as a welcome bonus.

Various: Another fine collection, including Schubert songs, Johann Strauss, Reger and popular song, comes from soloists of the Opéra National de Lyon (Erato).

Acknowledgements

Writing a book always turns out to be a greater undertaking than one remembers from the last time: a little like moving house, only the work will be longer, harder and better. The people and experiences contributing are always too numerous to list. I hope it will not be taken amiss if I severely limit those named here, while offering heartfelt thanks to all who played a part.

For early encouragement of my interest in Schoenberg, furthered by loans from her collection of scores and recordings, I must thank Sybil Pentith, my sixth-form music teacher. Subsequent discussion with Alexander Goehr left an enduring mark; so too did his lectures on the analysis of twentieth-century music, for which I would dash across to the Cambridge University Faculty of Music from my then home in History. Many are the performing musicians whose concerts, let alone recordings, have inspired over the years; special thanks should go to Daniel Barenboim, Maurizio Pollini and above all to Pierre Boulez.

I am immensely grateful to Reaktion Books both for initially commissioning me to write this book and for steering me so ably through the process of planning, writing and editing. Without an initial approach from Ben Hayes as Commissioning Editor and his subsequent encouragement, this project would most likely never have happened. Michael Leaman, Matt Milton, Rebecca Ratnayake and Phoebe Colley have all since proved generous with their time, patience and criticism. My readers and proofreader remained anonymous; they are equally deserving of thanks. The award of a British Academy Mid-Career Fellowship, during which most of the book was written, was equally crucial; thanks should therefore go not only to assessors and staff at the British Academy, but also to Jim Samson, who wrote a reference for my application at absurdly short notice. Support from colleagues at Royal Holloway, University of London is greatly appreciated. To Erik Levi, who read through the initial manuscript, generous yet incisive with his criticism, I owe a special message of thanks.

It is a commonplace in writing on Schoenberg to offer what might sound extravagant thanks to the Arnold Schönberg Center in Vienna and to the Schoenberg family. The only extravagance in this case would be of insufficiency. Nothing could have been too much trouble over a period of several years for Therese Muxeneder and Eike Fess, whose knowledge and understanding of Schoenberg's life and music puts mine to shame. Without their scholarly and personal friendship, this book would either not exist or, perhaps worse, would fall so far short as to deserve not to do so. Many thanks also to Angelika Möser, Karin Nemec, Bernhard Sieber and to the other ASC staff and fellow visitors who made my visits to Vienna and Mödling the inspiring, fruitful occasions that they were; likewise to the Avenir Foundation of Wheat Bridge, Colorado, for the grant enabling me to stay for a month in an apartment in Schoenberg's Mödling house and thus to begin to plan this book. That the ASC had suffered a fire a couple of months earlier, leaving its library unavailable for the first two of the four weeks turned out to be a blessing in disguise. I learned more than I could ever have imagined from an enforced period of twelve-note tourism, visiting as much as possible of Schoenberg's Vienna, learning how the city and its surroundings worked, how sites were connected, what was left and what was not.

Nuria Schoenberg-Nono was kind enough to grant me a Vienna interview, from which again I learned so much that could never have been gleaned from books, papers or indeed scores. Her generosity was fully matched by that of Ronald Schoenberg and Barbara Zeisl-Schoenberg, whose hospitality and invitation to their family home I shall not forget: not least on account of Barbara's peerless Sachertorte. Likewise by the generosity and hospitality of Lawrence and Anne Schoenberg: their presence that afternoon at the Rockingham Avenue house was followed by an equally valued invitation to Pacific Palisades, to their home and that of Belmont Music Publishers.

For introductions to the Schoenberg family in Los Angeles and for much else besides I am indebted to Alex Ross and to Lucy Schaufer. Of those who have assisted with particular advice and support, both specific and general, I should also name Leo Carey, John Deathridge, Greg Fullelove, Carrie Gibson, Paul Harper-Scott, James Helgeson, Sebastian Kokelaar, Phillip Koyoumjian, Oli Perry, Tamsin Rolls, Sebastian Smallshaw, Nicholas Vazsonyi and László Vikarius. For permission to reproduce images, fully detailed elsewhere, I thank Belmont Music Publishers, the Library of Congress, Universal Edition and Condé Nast. Last yet anything but least, I thank not only the community of Schoenberg scholarship, but the extraordinary breadth and depth of interest, encouragement and comradeship offered by friends and followers on social media, who have done much to assist, enrich and even on occasion to guide my work. Errors, lapses of judgement and all other shortcomings remain my responsibility alone.

Photo Acknowledgements

The author and publishers wish to express their thanks to the below sources of illustrative material and/or permission to reproduce it. Some locations of artworks are also given below, in the interests of brevity:

Courtesy Arnold Schönberg Center, Vienna: pp. 6, 20, 23, 40, 57, 78, 81, 86, 88, 97, 103, 105, 110, 122, 127 (right), 135, 149, 164, 167, 173, 178, 201, 203; Arnold Schönberg Center, Wien (Universal Edition Collection) / Arnold Schönberg © 1925, 1952 by Universal Edition AG, Vienna/UE 7669: p. 129; photo Max Munn Autrey: p. 168; permission given by Belmont Music Publishers, Los Angeles: pp. 37, 60, 68, 72, 75, 77, 79, 126, 127 (left); Ralph Crane/Vogue © Condé Nast: p. 186; photo Richard Fish: p. 200; photo Clyde Fisher: p. 158; courtesy Library of Congress, Washington, DC / Arnold Schönberg © 1912, 1940 by Universal Edition/UE 2994: p. 59.